LONGMAN SOCIOLOGY SERIES

Social Europe

edited by Joe Bailey

LONGMAN
London and New York

Longman Group Limited,
Longman House, Burnt Mill,
Harlow, Essex CM20 2JE, England
and Associated Companies throughout the world.

Published in the United States of America
by Longman Publishing, New York

© Longman Group UK Limited 1992

First published 1992
Third impression 1995

ISBN 0582 06810X CSD
ISBN 0582 068096 PPR

British Library Cataloguing-in-Publication Data

A catalogue record for this book is
available from the British Library

Library of Congress Cataloging-in-Publication Data
Bailey, Joe.
  Social Europe / Joe Bailey,
   p. cm. – (Longman sociology series)
  Includes bibliographical references and index.
  ISBN 0–582–06810–X : – ISBN 0–582–06809–6 (pbk.) :
  1. Europe – Social conditions – 20th century. 2. Social structure –
  Europe. 3. Social institutions – Europe. I. Title. II. Series.
  HN373.5.B36 1992
  306'.094 – dc20
                91–42750
                  CIP

Set by 9/10 in Times
Produced by Longman Singapore Publishers (Pte) Ltd.
Printed in Singapore

CONTENTS

vi *Social Europe*

LIST OF FIGURES AND TABLES

SERIES EDITOR'S PREFACE

The Longman Sociology Series is a new series of books which are written specifically for first and second year undergraduate students. Each title covers one key area of sociology and aims to supplement the traditional standard text.

The series is forward looking and attempts to reflect topics that will be included in syllabuses for sociology and social policy in the 1990s. It provides a range of volumes that bring together conceptual and empirical material. In addition, volumes in the series also examine key controversies and debates drawing on commentaries using conceptual and empirical material from a range of authors.

Each volume in the series whether authored or edited, will cover an area that would be commonly found in sociology and social policy syllabuses. The focus of each volume will be upon theoretically informed empirical work with policy relatedness.

The volumes are intended for an international audience and therefore comparative material is introduced where appropriate in a form that will be suitable for first and second year students.

The first volume in the series is an edited collection of papers on Social Europe. It brings together a distinguished group of contributors who all focus on ways in which sociologists can contribute to the analysis of European affairs. Altogether the essays in this volume provide a strong framework for sociological analysis of Europe and European societies in the latter part of the Twentieth Century.

December 1991
Robert G Burgess,
University of Warwick

PREFACE

This book is about modern western European societies. It is concerned both with the individual national societies that go to make up western Europe and with the potential unity of these societies.

The audience for this book will already be concerned with sociology. Readers will already be sensitised to the importance of understanding 'how these things are done elsewhere' – that is, to the significance of a comparative understanding of social phenomena. But the 'elsewhere' in question has rarely been so explicitly European and 'these things' rarely so clearly about changing social structures and responding institutions. These are not academic and rarefied views of social processes but are the very basis of everyday policy and practice. They concern the familiar organisations in which we work and live. This book of specially commissioned essays by British sociologists can be seen as contributing to a sociology of, for and in Europe. It does not attempt to be comprehensive; for instance, there is no explicit treatment of poverty or of culture. But it does try to lay out some of the most basic conditions and consequences of major social changes taking place now across Europe. These are the currency of any debate about Europe as a society and as a sociological entity. In this sense it is intended as a basic guide to the significance of the sociological data now available to us. These chapters contain materials helping to construct a comparative understanding of modern Europe beyond the oversimplifications we see in the flood of 'Euro-journalism' and the campaigning of self-interested politicians.

The book is by British sociologists, which may seem somewhat insular given the overall theme. This exclusivity is only for the subsidiary purpose of showing how pertinent and useful some of the material produced by sociologists in this country is to an analysis of Europe. Social scientists in general have a higher status in other European countries than in Britain. Yet the quality and relevance of contemporary sociological work, as illustrated here, shows how counter-productive this short-sightedness has been and will continue to be. Insularity and ignorance of other societies are deeply laid in British intellectual life, and sociology, as a foundation discipline of any social undestanding, has suffered because of this. These essays provide an example of the value of British sociology in a Britain which must increase its depth of understanding of its place in a changing Europe, an understanding which is accelerating in its rise up the political and popular agenda.

This book will be useful in a number of ways: as a resource for students now taking European studies courses; as a set of data and ideas which will help student projects take on issues conventionally addressed, but with a comparative European slant which is currently hard to find systematised; as focused information for those who sense that the social issues and problems they are familiar with in Britain need a wider European context for a real understanding; and finally as an aid to demystifying the welter of simplistic generalisations of social pundits on social affairs.

I am very grateful for all the thinking, talking and writing generously provided by my colleagues at Kingston Polytechnic, especially those with whom I have been teaching social science courses on Europe for the last ten years. Special thanks are due to Bob Burgess for his unfailingly good-humoured advice and encouragement and to Chris Harrison of Longman for his forbearance and support.

My greatest debt is to Caro Bailey.

ACKNOWLEDGEMENTS

We are grateful to the following for permission to reproduce copyright material:

Eurostat for table 2.2 taken from Rapid reports: Population and social conditions; table 2.3 taken from Social indicators for the European Community and *Eurostat Review 1977–86*; figure 4.1, table 4.3 and table 6.1 taken from Demographic statistics, 1990; Gower Publishing Company for table 2.5 taken from *British Social Attitudes* by R. Jowell, S. Witherspoon and L. Brook; Macmillan Press Ltd for tables 11.1, 11.2 and 11.3 taken from *Contrasting values in Western Europe* by S. Harding *et al*; NACRO for table 9.2; OECD for table 5.2 and figure 7.3; Sage Publications Ltd. for table 2.1; World Health Organization for tables 10.1, 10.2, 10.3, 10.4, 10.5 taken from Evaluation of the strategy for health for all by the year 2000: seventh report of the world health situation, and table 10.6 taken from the European Centre for the Epidemiological Monitoring of AIDS.

LIST OF CONTRIBUTORS

Joe Bailey is Head of the School of Social Sciences at Kingston Polytechnic and has taught courses on the sociology of Europe for ten years. His research interests are in urban sociology and the relation between social theory and forecasting. He is the author of *Social Theory for Planning* (Routledge 1975), *Ideas and Intervention* (Routledge 1980) and *Pessimism* (Routledge 1988). He is currently researching social judgements of progress and decline.

Lynne Chisholm is a Professor in Socialization and Inter-cultural Education at the University of Marburg. In her previous post at the University of London Institute of Education she directed the Girls and Occupational Choice project, and she has published widely in the fields of gender, education and the labour market and in youth transitions. Her current interests include the development of European research and policy perspectives on youth transitions. She is a founding member of the Centre for Youth Research Co-operation in Europe, (CYRCE) based in Berlin, and is a consultant to the European Commission's Task Force on Human Resources – Youth and Education through the Youth Research Matters Group at the EC Youth Exchange Bureau.

Stan Clark is a Lecturer in the Department of Sociology at the University of Liverpool. His previous research interest was in social class structure, and he is the joint author, with K. Roberts *et al.*, of *The Fragmentary Class Structure* (Heinemann, 1977). Since 1988 he has been engaged in a research project involving the universities of Liverpool, Surrey, Bielefeld and Bremen, which has been investigating the attitudes of British and German youth to work, leisure and employment training. The first part of the report has just been published by the Anglo-German Foundation for the Study of Industrial Society.

Grace Davie teaches sociology at the University of Exeter. She specialises in the sociology of religion and has published (with G. Ahern) *Inner City God: the Nature of Belief in the Inner City* (Hodder & Stoughton, 1987). She is currently involved in a collaborative project focusing on the religious factor in the construction of Europe.

Howard Davis is a Reader in Sociology at the University of Kent at Canterbury. His publications include *Beyond Class Images* (Routledge, 1979) and, with R. Scase, *Western Capitalism and State Socialism: an Introduction* (Basil Blackwell, 1985). He recently participated in an international study of the cultures of broadcasting in western Europe and is currently working on post-1989 changes in the media in the countries of eastern Europe.

Angela Glasner is Head of the School of Social Science at Oxford Brookes University. Trained in both sociology and computer science, she has worked at Middlesex Polytechnic, the Australian National University and the Canberra College of Advanced Education. Her current research interests include women and new technology, work and the industry, and gender relations in comparative contexts.

Christel Lane is a Lecturer in the Faculty of Social and Political Sciences in the University of Cambridge and is a Fellow of St John's College. Her main research interests are in industrial organisation and change and in employment and training in Europe. She has published *Management and Labour in Europe* (Edward Elgar, 1989) and numerous articles in *Work, Employment and Society*, *The Industrial Relations Journal* and *Sociology*.

Michael Levi is Professor of Criminology at the University of Wales College of Cardiff. His main specialism is in white-collar crime and policing, and his books include *The Phantom Capitalists* (Gower, 1981), *Regulating Fraud* (Routledge, 1988) and *Customer Confidentiality, Money-Laundering and Police–Bank Relations* (Police Foundation, 1991). He is currently carrying out research on money-laundering and cross-border crime generally and on the control of credit-card fraud.

Mike Maguire is a Lecturer in Criminology at the University of Wales College of Cardiff. He has conducted extensive research in the areas of policing, prisons, victims of crime, burglary and grievance procedures. His books include *The Effects of Crime and the Work of Victims' Support Schemes* (Gower, 1987), *Accountability and Prisons* (ed.) (Open University Press, 1988) and *A Study of the Police Complaints System* (HMSO, 1991). He is currently conducting research for the Royal Commission on Criminal Justice and is jointly editing a criminology textbook.

Ian Procter is a Lecturer in Sociology at the University of Warwick. He is the author of *Service Sector Workers in a Manufacturing City* (Gower, 1988). He has taught and researched in the areas of the sociology of labour and labour markets. His current research is on the work and family aspirations of young women.

John Rex is Professor Emeritus at the University of Warwick. He was formerly Professor of Sociology at the University of Durham and the University of Warwick. He was Director of the SSRC (ESRC) Research Unit on Ethnic Relations from 1979 to 1984 and Research Professor of Ethnic Relations at the University of Warwick from 1984 to 1990. He was President of the International Sociological Association's Research Committee on Racial and Ethnic Minorities, and is the author of many books and articles on race relations, including *Race Relations in Sociological Theory* (Weidenfeld & Nicolson 1970) and *Race and Ethnicity* (Open University Press, 1986).

John Simons is Head of the Centre for Population Studies at the London School of Hygiene and Tropical Medicine. A sociologist specialising in the sociology of reproductive behaviour, he has worked on the development of theory and methods of inquiry in this field. He has been particularly interested in cultural interpretations of fertility variation and change in Europe.

Bridget Towers is a Senior Lecturer in Sociology at Kingston Polytechnic, where she teaches health and social policy courses and is a member of the Gender Studies Group. Her research and publications are in the field of the political history of international public health. Her recent work has been on health screening in association with the AIDS and Contemporary History Unit at the London School of Hygiene and Tropical Medicine. She is currently working on the decline of the 'convalescent' sector of health-service provision.

CHAPTER 1

Social Europe: unity and diversity – an introduction

JOE BAILEY

Is Europe a society? Europe is a geographical unit with, increasingly, its own political and economic institutions. But Europe is not just the official 'European Community' or any particular political and administrative alliance. Within the obvious geographical limits, it is defined by our purposes. Specialist legal definitions and everyday, common-sense meanings are plainly different. It is what some writers would now call a 'discourse object' – something which is contested by interested parties all the time – and lately the meaning of 'Europe' has seemed to change almost weekly as the contest has been heated up by dramatic events.

Europe is now a major object of popular concern – both of anxiety and enthusiasm – in our everyday lives. It is the focus of enormous media coverage, of constitutional discussions, of political warnings, of ideological encouragement, of cultural fears. It is plainly the object of sociological investigation (and this is certainly one sense of the word 'society') in social surveys and research reports. But is it a social, as distinct from a political or economic, unit? Is it experiencing the same forces of social change, similar social structures, institutions and organisations?

Is Europe *becoming* a society? The current concern about Europe and our place within it may be an important marker of a profound social change taking place. The priority given to the political and economic dimensions of the European community should not deter us from examining the sociological significance of what is now happening. We should try to locate these dramatic shifts of social organisation in Europe within our understanding of social change generally within the world.

Sociology has been concerned with social change above all else. It came into existence as a discipline to make sense of the dramatic social changes taking place in Europe in the eighteenth and nineteenth centuries. Sociology's current relevance and importance is that it tries to understand the very profound shifts now taking place in social arrangements. It is somewhat odd, then, that it has neglected Europe as a focus for these concerns. Very little has been written, in English, by sociologists specifically about Europe as a unit over the last two decades (for example, Archer and Giner 1971; Giner and Archer

1978) and since the Second World War, at least, the significant comparator for British sociologists has been the United States, rather than Europe. The definition of Britain as part of Europe, at least in formal, legal terms, over this same period has pushed other social sciences – especially economics and political science – into an eager attention to Europe as a major focus for their work. The collapse of communism in central and eastern Europe has forced these same social scientists to concentrate on what Europe might mean in territorial and legal terms.

The need of the British to use the United States as their reference point is still there, of course: the power of the English-language community as a social entity *per se* should not be underestimated and is unlikely to decline. Europe, however, (whatever geographical limit is chosen) is now a rival for attention – but apparently less so for sociologists than other social scientists. Why? I will provide some reasons later in this introduction.

This book displays the very high quality and useful work that British sociologists are now doing on Europe. As the debate about how European countries are to be united begins to shift from the preoccupations with the single unified market coming into existence after 1992 (that is, a debate dominated by economics) to arguments about inter-governmental relations and forms of federalism (a debate about politics), the social and sociological structures which underpin economics and politics are becoming an obvious, attention-demanding issue. Politicians and the general public can see that both incompatibilities and connections between national organisations depend upon the 'fit', or the lack of it, between social structures and institutions in different European countries. This book shows how specifically sociological comparison is essential if we are to make sense of the social changes experienced in all European societies as they come to grips with the idea that they are connected with one another in a new way. All the work done by political scientists, economists, historians and social geographers depends upon assumptions about how social institutions and organisations work and how people continue to behave predictably (or not) within them; in other words, upon a sociology. This should not need saying, it is so obvious, but, plainly, it does as the lack of reference to sociological work by other social scientists attests.

Sociology and Europe

What do we mean when we speak of Europe? How is the object 'Europe' constructed in various 'discourses'? For some time now Europe as an economic entity and as a market has seemed dominant, with Europe defined as a set of political problems increasing in urgency. The social is seen as somehow attached and residual (Teague

1989). In fact the social – 'the social area' or 'social dimension' in EC-speak (Commission of the European Community 1988) – has been remarkably restricted to matters contained in the European Social Charter (1981); health and safety, equal opportunities and training – all treated as work-related issues.

This is certainly not a mistaken view of the social but it is a narrow official understanding of it. It is a consequence of the dominance in political debate of economic issues following the priority given to economic integration as the foundation of a genuine European community. The political and military dimensions of unity follow close behind the economic. Issues of cultural and historical difference are treated as separate and parallel matters, but again with little reference made, beyond the journalistic, to their sociological formation. The sociological nature of the different societies in Europe and the possibility of a European society itself is marginalised in all these debates.

This is another way of saying that a sociology of (or for) Europe has a very low salience in the current political discussions, which are likely to have profound effects on all our lives. The hierarchy of these discussions – economic-political-journalistic-cultural-sociological in sequence – is understandable. The dominance of markets and elections as the shapers of discourse and policy is undeniable. But all these issues are, of course, also sociological. It is impossible to talk of matters like the deregulation of European markets, taxation policy, federalism, common military organisation and nationalism without a sociological understanding of the formation and organisation of the societies which will face changes in all these areas. It is not that there is a shortage of data or thought. Whole sections of the quality press are devoted to Europe: publications are increasing rapidly in economics, political science and general cultural commentary. If anything, there is an overload of attention to Europe; but there is a distinct lack of fundamental understanding of Europe as a society – actual or becoming.

Political issues are made: they are not self-evident. That is to say that information and argument are deliberately selected by those engaged in publicising an issue in the public arena. In the (re)construction of the meaning of Europe sociology, as a primary form of both description and analysis, must have a much more prominent part. If this contribution is not explicitly demanded by the movers and shakers of European social change, the demand for it will break through by force of events. The sheer instability of our social institutions, as many of the chapters in this book show, will require a sociological understanding of them as unforeseen problems if we do not now begin to consider them as issues which can be influenced, shaped and, indeed, coped with.

Social change and comparison

The current moment is extremely significant. The sense that our societies are going through changes which are rapid, unpredicted, unsettling and potentially both dangerous and, perhaps, benevolent is almost palpable. The incantatory quality of '1992' as some sort of *annus mirabilis* in the history of western Europe is contrived and artificial but revealing none the less. We are all made aware of dramatic *events* happening – political revolutions and counter-revolutions, treaties and agreements, new laws, even physical constructions like the Channel tunnel. The understanding of social change is the analysis of the social *processes* behind these events and which gives them significance. We are unavoidably interested in the future (Bailey 1988, ch. 6) even if it appears to us just as a series of events. Our current uneasiness about what might or could happen in Europe (and indeed in the interconnected world as a whole) is informed by 'patterns' of social change. These patterns, attempts to see order within apparent confusion, are what many sociologists have been busy trying to delineate since the subject was formalised. Such patterns are essential to our sense that the world is comprehensible and not formless or arbitrary.

Western Europe has been seen as a set of advanced industrial societies which were the first industrialisers and modernisers (Giddens 1981a). Eighteenth- and nineteenth-century Europe gave birth to both industrial society and to the discipline of sociology which self-consciously examined it. Little wonder that Europe has been the test-bed of theories of social change – change seen as inevitable evolutionary 'progress' with some societies in the vanguard; change seen as the diffusion of culture or technology via military conquest or trade; change seen as repetitive cycles or as journeys to an inevitable Utopia or disaster. A whole range of theories (or perhaps 'patterns' would be better) have been used to account for the apparent similarities in direction taken by different nation states, and by extension, to explain their variations (Kumar 1978).

The most influential of the modern theories have stressed technological determinism in one way or another. Theories of 'convergence' stated that there was a logic of industrialism which forced political and cultural practices into line with it and which could not be stopped. Values, culture, political organisation and daily behaviour itself tended to develop, albeit by different routes, to the same final social formation required by industrial production (Dunning and Hopper 1966). Theories of 'post-industrialism' (Bell 1973) attempted to describe industrial societies as inevitably shifting to knowledge-based, service economies having solved the problems of production which inspired industrialism. In both cases the machine, whether the steam engine or the micro-processor, was privileged in understanding the source and sequence of change. Technology was seen as the prime mover of societies.

These were patterns which were useful as illuminating devices but which provoked considerable debate about their methodological adequacy and logical basis. They were without doubt creators of a sense of order within historical confusion, of a sequence of events elevated into a process which could be seen to operate across what is now western Europe and beyond. An understanding of social change is almost a psychological requirement. These two approaches with their strong message of social progress and optimism functioned to allow us to deal with the future of our societies as not only connected by trade and treaty but as, essentially, playing out together a benign logic of social development, dependent upon a shared technology.

The utility of these particular patterns has now declined. It is hard now to point to a theory of social change which commands majority support in our culture as a whole, let alone among professional sociologists. The retreat from grandiose prescriptions about the future has led to a more cautious approach to long-term change. The chapters in this book display a careful attempt to map sequence and direction in social changes taking place but do not attempt grand theories of social change itself. Several show that technology is by no means a clear magnet for change and is an unreliable basis for understanding its patterns. Towers' chapter on health and illness discusses the very uncertain effects of development in medical technology on health policy and the conflicts over its place in health improvement. Lane's discussion of 'industrial orders' demonstrates the dominance of institutional and political features in shaping the use of manufacturing technology in industrial competition between societies. Glasner shows that the new technology has not remedied persistent gender imbalances between men's and women's work.

The need to understand social change as a holistic pattern, however, is still there, but, as Archer commented some years ago, the best starting point is a historical examination of patternings rather than the dogmatic imposition of abstract theoretical models (Archer 1978). One of the most impressive current attempts to analyse the developmental trends and institutional features of modern industrial societies has been that in one section of the work of Anthony Giddens (1981b; 1985). For Giddens 'modernity', a new social order, emerged in Europe, characterised by four institutional dimensions: capitalism, industrialism, surveillance (the state control of information and monitoring) and military power. These dimensions are basic and irreducible to one another; that is, they are the fundamental social formations which we need to describe in order to understand how a particular society developed and to compare this development with other societies. They are a vocabulary for understanding social change and a description of the 'building blocks'. They are not an abstract theoretical model but rather a distillation and generalisation of actual historical patternings.

What is significant about Giddens' work – and there are other similar attempts; for instance, by Lash and Urry (1987) – is that it is a quintessentially sociological approach to understanding the similarities and differences between societies. It is directed not at the superficial appearance of economic and political behaviour, at the fluctuating and the transitory, at events, but tries to lay out the very basic forms of social organisation through which change or stability in different societies occurs. It is the language of the patterning of history. This is a significant part of sociology's job.

Similarities and differences

The intention of this book is to flesh out the significance of these categories, or similar ones, and to contribute to the empirical understanding of European social structure now, but against this categorial background. The chapters here describe and analyse particular social changes, not social change itself. Sociology makes sense of the world by linking levels of description and analysis in this way, and perhaps more coherently than any other social science.

If we wish genuinely to compare how, say, social control is accomplished, as Levi and Maguire do, or religious belief and belonging are still significant, as Davie does, in the countries of western Europe, we will arrive at a description of likenesses and differences. If we wish to go further and make sense of these similarities and divergences, we will need an account of the basic social formations which we can observe varying or converging and into which health and social control fit. This is what a comparative sociology of social change can do. It provides a template to make events and information understandable when seen together. The cost of not doing this is that we retreat into a naïve evolutionism whereby societies are treated as more or less advanced along some preordained path of development which is, somehow, naturally 'given' and visible through the data themselves. Recent writers on social change with an obvious political axe to grind have proposed exactly such a forshortened and self-serving account of change in eastern Europe (Fukuyama 1990), describing the 'end of history' and certainly the foreclosing of intelligent politics. There are plainly homogenising tendencies at work in Europe, such as the 'harmonisation' of legislation in the EC, and in the world as a whole, such as the 'globalisation' of the capitalist economy (Crompton *et al.* 1990). But a comparative sociology of Europe displays the resistance of national differences to this process. It locates these variable resistances within social forms which can be readily understood in the way that, for instance, Giddens suggests.

What we see in the descriptions of Europe in this book are the coexistence of pressures for both uniformity and difference, convergence and divergence, continuities and ruptures, connection and separation. This sounds rather rhetorical but it is, as the chapters show, real. The power of cultural and historical experience to resist new demands for control coming from 'outside' and the attempts by international agencies to overcome these resistances is the story of the European Community. National identities expressed in culture, language and ideology, seen through the prism of 'historical' memory and articulated through political organisations are powerful, and in eastern Europe, increasingly dominant. The pressures for interlinkage, commonality and even community between sovereign countries are extremely strong now in western Europe. The pressure for separation and the pressure for joining together meet in different geopolitical contexts. In western Europe national identity is resistant but not dominant and is probably declining. Here the running is made by the demand to unify. In the East the demand to separate has priority. In a Europe which will unite east and west it is unclear whether these opposed pressures will take the form simply of a dilemma (opposing demands to be absorbed by social institutions) or more seriously of a contradiction (a tendency to destroy the preconditions upon which unity depends) (Offe 1975).

Without doubt, making sense of the differences between countries and what they simultaneously share as advanced industrial societies is the most difficult and most important task of any social science with Europe as its focus. There remains a considerable problem for sociologists in clarifying how significant apparent differences really are. Are they different configurations of the same dimensions, as some writers have suggested is the case, with apparently different national values (Harding *et al.* 1986)? Davis' chapter on social stratification describes the variable effects upon social class of different combinations of the same two structuring dimensions of the market and the welfare state.

Is it possible to consider divergence within uniformity? These are analytical issues which can only make sense if informed by careful comparative analyses of relevant data, and this latter task is what the writers in this volume have attempted.

So this collection should be seen as fitting into a more extensive task which remains to be addressed. This first part is the bringing together of sociologically informed comparisons of the performance of particular social organisations in the face of clear changes in the underlying social structure. As Lynne Chisholm says at the beginning of her chapter on education and training, we can see coherence 'if we regard European societies as responding to sets of common problems with a range of different solutions, which themselves are structured by divergent forms of social and cultural organisation and relationships'. The next step will be to construct a general pattern.

Lest this sound too high-faluting it is important to stress the basic
practicality of the descriptions in this book. They perform a number
of very useful and pertinent services. First, they not only show *autres
pays, autres moeurs* but also clarify Britain's own position and
condition compared with those of its neighbours. Too often we are
vague about how, say, education or industrial relations are actually
conducted in Europe and we believe the facile generalisations of our
politicians, or, more usually, their lack of any systematic reference to
fellow Europeans' experience for fear of inspiring a sense of relative
deprivation in their audience. Selective ignorance of this kind is
exceptionally valuable at this juncture. Here Chisholm and Procter,
for example, have laid out in a conceptually clear way European
maps of these institutions.

Second, the chapters provide information to allow us to see newly
shared problems; Levi and Maguire set out the new problems of
crime control as physical borders become less significant; Rex does
the same sort of thing for immigration. The major social problems
emerging because of the extension of European social identity are, as
one writer describes them, 'peripheralisation', 'marginalisation' and
'dualisation' (Vadamme 1985). Significant variations in unemployment, citizenship rights, poverty and homelessness across the European continent are seen as leading to 'social dumping' (Betters 1989).
In turn, this will inspire social policy on a European scale hitherto
only hinted at. These chapters provide some of the sociological basis
for understanding the emerging policy debate.

Third, the overall effect of the book is to counterpoint the previous
concentration on the United States characteristic and traditional in
British sociology. This has been declining a little in recent years as
other parts of the world, especially Japan, have claimed our attention.
But the bulk of comparative material used is about America, and
over the last decade it is North American experience that has had the
most influence on Britain's national policy formation – ironically,
during the period of the greatest expansion in Europeanisation
elsewhere in the continent. A parody of Britain's recent stance on
European economic and political union might be that British politicians have championed deregulation and neo-liberalism over the
dirigisme, social cooperation and consensus more common among
our fellow Europeans and that our mentor in these views has been
the United States. Clear descriptions of the variety of west European
experience could not come at a more useful time.

Organisation of the book

The first section of the book is concerned with some of the basic
social structures which are the foundations of advanced industrial
societies. Demography, social stratification, industry, gender and race

are significant formative dimensions of social change. Social structures are enduring, deeply-laid social formations with a wide geographical reach. The social structures chosen in Part I are profound bases of European social order and social change. The fertility and age structure of the population, the ethnic and gender formations of that population, the patterning of inequality through the market and the state and the control and performance of industry are all quite fundamental to our understanding of any modern societies. These are the structuring forces at work now, however we wish to label them. Naturally they do not exhaust our categories of social structures, and issues of state formation could well merit separate treatment in a further volume (for example, Davis and Scase 1985). All the chapters deal with shifts and resistances in the operation of these structures and the potential meshing or friction as the separate national societies interact within a wider Europe.

Part II is concerned with the social institutions through which these structures operate as ongoing sets of social practices. Six categories of social institutions are described and analysed here; those dealing with education and training, trade unions, crime and policing, health, religion and leisure. Social institutions are standardised, rule-bound organisations affecting large numbers of people. This distinction between the levels of structures and institutions is intended to be of heuristic use; that is, as a useful aid to analysis in approaching social changes. The idea that structures give rise to institutions which in turn exist as organisations is simply a mapping device which allows us to approach the wide variety of social practices and behaviours in Europe and to begin the task of comparison.

The aim of the selection of institutions in Part II, as in Part I, is not to provide an exhaustive overview but to display some of the most obvious (and interesting) social organisations in our lives in a European context. It could obviously be extended.

Themes and continuities

It is important to understand the common threads running through the various chapters. The authors addressing their own specialisms from within the data available to them display issues which are the significant substantive topics for future analysis. They also exemplify some common methodological and theoretical matters and shared issues of values.

Common substantive issues

The most overwhelming obvious common preoccupation under this heading is the relationship between the diversity of national and regional experience and the pressure for uniformity which was mentioned earlier. Every contributor sets their work within this context because it unavoidably shapes the very appearance of all social changes. Thus in Simons' chapter on demography the shared forces of fertility and mortality decline meet different policy responses. In Lane's chapter on industry the deep roots of the distinctively different industrial structures in France, Germany and Britain resist the common pressures of international competition. In Rex's chapter the common issue of the relation between immigrant communities and their 'host' states is met in dramatically diverse ways depending upon the historical and political character of different societies. And so on. Every chapter addresses this issue of the widespread sharedness of social forces and the enduring distinctiveness of national responses.

An attached common issue is the power of the restructuring forces and the impossibility of separate societies avoiding them. The changes in market and welfare-state activity, described by Davis, and which have forced a massive change in social-class structure in western European societies are deeply laid. The shift to primary health care and the rising official level of health goals in the context of the need to ration resources is faced in all European societies, east and west, as Towers describes. The 'embeddedness' of national legal and political systems plainly resists this homogenising pressure, and successfully, as many authors show. Can this level of diversity and cultural distinctiveness continue? The inheritance of the past is massively resistant, but is it determinant? Procter, in his chapter on trade unions, points out that historical distinctiveness may, in fact, be renewed through the interaction of transforming forces from the wider world and strong national traditions.

A third common thread is the existence of 'groupings' of societies within Europe. It is possible to see historical 'blocs', as Davie describes the predominantly or officially Catholic and Protestant countries or those with other shared religious traditions. This idea of common cultural backgrounds is reinforced by Clark's chapter on the distinctive experiences of leisure in festivals and alcohol use still responding to the enduring Catholic/Protestant and urban/rural divides. But other groupings are also significant. The relatively rich countries of Germany and Denmark compare revealingly with the poor countries in the EC of Portugal, Spain and Ireland in the distribution of welfare. This has effects on social class formation and experience, as Davis shows. Legal traditions and policy priorities divide societies in respect of their criminal justice policies, and this could isolate some societies, as Levi and Maguire show. The point here is that it is possible to see Europe not as a collection of disparate societies but as groups of states with important shared features which will become very important, enabling or resisting potentials in the face of demands to unify or harmonise.

A fourth shared feature is the issue of what we might call 'mediation'. In the face of powerful external forces – for instance, for 'harmonisation' – adoption, adaptation and transformation, as Clark calls them, may be both the strategies and outcomes of countries' responses. That is, that national institutions and practices convert these pressures into forms which can be absorbed. Chisholm, in her discussion of education and training, shows how the classifying and preparing functions of educational institutions intervene differently in different societies in the transitions of youth into employed adults. National policy is made in a context of existing organisations and practices which interpret and bend outside demands. There are national characteristics in the definition of illness and treatment, as Towers remarks, which will condition what might otherwise be taken as perfectly unequivocal demands for 'health'. Her inclusion of the thirty-eight targets of the European Region of the World Health Organisation is an example of a pan-European agreement which will function only in a locally adapted way.

A final shared feature is the address to the role of the official Europeanising organisations, such as the EC, and the future. Sociologists are engaged in speculating about the likelihood of particular formally legislated standards becoming adopted in practice. Glasner provides a particularly convincing example of strong EC demands being made about the treatment of women in all institutions of society, demands backed up by a variety of vigorous national women's movements. But in practice this legislation is very slow indeed to have substantial practical effects. Levi and Maguire focus on cross-Europe policing and criminal justice policies as trans-European crime grows more obvious and serious. Both they and Rex note that one of the more vigorous (rather sinisterly) cooperative attempts to legislate change across Europe is concerned with border control and its implications for the regulation of immigration as well as illicit goods.

Prediction is not the function of this book. But all the contributors are concerned with the directions of social changes in their areas. Sociologists necessarily deal with the future in a conditional way by laying out the trajectories of change, the conditions and consequences of particular shifts and, most important of all, the data which help us to guard against the ignorant optimism or doom-saying which characterises so much popular discussion of the future of Europe.

Common issues of theory and method

This book is concerned with description and analysis, and this raises issues of both data and of analytical tools and terms. All chapters are descriptive and use data on a European scale. There are significant problems in the collection of regular, reliable and comparable data which make sociological comparison very difficult compared with, for instance, the description of economic performance, as Davis notes. Continuous and detailed monitoring is difficult with, at best, usually two or three societies being reliably comparable. Many of the chapters focus on a limited set of societies and aim for a deeper penetration of issues on a limited scale. So Lane focuses on Germany, France and Britain in the discussion of industry; Procter on Germany, Italy and France in describing trade unions. Elsewhere Eurostat data allow some broad-brush comparisons between EC countries, as in the case of Davis' report on social stratification or Rex's on race and ethnicity. The most extensive data – for instance, that used in Simons' chapter on demography – does allow reliable and ambitious generalisations to be made. But overall the limitations of the data are the most serious difficulty for sociologists working on Europe.

Sociology is an empirical discipline. The purpose of this book is to make sociological sense of the information. Other kinds of information than reliable time series of aggregate behaviour are, of course, highly relevant, and the sections by Davie and Clark make use of qualitative as well as quantitative information. But comparative research is hampered by the current paucity of hard data. What is presented here will be a useful data guide for students to use and extend where possible.

All the chapters are also analytical. Some emphasise analysis like Chisholm's account of education and training, which is a sophisticated account of the changing and problematic *functions* of these institutions. Davis also is concerned with conceptualising social mobility and social 'closure', among other issues, as outcomes of the operation of various levels of institution from the state and the market to the experience of the local workplace. Some chapters, by contrast, are extensive and detailed descriptions first, followed by analytical speculation, such as Simons' on the reasons for fertility changes and Procter's on the likely variability of trade-union response to market liberalisation. Yet other sections make clear that just *how* the relevant topic is to be defined, and hence just what *are* relevant data is itself an analytical issue which must be engaged immediately, testing out the available information against concept formation. Davie on religion and Towers on health both do this. Indeed, the whole volume is predicated on some sort of interplay between conceptual speculation and the revelations of data. As I said at the beginning of this introduction, the very nature of 'Europe' is a contested matter: the contest is as much conceptual as factual.

The tools of analysis of sociology are essentially terms which make sense of general patterns of data which would otherwise remain opaque. They are ideas or concepts which clarify the emergence of a pattern from a mass of apparently unconnected facts. The terms used by the contributors are conventional within the discipline of sociology: they are the terms used to describe the various parts of social structures, organisations and behaviours.

It is important to note the variety of what the separate authors have done. Within the remit of a 'social Europe' the contributors illustrate a range of approaches characteristic of British empirical sociology.

Further, no limiting geographical definition of Europe has been imposed beyond an intention to concentrate on 'western' Europe, though several chapters – for instance, those on education and training and on health – show how useful it is to see the hitherto communist societies in east and central Europe as both comparable and connected to EC and Nordic states. A flexible (and thus again contested) geographical definition of Europe is a feature of all social-science work which is aiming to come to grips with it as a social entity. Accepting official definitions of its unity can be useful for a particular purpose. But the nature of Europe is in the process of being decided as we write.

A systematic survey which asks the same questions of the same set of societies is certainly sociologically valid and is occasionally done (for example, Harding *et al.* 1986), but depends upon the sociological imagination being first applied to the issues – which is what is done here. These chapters are part of the effort to draft the pertinent questions to ask for the next stage of sociological inquiry.

Finally what all these chapters share is a respect for the diversity of values and practices which they describe and analyse. There is sometimes a nearly hidden sub-text in the official creation of a 'new' Europe that pluralism and the tolerance and even celebration of variety in social life is unworthy. This book illustrates the fascinating variation of social arrangements upon which the social science disciplines are predicated.

References

Archer, M. S. (1978) 'The theoretical and the comparative analysis of social structure', in S. Giner and M. S. Archer (eds) *Contemporary Europe: Social Structures and Cultural Patterns*, London: Routledge & Kegan Paul.

——and Giner, S. (eds) (1971) *Contemporary Europe: Class, Status and Power*, London: Routledge & Kegan Paul.

Bailey, J. (1988) *Pessimism* London: Routledge.

Bell, D. (1973) *The Coming of Post-Industrial Society*, New York: Basic Books.

Betters, L. (ed.) (1989) *The Future of European Social Policy*, Deventer (Netherlands): Kluwer.

Commission of the European Community (1988) *Social Europe: the Social Dimension of the Internal Market*, Luxembourg: Directorate General for Employment, Social Affairs and Education.

Crompton, R., Hantrais, L. and Walters, P. (1990) 'Gender relations and employment' *British Journal of Sociology*, 41 (3): 329–49 (issue on 'Britain in Europe').

Davis, H. and Scase, R. (1985) *Western Capitalism and State Socialism*, Oxford: Basil Blackwell.

Dunning, E. and Hopper, E. (1966) 'Industrialization and the problem of convergence: a critical note', *Sociological Review* 14 (2): 163–86.

14   *Social Europe*

European Social Charter (1981) Council of Europe Directorate of Press and Information, Strasbourg.

Fukuyama, F. (1990) 'Are we at the end of history?' *Fortune*, 15 Jan. 1990.

Giddens, A. (1981a) *The Class Structure of the Advanced Societies*, London: Hutchinson.

——(1981b) *A Contemporary Critique of Historical Materialism*, London: Macmillan.

——(1985) *The Nation State and Violence*, Cambridge: Polity Press.

Giner, S. and Archer, M. S. (1978) *Contemporary Europe: Social Structures and Cultural Patterns*, London: Routledge & Kegan Paul.

Harding, S. Phillips, D. with Fogarty, M. (1986) *Contrasting Values in Western Europe*, London: Macmillan.

Kumar, K. (1978) *Prophecy and Progress: the Sociology of Industrial and Post-industrial Society*, Harmondsworth: Penguin.

Lash, S. and Urry, J. (1987) *The End of Organised Capitalism*, Cambridge: Polity Press.

Offe, C. (1975) 'Legitimacy versus efficiency', in L. Lindberg, R. Alford, C. Crouch and C. Offe (eds) *Stress and Contradiction in Modern Capitalism*, Lexington, Ma: D. C. Heath & Co.

Teague, P. (1989) *The European Community: the Social Dimension*, London: Kogan Page.

Vandamme, J. (ed.) (1985) *New Dimensions in European Social Policy*, London: Croom Helm.

PART ONE

Changing Social Structures

CHAPTER 2

Social stratification in Europe

HOWARD H. DAVIS

The division of societies into social strata defined by differences of wealth, income, power and prestige is one of the most complex and fascinating problems of social and political analysis. Structured social inequalities are the key to answering the fundamental question: what kind of society is this and how is it changing? From a European perspective, the question concerns both the differences between countries and the structural features which they have in common. Are some more equal than others? Do they share similar characteristics because they have market economies? Do differences arise when they pursue alternative social policies? This chapter addresses these topics through a broadly comparative approach, beginning with a discussion of some of the concepts which are necessary for the analysis of social stratification. It then considers the patterns in a range of European countries using available economic and social data to show how these patterns are changing. Finally, the chapter considers some interpretations of major social divisions.

'Stratification' is a metaphorical term which refers to the hierarchical ordering of social relationships. It implies that social similarities and differences are systematic, not random, and that members of each social stratum have important characteristics in common such as occupation, income, life chances and culture. These social characteristics may be reflected in a sense of common identity, but this is not always the case. In European sociology (though not, significantly, in its North American counterpart) the usual way to describe large-scale social groupings has been through the vocabulary of 'class' and class analysis. This is because the most influential theories – namely, those of Karl Marx and Max Weber – emphasised the economic foundations of social stratification and the essential connection between industrial capitalism and social order since the Industrial Revolution. Marx's theory of class conflict was based on the assumption that the nineteenth-century owners and controllers of capital were segregated from the rest of the population, who lacked property and depended on selling their labour for an income. This fundamental difference was reflected in a class structure sharply divided between the bourgeoisie and proletariat, whose divergent interests created a high propensity for conflict. Although Marx's expectation that these conflicts would intensify and lead to proletarian revolution have seemed less and less relevant in western Europe as economic growth has continued and as political systems have matured, this has not diminished the value of certain aspects of his theory. The key assumption that organisation for capital accumulation through industrial market production shapes the social structure of modern societies is still applicable and useful in explaining the social condition, consciousness and culture of different groups. However, Marxist theories have rightly been criticised for overestimating material conditions, the system of property relations and the division of labour, and for underestimating the importance of social boundaries which derive from other characteristics such as ethnic origin, religion and gender. Any contemporary study of stratification has to take account of these other lines of cleavage which do not always have their origins in the economic circumstances of a particular group. Nationalism, ethnic conflicts and new social movements seem to have replaced class antagonism and workers' struggles at the centre of the political stage, creating a need for more complex models of social stratification. Some of these issues are treated at greater length elsewhere in this volume (see Chapters 6 and 8).

While Marxist and Weberian approaches to stratification identified the working class as a key actor in the shaping of industrial societies, and both were concerned with the socialist project for the transformation of society, Weber was also concerned with the social distinctions arising from status or prestige. Although he assumed that class relations were fundamental in industrial societies and that they were the main determinant of life chances through inequalities of access to the market, he also acknowledged that some distinctions arise because certain groups can impose values through religion, education, ideology, or customs which may exclude other groups or maintain a monopoly on social opportunities. In the twentieth century, the state has become the main alternative source of social structuration in European societies because of its powers to regulate and modify the market. The extent to which the formal equality of participants in the labour market or the equality of rights of citizens may be subverted by the status order or the mechanisms of the welfare state is particularly important for stratification analysis today, as the economic class system of the industrial societies is becoming more diffuse and differentiated.

Armed with a concept of stratification which includes economic, social and cultural aspects, it is necessary to specify the measures of social difference which will allow us to define the various social strata. First, however, it would be quite wrong to assume that boundary lines can be drawn like those on a map. On the one hand, the class boundaries of modern societies are highly permeable and allow for significant amounts of mobility between social groups. On the other, it is not possible to allocate all individuals to a particular class or status group because individuals are agents who actively combine characteristics like ethnicity or occupation or political allegiances in different degrees, which may 'contradict' the facts of their background. What the analysis of stratification involves is the identification of the shared economic and social circumstances which become a basis for action by groups. Not all class situations lead to collective action but they do have a tendency to generate *similar* reactions, even though it is possible for individuals to pursue their interests in widely different ways. The complex nature of stratification therefore creates the need for a number of measures which will allow social divisions to be compared from different angles. None of the measures suggested here is designed solely for the purpose of comparing stratification systems, and most data are collected for other purposes.[1] However, for general comparison they have to serve.

Three types of indicator are commonly used, which reflect the economic, social and cultural aspects of social differentiation. The first set of measures relates to market conditions and includes ownership and non-ownership of property and other forms of wealth, occupation or position in relation to the labour market including those who are not in employment, and income. The second type of indicator is related to consumption, and includes housing tenure and other forms of private and collective consumption such as education, health and the means of private consumption. The third set of measures tries to identify the variations in culture and consciousness through opinion and attitude surveys and establish the similarities and differences between strata in their subjective aspect.

The distribution of income, wealth and poverty

The way in which economic resources are allocated throughout society in the form of wealth and income is a basic indicator of the extent of social as well as economic inequality. A person's income, whether from earnings or from their ownership of capital, is almost invariably reflected in their social position, life-style, status and even state of health. Income is therefore a useful starting point for comparison between countries because it is easy to measure in principle, and is one of the forms of economic data which are collected continuously in the European countries. However, income is a continuous variable and it does not describe patterns of stratification as such, only the general range of income inequalities. It is in fact derived from several different sources, which can have important implications for social stratification. The first source of income is wages, salaries and earnings from self-employment. Working for an employer and working on one's own account represent two distinct types of employment relationship which may be reflected in social conditions, opportunities and consciousness. The issue of whether the 'petty bourgeoisie' (the stratum of small business owners and self-employed) has greater affinity with the bourgeoisie or the working class from which it springs has been a perennial issue in stratification analysis.

Income may also derive from ownership of assets such as property, land or shares. The rents, dividends and interest which accrue to the owners of these assets vary enormously between large-scale institutions and small private investors. Again, the distribution of these forms of wealth and income has profound implications for social and political analysis. Did the privatisation programme of the Thatcher government create a new kind of mass participation in the system of wealth creation, or did the increase in small-scale share ownership merely disguise a shift in economic power from state monopolies to private monopolies?

The third form of income, known as transfer income, is state pensions and state benefits of various kinds. This accounts for a large and rising proportion of total income because of the changing age profile of the European population (an increasing proportion above retirement age) and continuing poverty, unemployment and the need for social security and income support. The proportion of income accounted for by these transfer payments is a useful indicator of the boundaries between certain social strata.

Studies spanning several decades have shown that there is a very skewed pattern of income distribution in the European countries, which, for most of the postwar period, has been moving slowly towards more equality. However, the late 1970s saw a reversal in this trend in the United Kingdom and probably in many other European countries as a result of economic recession and the rightward shift in economic policy. In order to make comparisons across time and between countries, the total income at a particular time is divided up into the 'shares' which various sections of the population receive. Thus, in the 1960s, the share of the top 20 per cent was 44.2 per cent of total income in the United Kingdom, 52.9 per cent in West Germany and 53.7 per cent in France. The proportion in Sweden was 44.0 per cent (Atkinson 1983: 26). A decade later, the same differences could be found between these countries, but at somewhat lower levels. It appears then that Britain occupied an intermediate position in terms of income inequality. It still has a lower degree of inequality than France but a greater degree of inequality than Sweden. This is illustrated by the measure known as the Gini Coefficient, which summarises the overall distribution of income and wealth in a society by calculating a value between 0 (which represents complete equality) and 1 (which represents total concentration). This is a simple, rather crude index but it has been used as a guide by many authors, including Lane and Ersson (1987). Their analysis is based on four separate sources of data on the distribution of household and individual income, and it leads them to the estimates and ranking shown in Table 2.1.

These results for the early 1970s have a similar pattern of variation

Table 2.1 **Income inequality in European countries**

	Gini index	*Rank order*
Austria	0.369	8
Belgium	0.340	4
Denmark	0.380	9
FR Germany	0.383	10
France	0.417	13
Greece	0.460	14
Ireland	0.361	7
Italy	0.398	11
Netherlands	0.354	5
Norway	0.307	2
Spain	0.355	6
Sweden	0.302	1
Switzerland	0.401	12
UK	0.318	3

Source: From J-E. Lane and S.O. Ersson (1987: 83)

to those mentioned above, with the expected decline from the 1950s and 60s. In general terms, the countries of southern Europe have the most pronounced inequalities and the Scandinavian countries have the most even distribution. An interesting feature is that the larger countries with similar levels of economic development – namely, France, Germany and the United Kingdom – vary quite significantly. France has one of the highest levels of inequality and the United Kingdom one of the lowest; West Germany occupies an intermediate position.

According to these general comparisions, the postwar trend has therefore been in the direction of more equality, but a closer inspection of the effects of taxation and welfare shows that the benefits of redistribution have not been evenly spread throughout society. The Royal Commission on the Distribution of Income and Wealth examined this issue closely in the United Kingdom and found that, although the wealth of the top 1 per cent was much reduced by the 1970s, much of the redistribution occurred within the top 10 per cent. The intermediate groups have received a larger share of the redistribution than the poorest, whose position, according to a comparative study by Lawson and George (1980), improved only very slightly or not at all in the period up to 1980. In 1985 the top 1 per cent still owned 20 per cent of net personal wealth and the top 10 per cent more than half. The overall effect of economic growth on social inequality is, to use a familiar illustration, like the effect of a marching column: the column advances and the last rank (or most of it, at least) eventually passes the point which was reached by the vanguard some time before. The distance between the front and the rear does not change as the column moves forward. Although the rich have stayed rich or become richer, the position of the poor remains

Table 2.2   **Poverty in the EC, 1985, defined as households or persons receiving 50 per cent or less of the respective national average**

	% households	% persons
Belgium	6.3	7.1
Denmark	8.0	7.9
FR Germany	10.3	10.5
Greece	20.5	21.5
Spain	20.3	20.9
France	18.0	19.1
Ireland	18.5	18.4
Italy	12.0	14.1
Netherlands	6.9	9.6
Portugal	31.4	32.4
UK	14.1	14.6
EUR 12	14.1	15.5

Source: Eurostat, 1990; figures for Luxembourg unavailable

relatively unchanged. However they are defined, the poor continue to make up a large proportion of the European population, largely because of low incomes and unemployment. The 'poverty line' according to an EC definition, is an income half or less than half of the country's national average income per person. The countries which have levels of poverty above 15 per cent of the population include Portugal, Greece, Spain and Ireland, which are on the periphery of Europe and less developed. The lowest levels of poverty (below 10 per cent) are in Belgium, Denmark and the Netherlands. Italy and the United Kingdom are near average in the intermediate category. The United Kingdom has been moving in the direction of the 'peripheral' countries with a high level of poverty (18 per cent in 1990) through a combination of economic recession and rigid government policies on transfer payments.

Consumption

The rise of the 'welfare state' in the European countries in the postwar decades brought about a large-scale shift from private to collective forms of provision in housing, education, wealth and other key aspects of consumption. The scale of social expenditure is represented by Table 2.3, which shows a pattern of steady increase in all countries.

Although the growth in state expenditure has been universal, the effects of this on stratification have been more complex. Esping-Andersen (1990) has described the varieties of 'welfare capitalism' which affect the stratification system in different ways, and not always with egalitarian results. He concludes that 'the welfare system is not

Table 2.3   **Total social protection expenditure as a percentage of GDP, 1981**

	1970	1981	1983
Belgium	17.7	28.4	30.8
Denmark	19.6	30.1	30.2
FR Germany	21.5	29.4	29.1
France	19.2	27.5	28.5
Ireland	13.2	21.3	23.9
Italy	17.4	21.7	23.7
Netherlands	20.8	31.4	33.7
UK	15.9	23.5	24.1

Source: Complied using social indicators for the European Community: selected series, Eurostat (1984); Eurostat Review 1977–86, table 3.5 (1988)

just a mechanism that intervenes in, and possibly corrects, the structure of inequality; it is, in its own right, a system of stratification' (p. 23).

The first variety of welfare system is 'social democratic' and the most egalitarian because it embodies the principle of universal rights and universal solidarity. In this type, all are dependent, all can benefit and all have the obligation to contribute to the system of insurance. Such a system encourages a high level of participation in the labour market by both women and men and minimises the number of people dependent on transfer payments. It requires a high degree of political consensus and commitment to an egalitarian social philosophy.

The second type is 'corporatist', and is associated with those countries which have a strong state tradition and a history of granting privileged status and welfare provision to civil servants. In this case, welfare is not designed to make provision on the basis of universal criteria of need or to redistribute income but to maintain status differentials. Benefits and provisions vary for different social strata and serve to reinforce the social hierarchy. The social rights of each stratum are embedded in the conservative and usually religious traditions associated with corporatism.

The third variety is the 'liberal welfare state' which intervenes in the market as little as possible and gives low levels of benefit which are subject to strict entitlement rules. At the same time, it has mechanisms to encourage the market through subsidies for private medical schemes, housing and pensions. The political context for this is liberal individualism with a strong emphasis on the work ethic. The effect on stratification is to emphasise class dualism: the main recipients of welfare are the working class and the poor, while the middle class benefits from the system of subsidies to the private sector.

In practice, as Esping-Andersen is quick to point out, these varieties of welfare capitalism do not correspond perfectly with individual countries. Each country has elements of each type, although one may predominate. To see how they compare, Esping-Andersen made a detailed study of pensions, sickness benefits and

Table 2.4   **Rank order of welfare states: combined score based on pensions, sickness and unemployment benefits, 1980**

United States	13.8
Ireland	23.3
United Kingdom	23.4
Italy	24.1
France	27.5
Germany	27.7
Finland	29.2
Switzerland	29.8
Austria	31.1
Belgium	32.4
Netherlands	32.4
Denmark	38.1
Norway	38.3
Sweden	39.1

Source: Table 2.2 in Esping-Andersen (1990), de-commodification score based on SSIB data files

unemployment insurance, and derived a composite score based on the strictness of the rules which govern people's access to benefits, the levels of benefits relative to normal earnings, and rights to protection against the risks of unemployment, disability, sickness and old age. He calls this the 'de-commodification score' to indicate the degree of dependency on the market, a low score being typical of market-orientated countries and a high score being typical of countries with well-developed systems of social rights. The results are summarised in Table 2.4.

The pattern of variation illustrates the effect of the three welfare-state regimes. The lowest scores (which include the United States for comparison) relate to the countries which have a strong liberal market tradition. They include the United Kingdom because, in spite of the influence of the Labour party immediately after the war, the social democratic tendency was not maintained. Although the welfare state initially encouraged access to social consumption on the basis of need, this has been significantly eroded by the growth of private provision. The Anglo-Saxon countries are therefore closest to the 'liberal' welfare-state regime. The countries with intermediate scores include France, Germany, Italy and Switzerland, where the traditions of conservative corporatism and Christian democracy are relatively strong. Finally, the highest scores are found among the Scandinavian countries, and in Belgium and the Netherlands.

This analysis of welfare-state regimes therefore complements the analysis of inequalities of wealth and income, and helps to explain the relationship between the inequality-generating mechanisms of the market and the mechanisms of the welfare state which may either reinforce or counteract these mechanisms according to the priorities of social policy. It is important to note that the consequences for stratification are not directly related to the scale of social expenditure. Similar overall levels can accentuate or reduce the social cleavage between the working class and the middle class, between those groups which are most dependent on direct state support and those which benefit from subsidies to private consumption.

Arguments about the relationship between the welfare state and stratification have traditionally taken the line that economic growth and changing patterns of welfare and consumption have weakened the importance of class. It is said that this can be seen in the reduced significance of class voting, class awareness and industrial conflict. It is certainly true that industrial and occupational changes have enlarged the middle class at the expense of the working class, but the link between position in the labour market and consumption position is nevertheless very close. Neither 'affluence' nor 'welfare' have replaced the significance of class structure. They have contributed to it in new and distinctive ways.

Stratification and social consciousness

The extent and nature of awareness of social differences by the members of a population is an important question with political as well as cultural implications. The evidence for consciousness of social structure and social inequality reveals some interesting facts. First, at the most general level, the range of social inequality in European societies can be compared with the attitudes in that society to issues of social justice and the need for social change. One source of data is the Eurobarometer series of surveys carried out by the EC, which show that there are significant variations in public attitudes measured by simple questions on social organisation and the need for reform. Such data need to be handled with some scepticism because apparently similar questions may acquire different meanings as the culture and context changes. However, while there is a large majority in all the countries of the EC in agreement with the need for reform rather than revolution there is also some suggestion that attitudes are most polarised in the countries where the range of social inequality is greatest.

More precise investigations of attitudes to inequality and welfare have been carried out in several European countries through the International Social Survey Programme (Jowell *et al.* 1989). Using data from Austria, Italy, Netherlands, West Germany and the United Kingdom, they show how far attitudes to inequality are class-based. There is a positive relationship between attitudes and social class but this is combined with a high level of general agreement across nations and between classes. This is illustrated in Table 2.5, which uses

Table 2.5   **State welfare and class solidarity in four European countries**

	Britain	West Germany	Austria	Italy
% favouring . . .				
. . . more spending on health care:				
Poorest quartile	90	54	73	82
Wealthiest quartile	84	33	59	78
. . . more spending on pensions:				
Poorest quartile	87	51	61	79
Wealthiest quartile	63	32	50	75
. . . more spending on unemployment benefits:				
Poorest quartile	59	41	27	63
Wealthiest quartile	25	19	13	52
Government should reduce income differences between those with high and low incomes:				
Poorest quartile	58	63	70	79
Wealthiest quartile	37	52	62	64

Source: International Social Survey Programme, reported by P. Taylor-Gooby in R. Jowell *et al.* (1989: 49–51)

income levels defined as the top and bottom quarters of the population as an alternative to class proper.

The results show that the wealthy in Britain have less enthusiasm for redistribution than the wealthy in the other countries but that there is a broad consensus among both poor and wealthy in all the countries for improved levels of spending on health care. This corresponds with the expectation that a country with a 'liberal' welfare regime will express the divergence of interests between the middle classes and the poor (see Esping-Andersen 1990: 30–1; Halsey 1988: 29–33). However, these surveys show that cross-national variations are not particularly marked except in the valuation of inequality as an obstacle to advancement, or as the stimulus to personal gain. From this kind of evidence it is difficult to sustain the once-popular argument that Britain is a particularly class-conscious or class-ridden society compared with others in Europe.

Comparative studies of values show only small variations along class lines except with respect to values connected with work and occupation. The European Values Project, for example, found no great disparity between European value systems and encountered most variation in terms of moral, personal and religious values which cut across rather than conformed to the main cleavages of the stratification system (Harding *et al.* 1986: 217-18). This apparent lack of any strong connection between the objective features of stratification (income, occupation, access to welfare) and subjective attitudes to society has attracted the attention of researchers in a number of European countries. The core issue is that pronounced social inequalities are not necessarily associated with strong awareness of them or with political opposition to them as might be anticipated. In fact, where a correlation exists, it may be, as Lane and Ersson found, that the more even the income distribution between various strata the higher the class consciousness and the degree of unionisation (1987: 85–6). They interpret this by saying that equalisation of income is a product of a high level of class consciousness but, as they acknowledge, this fails to account for the origins of class consciousness in the first place. In a detailed comparison of class radicalism in France and Britain, Gallie (1983) looked for the causes in terms of income level, the technological character of the work setting, and the ideological influence of the trade unions. He found that none of these was the key to explaining the higher levels of radicalism in France, and showed that it was work grievances and the direct experience of more managerial control – more authoritarian in France than Britain – which provided the answer. In countries where the system of industrial relations is more institutionalised, the subjective response to inequalities of income and power may be more accepting or fatalistic. This and other empirical studies show that day-to-day experiences of social inequality are too complex and varied to allow for simple predictions of collective behaviour on the basis of positions in the stratification system. Everyday experience in the 'workplace' (which may of course be the home as well as the office or factory) is where the objective and subjective aspects of social stratification combine and interact. This is why occupational categories are most commonly used to describe the system of stratification. They are one of the best indicators available of position within the productive system and the social and political characteristics which are likely to be associated with typical positions.

We can now integrate the analysis of the market situation of each stratum (defined by the source and amount of wealth and income) with their social situation (defined by their occupation or position within the division of labour and system of authority relations). These are connected in turn with differences of status and life-style. A composite classification which is relevant to most European societies will include the following categories:[2]

1 A capitalist class, comprising business proprietors, and owners of large-scale shareholdings, land and property.
2 A service class, comprising two strata: directors, managers and higher-grade professional employees; and lower-grade professionals, managers and technical workers.
3 A working class, comprising two strata: clerical, secretarial and routine non-manual workers; and skilled manual workers.
4 A lower working class: comprising semi- and unskilled manual workers and those who regularly depend on state benefits because of low wages or unemployment.

The 'capitalist class' is the smallest but the most powerful of the categories. In modern industrial societies this stratum, which includes members of the economic, political and cultural elites, forms about 1 per cent of the total population. Although much of their wealth and power is hidden from general view, their importance is not diminished by their lack of conspicuous consumption. The character of this stratum varies between countries according to their patterns of history and social development. In Britain, the term 'establishment' is often used to describe the typical relationships and patterns of influence which operate within the ruling group. The oldest of the industrial societies, Britain has long since combined the features of the old aristocracy with the capitalist class to form a relatively cohesive ruling group defined by its control over the industrial firms and banks which dominate the economy, its monopoly of social privilege, and its capacity to steer the political system. Although it is no longer entirely based on leading families, there are closely interlocking social networks which are reinforced from one generation to the next by the exclusive mechanisms of private education. It has a cohesive culture which is based on a shared conception of the 'nation' and the identification of the national interest with its own interests. It exercises its power in subtle ways, as Coates says, protecting itself through 'its own exclusivity, low public profile, and astute public orchestration of the pre-capitalist institutions of monarchy and aristocracy' (in Bottomore and Brym 1989: 43).

The character of the capitalist class in France derives from the structure of capital and the distinctive role of the state in promoting a technocracy in public administration. The relatively late arrival of industrialisation in France meant that even as late as the 1970s, half of the 200 largest companies were still family-controlled. Marceau (1989) has described how the restructuring of capital in the subsequent decades brought about a convergence between owners and controllers of capital so that, through family ties, similarities of education, and parallel career paths in public administration or industry, the distinction between ownership and control has become relatively unimportant. The *grandes écoles*, the elite institutions of higher education, are the proving grounds for talent and sustain a modern form of legitimacy for the ruling class, namely 'technocracy', which is sufficiently broad to include the exercise of power through both private and public institutions. The Paris-based elitist technocracy of France complements the inegalitarian social system and has at least as much social and political homogeneity as its parallel stratum in Britain. It retains its legitimacy not through the acceptance of tradition but because the mechanisms of exclusion are ostensibly designed to create professional rulers rather than privilege for its own sake.

In contrast to both Britain and France, which have distinctive capitalist classes, Germany has no easily identifiable ruling group. There are several reasons for this, including the discontinuities resulting from the Second World War, the enhanced opportunities for mobility into the economic elite during the postwar boom period, and the attempt systematically to integrate all social strata into the social market economy. This does not mean that there is no capitalist class in Germany, only that it has greater fluidity and less social and political cohesion than in Britain and France. As Ardagh observes, its prosperity and lack of inherited privilege makes the stratification of German society more like that of the United States than any other country in Europe (1988: 146).

This comparison between the capitalist classes in three European countries illustrates the fact that countries with a broadly similar range of social inequality may exhibit varying degrees of permeability across their social boundaries. In an extreme case, a highly unequal and elitist social system could nevertheless be called 'open' if it encouraged a high rate of social mobility. In contrast, a relatively egalitarian society could be called 'closed' if it had powerful exclusionary mechanisms to discourage movement between strata. Studies of social mobility have to contend with some of the most intractable problems of international data comparison, and it is impossible to do justice to this question here.

However, it is possible to draw two general conclusions – which are presented in a useful summary by Heath (1981: 193–223). First, the overall or mass mobility rate depends on the changing pattern of occupations. If, for example, the number of non-manual jobs increases at the expense of manual jobs, this will be reflected in the mobility rates within and between generations for the two strata. Countries which have experienced recent rapid industrialisation tend to have high structural mobility rates, and it is usual to find conspicuous inequality linked with rising egalitarian expectations. On the other hand, in the mature industrial societies, where occupational shifts are more moderate, mobility of this type will necessarily be limited. Second, social and cultural factors can make a difference. Heath's comparison shows that, after allowing for the pattern and rate of change in the occupational structure, European societies can be grouped in two ways: according to their relative maturity (the 'newer' societies are more open than the 'old'); and according to their political experience (countries with long periods of socialist government are more open than those with a history of mainly conservative or right-wing governments). Thus Sweden is most open, Britain is in an intermediate category, and France, Germany, Italy and Spain are more closed. Careful analysis permits a distinction to be made between structures of inequality and their relative openness, which can vary independently, but the results in practice show that there is usually a close connection between equality and openness in social structures. As Heath points out, this should not come as a surprise, because national characteristics do not vary randomly, 'they come as more or less firmly tied bundles whose individual components cannot easily be pulled apart or altered at will', even by governments (1981: 223). The system of social stratification and the policies of government are inextricably linked.

The most striking development in the stratification system in recent decades has been the growth of the professional and managerial strata and the corresponding decrease in manual occupations in manufacturing industry. The rise of what is often called the 'service class', with a vast array of new occupations, creates problems of definition as well as difficulties in interpreting its political significance. It is not simply a question of the expansion of the 'middle classes' or white-collar employment generally, although on average nearly two-thirds of all workers in western European economies are in service occupations (that is, not in agricultural or industrial occupations). It concerns the emergence of a new and powerful stratum within the broad category of services with its own distinctive economic position and social identity. According to Goldthorpe's definition, the service class includes professionals, administrators and managers whose positions involve the application of specialised knowledge within the framework of bureaucratic organisations, whether public or private (Goldthorpe 1982). The increasing scale, complexity and rationalisation of the capitalist productive system has created the need for this stratum to control and coordinate the functions of capital on behalf of the capitalist class. It typically accounts for between 10 and 25 per cent of all employees. Their distinctiveness comes from a strong market situation owing to their professional expertise, combined with a work situation which allows a high degree of autonomy and discretion.

Previous arguments about the service class (for example, Dahrendorf 1963) were naturally concerned with its political orientation, yet they found it difficult to reach a conclusion. The service relationship to capital implied that their chief loyalty would be to the ruling group but the influence of advanced education, the experience of mobility and the ideology of rationality and progress appeared to give the service class a certain independence from the conservative culture and politics of the superordinate stratum. More recent evidence of service-class formation in three European countries (Erikson *et al.* 1979) points to other reasons for divided loyalties. The very rapid growth of the service class has encouraged recruitment from a wide range of social strata, including the working class. Their closeness to working-class origins and social heterogeneity suggests that a new class identity has not had sufficient time to develop. The 'demographic' and 'socio-cultural' identity of the stratum has so far been inhibited (Goldthorpe 1982: 174–5). This tends to be confirmed by studies carried out in individual countries. In France, for example, Boltanski (1987) made a study of *cadres* but found it impossible to identify precise boundaries or collective action based on common attributes and shared interests. What is likely, as the service class matures, is that it will find a place which is more than simply an appendage of the capitalist class but one which is unlikely to bring it into conflict with the class above. As the process of economic and political integration in Europe develops, the role of the service class will be enhanced through its characteristics of expertise, mobility and relative lack of commitment to traditional or national culture.

The fate of the working class across Europe has provoked writers in many countries to pronounce on its demise, its transformation or even its reincarnation. The universal and incontrovertible facts are these: that the mass-employment manufacturing industries which were the backbone of working-class communities and labour organisations have either been eliminated through global competition or altered out of recognition by the application of new technologies; that there has been a numerical decline in the main categories of working-class occupations; and trade unions have suffered a significant decline in membership. This has radically altered the framework for the interpretation for the sociology of this stratum. In the 1950s and 1960s the participation of workers in the new prosperity seemed to be a part of the process of integration of the formerly dichotomous and conflictual class structure. For more than a decade, research focused on the evidence for '*embourgeoisement*' and indicators of change or decline in the patterns of industrial and class conflict (Goldthorpe *et al.* 1969). Today, the themes of fragmentation and even destruction of the working class are ascendant, as economic recession, technological change and the collapse of socialism in eastern Europe have created a radically different set of conditions.

The changing industrial structure has undermined the once fundamental boundaries between skilled and semi-skilled workers and the status distinction between 'white-collar' and 'blue-collar' work. Each stratum had its own typical patterns defined by the type of income and employment contract (wages or salaries), the type of skill (manual or non-manual), and working conditions (the shop floor or office). These all contributed to distinctions in the pattern of consumption, housing, life-style and culture. Today, the internal divisions of the working class relate to the new features of the capitalist production system which responded to the competitive pressures of the 1970s and the 1980s by 'snaking out' large numbers of workers from the key industrial sectors. Production has been reorganised into 'core' and 'peripheral' activities in order to achieve maximum flexibility at minimum cost. Instead of a division between types of work and occupation, this creates a new division between workers with strong contractual and social ties to their employer and workers with relatively loose ties. The core consists of qualified workers on permanent contracts, with higher levels of earnings and commitment to the organisation. Skilled workers who have survived the recession have seen their earnings increase in real terms. Under 'flexible specialisation', as it is often called, the much larger group of peripheral workers has less security and is more likely to be self-employed or on temporary or part-time contract. One of the advantages for the employer is that job demarcations are removed and working practices are made more flexible. The position of the employee is likely to deteriorate into one of low security, low wages and low opportunity.

There is no sharp boundary between relatively disadvantaged workers and the unemployed. There is a case for describing the latter (and the poor generally) as an 'underclass' because they are not fully integrated into the class structure. (Dahrendorf 1987). The case against describing them in this way is that the condition of unemployment is, for the majority who escape long-term unemployment, intermittent, and there is constant movement up and down the lower ranks of the working class. The fact that poverty may be a result of low wages, stage in the life-cycle or single-parent status as well as unemployment suggests that the new poor are part of a working class which has become increasingly fragmented. Dependency on income from employment may be exchanged for dependency on the state, but this does not always involve a radical transition in income or status.

The impact of recession and economic change in Europe in the 1980s led to a number of studies of the relationship between formal employment and informal economic activity, whether of the self-service variety (for example, self-build or do-it-yourself) or work in the semi-legal or black economy (see Pahl 1989). Pahl and other researchers had expected to find an increase in self-provisioning and informal economic activity to cope with growing insecurity at the margins of the labour market. This was only partly confirmed. The evidence shows that unemployed people are the least likely to be engaged in informal work, and low wage households have few of the resources needed to make the most of opportunities for such work. The effect is to polarise households into 'work-rich' and 'work-poor', that is, households which have multiple earners and which can use their own labour, skills and tools to improve their position, and households which are denied these opportunities because of age, disability or because they only have a single earner.

The detailed study of social stratification in European societies has usually been carried out in the context of single societies. Some studies compare two, or not usually more than three, countries. There are certainly no equivalent social data to match the continuous and detailed monitoring of economic performance throughout Europe. This makes it difficult to draw general conclusions. However, there is a family resemblance between the systems of social stratification in the European countries because they have in common the same, and increasingly internationalised, capitalist production and market system. They also have in common the features of state welfare. These two aspects of contemporary society create the framework for social differentiation. We have seen that within this framework there is considerable room for variation both in the objective features which divide the strata and in the subjective responses and collective action which they may inspire. In thinking about comparative stratification it is prudent to bear in mind the following advice from a discussion of the do's and don't's of class analysis (Giddens 1982: 164–6).

The first rule is not to extrapolate from short-term trends. Each decade of the postwar period has brought its own style of sociological analysis and interpretation: from the promise of 'classlessness' in the years of the economic miracle to the resurgence of class and class conflict in the 1970s, and the 'recomposition of class' in the 1980s. Too much emphasis on the short term leads to perceptions of change which overlook the continuities of social structure and exaggerate the speed of current developments.

The second rule is not to generalise from a single society. The United States can hardly be used today, as it was in the past, as the prototype of industrialism, and as a symbol of the European future, because Japan and the European societies themselves show the possibility of viable alternative paths of development. Perhaps the contemporary illusion for Europeans is the idea of an integrated 'European society' to which all the individual countries will converge. Whether this seen in a positive or a negative light, the evidence does not support the idea that national societies will be rapidly subsumed into a common type.

The third rule is to accept the contingent character of social change, not to assume that there is a single force or tendency causing societies to develop along a predetermined path. The interaction between the class dynamic of the economic system and the citizenship dynamic of the state welfare system best illustrates this point in the European societies. The interplay of similar structures and processes can lead to a variety of outcomes.

Finally, there is an increasingly important rule, which is to recognise the international context of social change and to use comparative evidence as far as possible. Social analysis has been no less insular and national in its concern than most other aspects of society. The dearth of good comparative social data is an obstacle which will have to be removed if we are to gain a better understanding of the divisions and conflicts within social Europe.

Notes

1 In fact, there are very few measures, whether economic, social or cultural, which are completely standardised between the European countries. Measures of income, employment, occupation, consumption and so on are constructs which vary according to the conditions of each country and are collected by organisations at the national level. For a discussion of some of the problems involved in comparing labour market data from many countries, see Bean (1989) or Hakim (1991).

2 This is applicable to the capitalist societies of western Europe, not to state socialism in eastern Europe, where the boundaries of stratification were defined by the party-state system and not by the market. Recent changes in these countries are likely to bring about some convergence towards the western types of stratification. For a discussion of the contrasts between the capitalist and state socialist forms of stratification, see Davis and Scase (1985).

References

Ardagh, J. (1988) *Germany and the Germans*, London: Penguin Books.

Atkinson, A. B. (1983) *The Economics of Inequality*, 2nd edn, Oxford: Oxford University Press.

Bean, R. (ed.) (1989) *International Labour Statistics: a Handbook, Guide and Recent Trends*, London: Routledge.

Boltanski, L. (1987) *The making of a Class: Cadres in French Society*, Cambridge: Cambridge University Press.

Bottomore, T. and Brym, R. J. (eds) (1989) *The Capitalist Class: an International Study*, Brighton: Harvester Wheatsheaf.

Dahrendorf, R. (1963) 'Recent changes in the class structure of European societies', in S. Graubard (ed.) *A New Europe?*, Boston: Beacon Press.

——(1987) 'The erosion of citizenship', *New Statesman*, 12 June, pp. 12–15.

Davis, H. and Scase, R. (1985) *Western Capitalism and State Socialism*, Oxford: Basil Blackwell.

Erikson, R. Goldthorpe, J. H. and Portocarero, L. (1979) 'Intergenerational class mobility in three western European societies', *British Journal of Sociology*, 30 (4): 415–41.

Esping-Andersen, G. (1990) *The Three Worlds of Welfare Capitalism*, Cambridge: Polity Press.

Gallie, D. (1983) *Social Inequality in France and Britain*, Cambridge: Cambridge University Press.

Giddens, A. (1982) *Profiles and Critiques in Social Theory*, London: Macmillan.

Goldthorpe, J. H. (1982) 'On the service class, its formation and future', in A. Giddens, and G. Mackenzie (eds) *Social Class and the Divison of Labour*, Cambridge: Cambridge University Press.

——Lockwood, D., Bechhofer, F. and Platt, J. (1969) *The Affluent Worker in the Class Structure*, Cambridge: Cambridge University Press.

Hakim, C. (1991) 'Cross-national comparative research on the European Community: the EC Labour Force Surveys', *Work, Employment and Society*, 5 (1).

Halsey, A. H. (1988) *British Social Trends since 1900*, London: Macmillan.

Harding, S. and Phillips D. with M. Fogarty (1986) *Contrasting Values in Western Europe*, London: Macmillan.

Heath, A. (1981) *Social Mobility*, London: Fontana.

Jowell, R., Witherspoon, S. and Brook, L. (1989) *British Social Attitudes: Special International Report*, London: Gower.

Lane, J-E. and Ersson, S. O. (1987) *Politics and Society in Western Europe*, London: Sage.

Lawson, R. and George, V. (1980) 'An assessment', in V. George and R.

Lawson (eds) *Poverty and Inequality in Common Market Countries*, London: Routledge & Kegan Paul.

Marceau, J. (1989) *A Family Business? The Making of an International Business Elite*, Cambridge: Cambridge University Press.

Pahl, R. E. (1989) 'From "informal economy" to "forms of work": cross-national patterns and trends', in R. Scase (ed.) *Industrial Societies: Crisis and Division in Western Capitalism and State Socialism*, London: Unwin Hyman.

CHAPTER 3

Industrial structure and performance: common challenges – diverse experiences

CHRISTEL LANE

The advent of the Single European Market (SEM) has focused our attention on Europe as a new industrial unit which will also bring in its train trends towards common social and political patterns of organisation. It is intended that this larger entity will combine the industrial strengths of the various member states and cancel out their individual weaknesses. It is thus designed to create the industrial competitiveness *vis-à-vis* American and Asian rivals which at present eludes individual economies. But at the present time, economic and social unity is still a remote goal, and diversity between member states is more striking than homogeneity.

This enduring diversity of industrial structure and organisation is seen as having been shaped by the social and political institutional framework of each society, giving rise to industrial orders. The moulding of national industrial orders has occurred throughout the period of modern industrial development, but the distinctive cast of each order was forged at the very beginning of the industrialisation process. An examination of the industrial structure and organisation of the three largest member states – Germany[1], France and the United Kingdom – will serve to illustrate the existing diversity and focus attention on the different ways in which common challenges are being faced. Such challenges emanate both from the changing world economic framework, particularly from shifts in markets for industrial products and the accompanying intensification of competition, and from the acceleration of technological change, as experienced in the 1980s.

Industrial development and structure

In all three countries, the pace and the nature of industrial development was determined by the way the necessary capital was provided and by the origins and industrial orientations of the early entrepreneurs. Britain's industrialisation started almost a century before that of its continental rivals. The early stage of development was dominated by the large merchant entrepreneurs (Fox 1985) and entailed the parallel weakening of artisan craft producers. This ensured the early dominance of a merchant ethos over a productivist one. All through the nineteenth century, the connections between industry and the banking sector remained underdeveloped and held back the emergence of large firms. The first impulses towards the industrial concentration at the turn of the last century resulted in only very partial large-firm development in the more traditional industrial sectors.

The creation of a significant sector of large, publicly quoted companies came only at the end of the 1920s and embraced also the then more modern industries, such as chemicals, electrical engineering and vehicle building. The new ease of raising capital on the stock market led to a rapid expansion of the corporate sector and the simultaneous shrinkage of the small and medium-sized enterprise (SME) sector, giving Britain a somewhat unbalanced industrial structure. Also notable in the British case is the early emergence of multinational companies (MNCs), taking advantage of the easy access to foreign markets, created by Britain's imperial status. This was, however, paralleled by the early entry into Britain of American MNCs, particularly in the more modern industrial sectors.

Since the early 1970s, there has occurred a halt in this trend towards industrial concentration, and the 1980s have witnessed a significant revival of the SME sector. But even today, Britain's industrial structure remains the most highly concentrated in Europe, and its SME sector is still among the least developed.

In Germany, large and giant firms evolved during the first decades of its industrialisation period: that is, in the decades around the turn of the nineteenth century. The fast pace of industrialisation meant that merchant capital was never accumulated in sufficient quantity to finance expansion, and capital was instead made available by the large universal banks, also created during the early industrialisation period (Kocka 1975). Large firms have decisively shaped industrial organisation and structure ever since. But the SME craft sector of the economy, due to early state protection and promotion of the craft form of production, survived the onslaught of the industrial giants relatively well (Streeck 1986). This has meant that, in Germany, large industrial firms have always existed side by side with smaller family-owned and managed craft enterprises and that interaction between, and reciprocal influence of, the two has been common. This long coexistence explains why the craft ethos – namely, a production orientation and an emphasis on skill and product quality – has remained much more prominent in Germany than in the other two European countries (Piore and Sabel 1984).

At the end of the Second World War tough anti-trust laws, introduced by the Americans, led to some industrial deconcentration, but merger activities during the 1960s and 70s restored the old pattern of concentration and industrial structure. The SME sector, after some decline in the postwar period, has nevertheless remained a vigorous and important part of German industry (Doran 1984). Despite this early evolution of industrial giants, MNCs were slow to develop in Germany, and internationalisation was attained through the cultivation of a strong export orientation.

France's pattern of industrial development has differed significantly from that of both of its European rivals. Although industrialisation started in the second half of the nineteenth century, development occurred unevenly and haltingly. Notwithstanding the creation of a few large firms in the more modern sectors, France remained essentially a country of petty entrepreneurs until the 1950s. Family-owned SMEs, dedicated more to the preservation of family patrimony and control than to a quest for expansion, gave their indelible stamp to French industrial culture and structure (Trebilcock 1981; Landes 1969). Although pockets of artisanal producers have remained in some sectors of industry the craft culture and its organisational forms had essentially been destroyed in the wake of the French Revolution, through politically motivated legislative intervention by the state (Schriewer 1986). Explanations for French relative economic backwardness range from the downward pull of a large agricultural subsistence sector, coupled with slow population growth and fragmented home markets, to the shortage of capital for industrial expansion, resulting from the underdevelopment of both bank lending and of a stock market.

A significant corporate industrial sector came into existence only from the late 1950s onwards, particularly during the 1960s and early 1970s. Industrial concentration ensued under pressure and guidance from a modernist state, concerned to equip French industry with large firms, sufficiently strong to compete on increasingly more open and expanding world markets. Extensive state control of the financial system made it possible to channel the necessary expansion capital into targeted industrial sectors and firms. The group structure of the French economy, whereby several large firms are combined in the form of a financial holding company to pool resources, dating from the early period of industrialisation (Scott 1985: 133), became perpetuated also at this modern stage. Further concentration occurred during the early 1980s when nationalisation was accompanied by injection of new capital and further merger activities. The slow evolution of large corporations also meant that MNCs developed late in France and never acquired the significance that they possess in the British context.

Thus, from the 1960s onwards, a few large industrial groups came to dominate the French economy and to pose a severe threat to the many SMEs, nurtured in a less competitive industrial environment. The late emergence of the corporate sector meant that interaction with the SME sector never became very close and that, instead, two disparate industrial sectors came to exist side by side. This dualism

Table 3.1 **The distribution of number of enterprises* and of share of employment and gross value added* by employment size in the early 1980s**

Small enterprises (20–99 employees)

	No. of units		Employment		Value added	
	1981	1983	1981	1983	1981	1983
Germany	69.1	69.8	14.7	15.2	12.5	12.6
France	75.5	75.8	19.7	20.2	17.1	18.0
UK	76.6	77.4	13.8	14.9	10.5	11.1

Medium enterprises (100–499 employees)

	No. of units		Employment		Value added	
	1981	1983	1981	1983	1981	1983
Germany	25.1	–	24.6	25.6	22.5	–
France	19.9	19.7	25.4	27.1	22.8	23.3
UK	17.5	17.1	14.5	15.7	13.0	13.8

Large enterprises (>500 employees)

	No. of units		Employment		Value added	
	1981	1983	1981	1983	1981	1983
Germany	5.8	–	60.7	–	65.0	–
France	4.6	4.5	55.0	54.1	47.0	43.0
UK	5.8	5.5	71.6	69.4	76.6	75.0

* As a percentage of enterprises employing more than 20 people

Source: Eurostat, *Structure and Activity of Industry Data by Size of Enterprise* various issues. Quoted by Dunne and Hughes (1990: 64), extracts from table 27.

has been further accentuated by the heavy involvement of the state in the expansion and shaping of the corporate sector, and the continuation of family domination in the SME sector. From the 1980s onwards, however, more state support was extended also to the latter sector which, as in Britain and Germany, experienced a period of revival (Vickery 1986).

Table 3.1 sums up the outcomes of a century of industrial development and provides figures for the early 1980s, affording a comparative perspective on industrial structure in Europe. These figures show that, despite the recent revival of smaller firms, Britain's industrial structure remains less balanced than those of its continental competitors. This difference, as noted by Hughes (1990), is particularly marked when we consider also medium-sized enterprises. It is in this area that the main difference between British and German industrial structure is now located which is otherwise quite similar. In the French case, a markedly lesser degree of concentration remains notable also in the early 1980s.

The remaining differences in the degree of concentration are well

Table 3.2   **Decline in manufacturing employment between 1980 and 1986 (%)**

France	Britain	Germany
−14.1	−25.2	−7.2

Source: OECD statistics, quoted by Boyer (1986)

illustrated by the following focus on the industrial giants: of the 100 largest firms (in terms of turnover) in Europe in 1988, twenty-eight were British (including the two Anglo-Dutch firms), twenty-four German and seventeen French. Of the twenty largest, four were British (two Anglo-Dutch), seven German and four French (*L'Expansion*, Dec. 1989/Jan. 1990: 149). These figures show Britain leading in the number of large firms, Germany in the number of giants and France coming third and joint second respectively. They also make clear that the large firms of all three countries are important players on world markets. All these statistics on industrial structure in terms of firm size show that differences in historical development have given way to more convergent trends during the last few decades. But such purely quantitative indicators of growing similarity still hide important enduring divergencies in more qualitative aspects of manufacturing industry. These will receive consideration in the following profile of contemporary industry in our three European countries.

Industrial organisation and performance in the 1980s

There are significant differences in the importance of manufacturing industry both among the three societies and within each over time. All three have experienced a significant decline of manufacturing industry during the 1970s and 1980s, with Britain being by far the most seriously affected and Germany the least affected of the three. (See Table 3.2 on changing employment figures.) This decline has been due to world recession but also signals a loss of competitiveness in both traditional industries and the more advanced industries, *vis-à-vis* the newly industrialising countries of South-east Asia and *vis-à-vis* Japan, respectively. The 1980s have thus been a period of industrial decline and of sustained attempts to halt or reverse that decline through the adoption of a new manufacturing policy, moving away from mass production of standardised goods.

By 1986, employment in industry (including construction) had reached the following level: in both France and Britain, 30.5 per cent of all employed were in industrial employment, whereas in Germany the proportion was a significantly higher 40 per cent (Eurostat 1988, Industry: 9, Fig. G4). The differential performance of the three manufacturing sectors are indicated by the following comparative figures on value added, output and export. By 1986, industry's share

Table 3.3 **Share in EC external trade in manufactured goods, 1987 (%)**

Germany	38.0
France	14.5
Britain	13.9

Source: Eurostat 1988, Industry: 86

of value added was 41 per cent in Germany, 39 per cent in Britain and 32 per cent in France (Eurostat 1988, Industry: 8, Fig. G2). Of net manufacturing output in the European Community (EC), 35 per cent was contributed by Germany, 21 per cent by France and only 19 per cent by Britain (*ibid*: 38). The disparity in industrial performance is most strongly manifested in export activity, as is indicated by Table 3.3.

These general quantitative indicators need to be supplemented by data showing how the various strengths and weaknesses are constituted. Germany's relative industrial strength lies in the following facts: it has achieved an international position in a very broad range of industries and, in each of these, can rely on a large cluster of mutually reinforcing industrial segments (Porter 1990). Successful industrial segments include mechanical and electrical engineering, chemicals and pharmaceuticals, cars, printing and precision optics. Firms tend to concentrate on technologically sophisticated goods, often produced in short runs or to special order. They draw on a deep knowledge base, as well as on a large pool of highly skilled labour. The productivist ethos and the cooperation between craft and industrial producers outlined earlier contribute strongly to the attainment of these goals.

The German drive for excellence in engineering design has also had a retarding influence. Germany lacks competitive advantage in semiconductors/computers and most goods heavily reliant on electronics. But German firms have been adept at incorporating electronic components into a wide range of products. In the more traditional and crisis-ridden industries, extensive restructuring and modernisation has taken place and most have managed to return to a satisfactory competitive position (Katzenstein 1989, various chapters).

The French economy displays a more uneven development and less balanced industrial composition. Thus, we find some sophisticated high-tech sectors, such as weapons technology, the nuclear industry and electronic communication, existing side by side with industries like textiles and mechanical engineering where technological sophistication and skill intensity have remained low. French strengths in the high-tech sectors lie in sophisticated technological design and less in efficient production organisation, and it is uncertain whether the high-tech industries could remain competitive without extensive state support in the form of R & D subsidies and export diplomacy. France also retains a strong position in traditional industries, such as food and drink and beauty products. Restructuring of crisis industries started later than in the other two societies and has not yet been completed.

Britain has continued to lose ground in all the modern industries and cannot boast of across-the-board strength in any one of the core industries, although pockets of excellence remain in such industries as chemicals and pharmaceuticals (Porter 1990). Competitive strength is now found only in traditional industries, such as food (biscuits and confectionery) and drink and tobacco. Generally, too many enterprises have retreated from competitive markets for technologically sophisticated goods and have instead concentrated on low-skill and low-value goods (Williams *et al.* 1990). Restructuring of the crisis industries appears to have succeeded only in the steel industry. Despite extensive improvements in areas like labour relations and work practices, core weaknesses remain, and the transition to a new manufacturing policy has only been imperfectly accomplished (Lane 1989: ch. 7).

Aspects of industrial order

It has repeatedly been indicated that the social institutional framework in which industry is embedded has a strong influence on its organisation. Interaction between production organisation and its social-institutional environment is referred to as industrial order (Herrigel 1989). A focus on industrial order examines the support systems available to industry and analyses both their degree of availability and the nature of their impact. Of the different social and political institutions with an impact on industrial organisation, four will be singled out for discussion: the state; the financial system; the educational system; and the support structures resulting from industry's self-organisation, such as trade associations and chambers of various kinds. Space available dictates that only outline features of the three industrial orders can be indicated.

The state–industry relationship is shaped both by the political philosophy guiding intervention and by the structure of the state, most notably by whether a country has a highly centralised or a more decentralised political structure. In the case of France, there is a long tradition of a highly directive state and of a marked concentration of power at the centre. During the early decades of the postwar period, this *dirigiste* and highly centralised stance on the part of the state was well suited to a far-reaching modernisation of industry, targeting particularly large firms in the most advanced industrial sectors. The preferred instruments of intervention have been indicative planning, nationalisation and extensive state control over credit allocation. Such policy has, at the same time, often bypassed the large family-owned sector of SMEs, particularly in the more traditional industries and has indirectly undermined their viability. The centralisation of economic decision-making and resource allocation made it difficult for SMEs to get access to state-sponsored support structures. During the second half of the 1980s, faith in the effectiveness of *dirigisme* has greatly declined and the market has received greater emphasis. The move, during the early 1980s, towards more decentralised economic decision-making has resulted in improved access to resources by smaller enterprises (Amadieu 1990: 93). By comparative standards, however, the French state remains both directive and centralised, and its influence in industry remains ensured both through relatively tight control over capital allocation and through the system of *pantouflage* – that is, widespread mid-career change by high state officials into top management positions in industry. The latter has had multiple consequences, such as exceptionally high elite cohesion, a hierarchical business structure and bureaucratic management style. The overall effect is that in the French industrial order, state-sponsored support structures have a strong weight and weaken self-organisation. But a high degree of state regulation of industry does not necessarily equal high effectiveness, and state penetration of the SME sector is much weaker than in the large-firm sector.

The German pattern of state–industry relations is very different from the French. The philosophy of the social market economy emphasises competition in the free market and eschews detailed state intervention in industry, except in its acknowledgement of responsibility for the social costs to labour, resulting from economic restructuring. At the same time, the central state provides a uniform and strong regulatory framework in such spheres as industrial relations and training, and thus contributes to relatively homogeneous forms of industrial organisation, both across industries/regions and size categories of firms. The federal political structure grants local states (the *Länder*) significant economic resources and competencies and thus ensures that state-sponsored support structures are relatively well attuned to local needs and to the requirements of SMEs which operate more strongly at this lower level. Thus the German state has considerable involvement in industry, but the strong degree of self-organisation established by industry ensures that this involvement does not turn into direction and interference.

In Britain, yet a different pattern of state–industry relations prevails. The philosophy of *laissez-faire*, dominant during most of the postwar period but compromised in times of pressing economic crisis, has made for a patchy and ineffective industrial policy. State reluctance to intervene is paralleled by industry's insistence on a hands-off relationship. Comprehensive regulatory frameworks on aspects of industrial organisation were never developed, and variation between regions, industries and types of firms has remained pronounced. This is particularly notable in the fields of industrial relations and training. The dominance of market criteria, together with a relatively centralised political structure, has meant that, for a long time, state help for the sector of SMEs was underdeveloped and failed to check the decline of this sector. Although the last two decades have seen a reversal of this policy of neglect, there still remain numerous problems in the targeting of aid to the small-firm sector. In the British context, neither large firms nor SMEs can rely on a consistent and dense system of state-sponsored support systems.

The manner in which industrial enterprises raise their capital and the way their relation to the financial system is structured constitute a second important dimension of industrial order – an excellent comparative discussion of bank–industry relations is provided by Vittas (1986). British firms mostly raise capital by issuing shares on the stock market, and the stock exchange forms the centre of the British financial system. The banking system, divided between investment and clearing banks, is highly centralised, and bank lending – where it occurs – has never led to close bank–industry relations. Thus British relations between the financial system and industrial firms are purely market relationships. They impose both constraints of high, short-term financial returns on industrial management and obviate the performance of support and control functions on the part of the financial institutions. The absence of the latter has been particularly detrimental to the development of smaller firms. The pressure for quick financial returns is widely held to have shaped managerial investment behaviour in a negative fashion. It is connected with insufficient investment in both skill development and technological innovation. Lastly, the relative ease of mergers and takeovers, facilitated by the British financial system, militates against the development of medium-sized firms and hence of a balanced industrial structure.

The French financial system has the following characteristics: it is a credit-based system, centred on intermediary financial institutions, and the availability and price of credit is strongly influenced by the state. The stock market remains underdeveloped, and, until the 1980s, the deposit-taking banks have not been prominently involved in industrial lending. Although such a system has made it possible for state-directed industrial restructuring and modernisation to take place it has also, until recently, made it difficult for smaller firms to get access to credit. The political decentralisation of the 1980s has, however, brought industrial funding closer to the SMEs. The relations between financial institutions and enterprises tend to be purely functional and do not extend into the areas of consultancy and control. In the 1980s, however, some of the large French banks have begun to copy the German model and have started to acquire substantial industrial portfolios (*The Economist*, 4 August 1990: 67–8).

The German financial system is mainly credit-based, and the cost of credit is determined purely by the market. The stock market remains underdeveloped. The large universal banks form the centre of this system, and their relations with industry, are exceedingly close. Long-term relationships are built up between a given firm and its house bank, and lending is normally accompanied by supportive supervision and informed consultancy. Banks own substantial amounts of industrial equity and also act as proxies for smaller investors. They are represented on the boards of most large companies, and the latter do, in turn, have seats on the banks' boards. Groups of banks sometimes form 'crisis cartels' to assist in the restructuring of traditional industries, such as steel, and of ailing giants, such as the electro-technical firm AEG in the 1980s. In addition to the 'Big Three' banks there are countless regional and local banks which cater very satisfactorily to the needs of SMEs.

These long-established close ties between German industry and banking have left a strong imprint on industrial culture. They have contributed to the maintenance of long-term investment horizons and, coupled with the engineering orientation of German industry, have resulted in steady technological updating and the parallel development of the necessary skill resources. The active industrial involvement of banks has facilitated the formation of a self-regulating industrial community which justifies the non-interventionist stance of the state, discussed above.

Industry depends not only on the easy availability of capital but also on an ample supply of suitably educated and trained human resources. Hence the educational system forms another crucial component of industrial order. For reasons of space, consideration of the university-educated minority will be omitted, although it is important both for the areas of management and of R & D. Instead, the focus will be on the vocational training of the majority of the labour force. The issues at stake are both the levels of education and training possessed by a given population and its content which, in turn, depends on the closeness of ties between industry and institutions of education and training.

A highly trained labour force equips industry not only with the necessary technical skills but also has a decisive impact on attitudes and orientations which shape industrial organisation and culture. (For details, see Lane 1989: ch. 2–4). Among the many areas affected are length of hierarchy and ease of vertical and horizontal communication, attitudes towards, and capabilities in, the field of technological innovation, adaptability to change, as well as the balance between extrinsic and intrinsic employee motivation and the resulting standards in the quality of products and services.

Germany's strong craft tradition is manifested in a highly developed system of vocational education and training (VET), and the social prestige of that system rivals that of general education. The highly standardised dual system (that is, both college and industry based) provides courses for manual and non-manual occupations from the apprenticeship level upwards to that of master craftsman. It thus offers career ladders as well as ensuring homogeneity of standards at various levels. The strong role taken by industry in determining the content and supervising the implementaton of training ensures that the practical component remains prominent. The involvement of the Chambers of Craft and Industry in monitoring the system keeps craft standards diffused throughout industry. State involvement means both a financial contribution (one-third of the costs) towards the more theoretical college-based part of VET and the maintenance of the general regulatory framework, while union participation ensures some input also from labour. The high participation rate – around 65 per cent of those eligible have at least a Skilled Worker Certificate – has decisively shaped all aspects of industrial organisation.

The features of continuity, homogeneity and achievement of high and widely diffused standards, characteristic of the German system of VET, are all sadly lacking in the British system. VET was developed relatively late in a 'feast and famine' fashion and has never achieved the same importance and social recognition as general education. There exists a confusing variety of training and validating bodies and a wasteful overlap between them, and continuity between the various levels of VET is not ensured. The weaknesses of the British system are now widely recognised, and the whole area has been under review throughout the 1980s. The initiative for remodelling the system has come from the state, but the latest stage in this process – the formation of Training and Enterprise Councils (TECs) – signals the realisation that schemes will only succeed with the active participation of industrial employers.

The two main components of the system of VET are the traditional apprenticeship and the Youth Training Schemes. The latter, introduced and organised in different forms during the 1980s, have expanded at the expense of the former. The YTSs have overcome some of the rigidities of the union-administered apprenticeships and have reached a larger proportion of young workers, but they have not yet managed to reach the same high levels of training standards. Although progress has been made in the standardisation of training levels to be reached, standards remain low by comparison with Germany, and the gap between the two countries in skill resources available to industry stays large.

In France, VET was first systematically promoted in the late 1950s although, until recently, it stayed at a low level both in terms of social prestige and in the degree of currency it achieved. During the 1980s, big efforts have been made to extend both the reach of VET, and to raise levels of skill at intermediate and advanced levels. The main part of VET is provided in the state-administered and -financed educational system, while a compulsory levy on industry ensures that employers provide further training for their employees. The relative availability of skilled employees at various hierarchical levels in the

Table 3.4 **Numbers qualifying in engineering and technology, 1985 (per 100,000)**

	Britain	France	W. Germany
Doctorates	1.2	0.5	1.6
Masters and enhanced degrees	4.0	11.0	7.0
Bachelor degrees	25.0	27.0	34.0
Technicians	51.0	63.0	72.0
Craftsmen	62.0	167.0	197.0

Source: National Institute of Economic and Social Research, quoted by *The Economist*, 13 Jan. 1990. Extract from table

three societies is indicated by Table 3.4. It indicates that France has advanced much further than Britain in catching up with Germany.

A last feature of industrial orders in Europe to be discussed is the degree of self-organisation of enterprises in industry-wide and/or regional associations of a formal and informal kind. Such permanent and temporary producer associations can facilitate cooperation, regulate competition and undertake representation *vis-à-vis* political authorities and labour organisations. They execute an important role *vis-à-vis* other social and political institutions, such as the ones discussed above. They ensure that supplies of capital, skills and knowledge are of the right kind of quantity and that they are made available on advantageous terms and targeted in an appropriate manner. Such intermediary organisations are particularly vital for SMEs.

The prevalence of intermediary organisations in our three societies will be densest where, as in Germany, the craft form of production has endured but may also be sustained by family and neighbourhood networks, as in France. In the British case, where neither craft-based nor family/neighbourhood-based organisation has been preserved, intermediary organisations have remained weak and fragmented. This may be illustrated by looking at the role of chambers in the three societies. In Germany, Chambers of Craft and Industry are statutory bodies with compulsory membership contributions. They not only provide the usual range of business services but also perform a central role in the provision of a skilled labour force and the maintenance of skill standards. In France, chambers can also rely on a compulsory levy to finance a range of business services, but their lack of involvement in the field of training deprives them of the key position they occupy in German industry. The British Chambers of Commerce, relying on voluntary membership, have insufficient financial and organisational resources to have a strong impact in any area of business organisation.

The picture is similar when we turn to industry-based trade organisations. Whereas in Britain they tend to be weak and fragmented and thus unable to regulate sectoral competition or provide the more costly services, such as the provision of scientific knowledge by research institutes, in Germany the opposite is the case. The lack of influence of British associations over their members makes them unfit to assume the role of interlocutors between government and firms. In the German context, in contrast, trade associations perform the functions of 'private government', regulating their members on behalf and in lieu of the state (Grant *et al.* 1987: 39) and thus shield them from direct political intervention. In France, where state intervention is more accepted, the role of intermediary trade organisations is consequently much weaker. The state is most likely to deal directly with large firms. SMEs have traditionally been out of the state's reach and have thus often formed their own, more informal self-help groups. Such networks of mutual assistance are said to have increased notably during the 1980s (Amadieu 1990).

Conclusions

This review of the industrial structure and organisation in three large European societies has outlined a picture of enduring diversity. This diversity is not simply one of structure and performance which can be altered by the adoption of appropriate policy measures. It has deep roots in the social-institutional framework of each society and is mainly the result of complex historical processes. This is not to say that national moulds have been cast for ever and that industrial change is impossible. Indeed, the German pattern of industrial organisation owes some of its features to fundamental social and political changes, initiated – partly on the instigation of the Allied victors – only in the postwar period. Similarly, France has fundamentally adapted its pattern of industrial organisation during the last thirty years and has slowly moved closer to that of its German neighbour. But convergence towards a single pattern of industrial organisation in the wake of European integration is not likely to occur in the near future.

Note

1 All information in this paper refers to the former Federal Republic of Germany.

References

Amadieu, J-F. (1990) 'France', in W. Sengenberger, G. Loveman and M. Piore (eds) *The Re-emergence of Small Enterprises*, International Institute for Labour Studies, Geneva.
Boyer, R. (1986) *La Flexibilité du Travail en Europe*, Paris: La Découverte.
Doran, A. (1984) *Craft Enterprises in Britain and Germany*, A study for the

Anglo-German Foundation by the Economists Advisory Group, London: AGF.

Dunne, P. and Hughes A. (1990) *Small Businesses: an Analysis of Recent Trends in their Relative Importance and Growth Performance in the UK with some European Comparisons*, Small Business Research Centre Working Paper No. 1, Department of Applied Economics, University of Cambridge.

Fox, A. (1985) *History and Heritage: the Social Origins of the British Industrial Relations System*, London: George Allen & Unwin.

Grant, W., Paterson, W. and Whitson C. (1987) 'Government–industry relations in the chemical industry: an Anglo-German comparison', in S. Wilks and M. Wright (eds) *Comparative Government and Industry Relations*, Oxford: Clarendon Press.

Herrigel, G. (1989) 'Industrial order and the politics of industrial change: mechanical engineering', P. Katzenstein (ed.) *Industry and Politics in West Germany: Towards the Third Republic*, Ithaca, NY: Cornell University Press.

Hughes, A. (1990) *Industrial Concentration and the Small Business Sector in the UK: the 1980s in Historical Perspective*, Small Business Research Centre, University of Cambridge. Working Paper No. 5.

Katzenstein, P. (ed.) (1989) *Industry and Politics in West Germany: Towards the Third Republic*. Ithaca, NY: Cornell University Press.

Kocka, J. (1975) *Unternehmer in der Deutsche Industrialisierung*, Goettingen: Vandenhoek and Ruprecht.

Landes, D. (1969) *The Unbound Prometheus: Technological Change and Industrial Development*, Cambridge: Cambridge University Press.

Lane, C. (1989) *Management and Labour in Europe*, Aldershot: Edward Elgar.

Piore, M. and Sabel, C. (1984) *The Second Industrial Divide*, New York: Basic Books.

Porter, M. (1990) *The Competitive Advantage of Nations*, London: Macmillan.

Schriewer, J. (1986) 'Intermediaere Instanzen, Selbstverwaltung und berufliche Ausbildungsstrukturen im historischen Vergleich', *Zeitschrift für Paedagogik*, 32: 69–90.

Scott, J. (1985) *Corporations, Classes and Capitalism*, 2nd ed, London: Hutchinson.

Streeck, W. (1986) *The Territorial Organization of Interests and the Logics of Associative Action: the Case of Artisanal Interest Organizations in West Germany*, Research Unit on the Labour Market and Employment, Berlin: Wissenschaftszentrum.

Trebilcock, C. (1981) *The Industrialization of the Continental Powers 1780–1914*, London and New York: Longman.

Vickery, L. (1986) 'France', P. Burns and J. Dewhurst (eds) *Small Business in Europe*, London: Macmillan.

Vittas, D. (1986) 'Bankers' relations with industry: an international survey', *National Westminster Bank Quarterly Review*, Feb.

Williams, K., Williams, J. and Haslam, C. (1990) 'The hollowing out of British manufacturing and its implications for policy', *Economy and Society*, 19: 456–90.

CHAPTER 4

Europe's ageing population – demographic trends

JOHN SIMONS

One feature of Europe's population in the 1990s dominates all the others: its reluctance to reproduce itself. A recent United Nations review comments 'Europe is literally melting away like snow in the sun' (United Nations 1989a: 8). Taking a similar view, the former French Prime Minister, Jacques Chirac, says, 'In demographic terms, Europe is vanishing. Twenty or so years from now, our countries will be empty, and no matter what our technological strength, we shall be incapable of putting it to use' (quoted in the Paris daily, *Libération* in October 1984, in an interview from which excerpts are printed in *Population and Development Review*, 11 (1): 163).

The faltering of reproduction, and the consequent ageing of the population, will be the main theme of this chapter. It starts with a review of the main features of Europe's demography. This is followed by a section on interpretations of the fertility decline as the principal cause of population ageing. The final sections deal with the social consequences of population ageing and its policy implications. For the purposes of this chapter, Turkey and the USSR are not included in Europe. The countries that are included are listed in Table 4.4.

Main demographic features

Growth

Europe's population of around 500 million is still growing, but slowly. Its share of world population is falling, steadily. In Table 4.1 the trend in the population of Europe since 1950 is contrasted with figures for the world as a whole, for developed countries and for developing countries. Europe's share of world population falls from 15.6 per cent in 1950 to an estimated 6 per cent in 2025. Over the same period the developing countries' share increases from two-thirds to 84 per cent. Population barely increased in Europe in the 1980s, and is expected to start declining in the early decades of the next century. Within the continent, the population of western Europe leads the downward trend, and is expected to start declining after the year 2000.

Table 4.1 **Population trends in Europe and the world, 1950–2025: population (millions), share (%) of world population (in parentheses), and growth rate (%) (UN medium variant projections)**

| | Population | | | | Growth rate | | | |
	1950	1985	2000	2025	1950–55	1980–85	1995–2000	2020–2025
Europe	393	492	509	512	0.79	0.32	0.21	−0.06
	(15.6)	(10.1)	(8.1)	(6.0)				
Eastern	89	112	117	123	1.02	0.41	0.33	0.12
Northern	72	83	85	86	0.37	0.17	0.13	−0.03
Southern	109	142	149	150	0.84	0.50	0.29	−0.06
Western	123	155	158	153	0.83	0.16	0.11	−0.22
Developed								0.18
countries	832	1,174	1,262	1,352	1.28	0.65	0.45	
	(33.1)	(24.2)	(20.2)	(16.0)				
Developing								
countries	1,683	3,680	4,989	7,114	2.05	2.10	1.92	1.13
	(66.9)	(75.8)	(79.8)	(84.0)				
World	2,515	4,854	6,251	8,467	1.80	1.74	1.62	0.98

Source: United Nations (1989b: 74–5)

Mortality

Because population growth depends on the excess of births over deaths (ignoring the effects of migration), population decline can occur if mortality is high enough. In the event, the substantial decline in mortality during this century has considerably reduced the level of fertility required for population replacement (Sardon 1990: 17).

A commonly used measure of a country's mortality is life expectancy at birth, which is a summary measure of mortality across all ages in a population. Life expectancy at birth is independent of the age structure of a population, and can therefore be used to compare one population with another. (Differences in age structure, such as large differences in the proportion of the elderly, can yield large differences in crude death rates even between populations with the same expectation of life at birth). Another important measure of mortality is a country's infant mortality rate, which is usually measured as the number of deaths of children under 1 year of age per thousand live births. Shown in Table 4.2 are trends and projections for both life expectancy at birth and infant mortality rates for Europe and for regions of Europe separately. Also shown are trends for developed and developing country groups, and for the world as a whole.

For Europe as a whole, life expectancy at birth reached 70 years for males and nearly 77 years for females in the early 1980s, and is expected to reach nearly 77 years for males and 82 years for females in the second decade of the next century. Eastern Europe has lagged behind the rest of Europe in extending the life span, but the gap

Table 4.2   **Life expectancy at birth (years), males and females, and infant mortality rate (infant deaths per thousand live births), Europe and the world, 1950–2025 (UN medium variant projections)**

| | Life expectancy | | | | | | | | Infant mortality rate | | | |
| | 1950–55 | | 1980–85 | | 1995–2000 | | 2020–25 | | 1950–55 | 1980–85 | 1995–2000 | 2020–25 |
	M	F	M	F	M	F	M	F				
Europe	63.2	67.6	70.0	76.7	72.8	79.2	76.2	82.1	62	15	9	66
Eastern	60.9	65.5	67.3	74.3	70.0	76.7	74.5	80.6	83	19	13	7
Northern	67.1	71.8	71.3	77.5	74.2	79.9	77.0	82.5	28	10	6	5
Southern	61.3	64.9	70.8	76.9	73.7	79.6	76.7	82.4	79	18	11	6
Western	65.3	70.1	70.9	78.2	73.7	80.5	76.7	82.9	44	10	7	5
Developed countries	63.0	68.7	68.5	76.3	72.0	79.0	75.6	82.0	56	16	11	6
Developing countries	40.3	41.9	56.6	58.7	61.8	64.5	68.5	72.4	180	89	64	33
World	44.8	47.1	58.2	61.1	62.9	66.2	69.3	73.5	155	79	68	30

Source: United Nations (1989b: 166–86, 190, 194–5)

appears to be narrowing. Until recent years, the sex differential in mortality had widened over several decades. The differential now seems to have stabilised, though it is still widening in some countries. The relative advantage of women has been attributed to various factors: greater congenital robustness, behavioural factors (such as less consumption of alcohol) and less exposure to hazardous environments.

The increase in life expectancies means that higher proportions of the population are to be found in older age groups. For Europe as a whole, the percentage of the population aged 60 years or more rose from 13 per cent in 1950 to 18 per cent in 1985, and is projected to rise to 21 per cent by the end of the century.

The increase in life expectancy is largely attributable to the decline in mortality associated with cardio-vascular disease, especially coronary diseases. However, these remain the main cause of death among men over the ages of 35 or 40, followed by cancer in the age group above 40. On the other hand, cancer is the main cause of death among women between the ages of 25 and 60, and circulatory disease after the age of 60 (United Nations, 1989a: 101).

Over the past three decades, infant mortality in Europe has declined substantially, from 62 per thousand live births in the early 1950s to 15 in the early 1980s. Infant mortality still accounts for high proportions of total mortality in the developing countries, but a negligible amount in the developed countries.

Defining its strategy for the achievement of 'Health for all by the year 2000', the European Region of the World Health Organisation declared that 'The first aim of the European Strategy is to ensure equity in health between and within countries' (Quoted in United Nations 1988a: 395). It seems likely that equity within countries will be harder to achieve than equity among them. Although mortality rates have declined in all social categories, the pattern of social differentials seems to have remained largely unchanged.

According to a review of recent studies in several European countries presented to a European Population Conference in 1987 (Valkonen 1987), mortality for adult men is higher among manual workers (especially unskilled manual workers) than among non-manual workers. The mortality of those with basic education only is approximately double that of university graduates. The inverse association between mortality and status still applies, almost always, when deaths are subdivided by cause. For women, differences in mortality are generally smaller than for men. This is said to be because mortality caused by some cancers (such as breast cancer and cancer of the uterus) and by accidents or violence is either positively or irregularly associated with social status.

The studies reviewed suggest that, for both men and women, social class differences in mortality had increased in the preceding ten to twenty years in some countries and remained constant in others. In the case of infant mortality there appeared to have been some improvement in the inverse association between social class and mortality. In Denmark and Sweden, socio-economic differences in the components of infant mortality had been almost eliminated.

Although much of the research in this field has been concerned with specific risk factors, it is believed that the greater part of socio-economic differentials in mortality is caused not by specific risk factors or inequalities in health care but by the general inequality of living conditions and related differences in life-style (Valkonen 1987: 245).

Marriage, cohabitation, divorce

Figure 4.1 shows the trend in the marriage rate in European Community countries (which account for 60 per cent of Europe's population) since the 1960s, when the proportion of people who were or had been married reached an historically unique peak in Europe. Evidently the popularity of marriage went into steep decline in the 1970s, levelling in the late 1980s at a rate well below that of the 1960s. The trends for most European countries outside the EEC have been broadly similar (Monnier 1990: 929; Council of Europe 1990: 109; Sardon 1986). While the decline is partly due to postponement of marriage, there can be little doubt that the proportion who will remain unmarried has increased significantly.

One issue raised by the change in the propensity to marry is the extent to which formal marriage is being replaced by less formal alternatives. In the event, there is evidence of an increase in the popularity of cohabitation. Data assembled by Höpflinger (1985: 50) for four European countries show that, in the younger age groups, decreases in the proportion married are generally offset by increases in the proportion cohabiting.

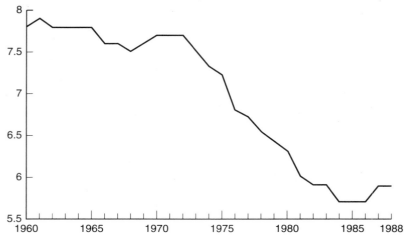

*Figure 4.1   **Marriages per thousand population, European Community, 1960–1988***
Source: Eurostat (1990: 182)

A growing reluctance to get married has been accompanied by an increasing reluctance to stay married. Changes in the law have made divorce much easier in northern and western Europe. Table 4.3 shows, for selected EEC countries, the trend in number of divorces per thousand marriages. Sardon (1986: 478) has estimated, for seven European countries, the trend between 1947 and 1975 in the proportion of couples marrying in a particular year whose marriages were destined to end in divorce, and the average duration of these marriages. Apparently recent rates imply that around a third of marriages end in divorce, and that there has been a marked reduction in the length of these marriages.

*Table 4.3   **Divorces per thousand existing marriages, selected European countries, 1965–88***

	1965	*1975*	*1985*	*1988*
Belgium	2.3	4.4	7.3	8.4
Denmark	5.4	10.6	12.6	13.1
France	3.1	4.5	8.4	8.4
Italy	–	0.8	1.1	2.1*
Netherlands	2.2	6.0	9.9	8.1
UK†	3.1	9.6	12.9	12.3

* Provisional data
† Data before 1983 relate to England and Wales only

Source: Eurostat (1990: 189)

Fertility

The change that has had, and will continue to have, the greatest impact on European demography (and much else) is the decline of fertility to levels insufficient to replace populations.

A commonly used measure of current fertility is the total fertility rate (TFR), which is the average completed family size implied by the age-specific fertility rates achieved by a population in a specified year. In most European countries the rate fell from around four children per woman at the beginning of the century to a level well below that required for required for renewal of the population throughout the period 1925–45 (Sardon 1990: 17). After the Second World War, the TFR rose again to above the replacement level in most countries and appeared to be stabilising. In the mid-1950s there was a widespread rise, which reached a peak in 1965 in most countries.

The behaviour of the TFR over recent decades in European countries is shown in Table 4.4. Also shown are projections for the period 1995 to 2025. With the mortality pattern of modern Europe, the TFR needs to be about 2.1 to ensure population replacement. The only European countries shown in the table with fertility above this level in 1988 are Iceland and Ireland, but the projections assume that these populations too will join the below-replacement majority.

Between the mid-1960s and the mid-1970s, fertility declined rapidly in north, west and central Europe. In Italy, Portugal and Spain, the decline from the mid-1960s was continuous; it was more moderate than elsewhere in Europe for the first ten years but became much steeper after 1974. Since the mid-1970s, European fertility rates have declined less rapidly in a number of countries or have stabilised, and there has been a modest recovery in some.

Analyses of the demographic statistics reveal that the fertility decline has been caused largely by a decrease in third and higher-order births, together with an increase in the proportion of childless women. Changes have also occurred in the age at which women start childbearing. For European Community countries, the average age fell from 25.5 years in 1960 to 24.4 in 1970, and has since risen steadily; in 1987 it was 25.9 years (Eurostat 1990: 169).

Reporting in 1982 on an analysis of the fertility decline, Calot and Blayo (1982) offered two alternative characterisations of the phenomenon. One of these saw the decline as the first down-swing of an infinite series of oscillations of fertility somewhere near the level required for population replacement. The alternative characterisation saw the decline as the resumption of the historical decline of fertility to levels well below the replacement level, after an accidental upturn that was a consequence of two world wars. It is too early to say whether the recent upturns in the TFR observed in a number of countries firmly support the first of these alternatives. The TFR can be a misleading index of potential family size because it is affected by

Table 4.4   **Total fertility rate, Europe, 1965–2025 (UN medium variant projections from 1995)**

	1965	1975	1985	1988	1995–2000	2010–15	2020–25
Eastern Europe							
Bulgaria	2.07	2.23	1.95	1.96	1.80	1.90	1.90
Czechoslovakia	2.37	2.43	2.07	2.02	1.90	1.90	1.90
Germany (GDR)	2.48	1.54	1.74	1.67	1.70	1.80	1.80
Hungary	1.82	2.35	1.83	1.81	1.80	1.80	1.80
Poland	2.52	2.27	2.33	–	2.05	2.05	2.05
Romania	1.91	2.60	–	–	1.90	1.90	1.90
Northern Europe							
Denmark	2.61	1.92	1.45	1.56	1.55	1.70	1.70
Finland	2.47	1.68	1.64	1.59	1.70	1.78	1.80
Iceland	3.71	2.65	1.93	2.27	1.85	1.87	1.90
Ireland	4.03	3.41	2.49	2.17	2.20	2.05	2.05
Norway	2.93	1.98	1.68	1.84	1.73	1.80	1.80
Sweden	2.42	1.77	1.73	1.96	1.70	1.78	1.80
UK	2.83	1.81	1.80	1.83	1.82	1.90	1.90
Southern Europe							
Albania					2.55	2.25	2.20
Greece	2.32	2.33	1.68	1.52	1.70	1.85	1.90
Italy	2.55	2.19	1.41	1.33	1.55	1.70	1.70
Portugal	3.07	2.57	1.71	1.53	1.75	1.90	1.90
Spain	2.97	2.80	1.61	1.43	1.70	1.85	1.90
Yugoslavia	2.71	2.27	2.05	1.98	1.82	1.90	1.90
Western Europe							
Austria	2.70	1.83	1.47	1.44	1.55	1.70	1.70
Belgium	2.60	1.73	1.50	1.56	1.70	1.80	1.80
France	2.84	1.93	1.82	1.82	1.85	1.90	1.90
Germany (FR)	2.51	1.45	1.28	1.40	1.50	1.70	1.70
Luxembourg	2.41	1.63	1.38	1.51	1.55	1.70	1.70
Netherlands	3.04	1.66	1.51	1.54	1.50	1.65	1.70
Switzerland	2.61	1.61	1.51	1.51	1.57	1.70	1.70
Developed countries*	2.69	2.20	1.93	1.90	1.90	1.93	1.94
Developing countries*	6.08	5.41	4.19	3.92	3.45	2.70	2.33
World	4.97	4.45	3.61	3.44	3.13	2.58	2.27

* Data for 1965–88 refer to the following periods: 1960–65, 1970–75, 1980–85, 1985–1990 (United Nations 1989b: 150)

Sources: Data for 1965–88 – Monnier (1990: 928); data for projections – United Nations (1989b: 150 and 155)

shifts in the timing of births – short-term shifts and shifts caused by a systematic change in the age of women at first and subsequent births (Brass 1989: 17). For example, it has been shown that when the age at maternity was declining, the TFR misrepresented the underlying trend to an extend that was sufficient to mask the onset of the fall in completed fertility in the generations producing children during the period (Sardon 1990: 21).

One of the most striking new trends in recent years has been the increase in the proportion of births that have occurred outside marriage. For EEC countries the proportion rose from 5.5 per cent in 1975 to 16.1 per cent in 1988. In Denmark it rose from 21.7 per cent to 44.7 per cent, and in the United Kingdom, from 9.0 per cent to 25.1 per cent, in the same period (Eurostat 1990: 172–3). Nevertheless, for the present, the great majority of European couples still prefer to be married when they become parents.

Ageing

Largely as a consequence of fertility decline (which has shifted the age distribution upwards) but partly as a consequence of mortality decline (which has meant more survivors in the older age groups) the population of Europe has been ageing. This is not a new phenomenon. It started with an historical fertility transition a century ago, accelerated when fertility dropped to a low level during the Depression years of the 1930s, slowed down as a result of the baby boom after the Second World War, and finally accelerated again as a result of the fertility decline in the mid-1960s. Although the process could be reversed by an upturn in births, this would have to be a remarkable one: a speedy and sustained (and very unlikely) return to a total fertility rate of around 2.5 births per woman (United Nations 1989a: 102).

One measure of ageing is change in the median age. For Europe as whole, the median age – 31 years in 1950 – is expected to increase to 38 years by the end of the century and to 43 years by 2025. In contrast, the corresponding figures for Africa are 19, 18 and 23 (United Nations 1989b: 53). The trends in age structure, median age and dependency ratio are shown in Table 4.5. The proportion of the population in the economically active age range is expected to increase until the end of the century as the high-fertility generations of the 1950s and 1960s reach working age. Subsequently the proportion of dependants is expected to increase, owing largely to the effect of the low-fertility generations which arrived after the baby boom, but also to the effect of declining mortality.

Household structure

Along with other demographic changes reviewed above, there has been a substantial change in household structure in European countries.

The proportion of one-person households rose, and average household size fell throughout Europe. From around 1960 to around 1980, the proportion rose from 20 to 25 per cent in France, from 21 to 31 per cent in the Federal Republic of Germany, from 11 to 18 per cent in Italy, and from 14 to 20 per cent in Hungary (Wall 1988: Table 7).

Table 4.5   Age structure (% in different age groups), median age and dependency ratio (population aged 0–14 and 65+ as % of population aged 15–64), Europe, 1950–2025 (UN medium variant projections from 1990)

	1950	1970	1990	2010	2025
Age group					
0–4	9.2	8.3	6.4	5.7	5.5
5–14	16.2	16.6	13.3	11.9	11.1
15–25	16.2	15.5	15.1	12.3	11.6
60+	12.9	16.7	18.6	22.0	27.0
65+	8.7	11.4	13.4	16.1	20.1
Median age	30.5	32.3	35.0	40.3	42.9
Dependency ratio					
0–14	38.5	39.2	29.3	26.6	26.2
65+	13.2	17.9	20.0	24.3	31.7
Total	51.7	57.2	49.3	50.9	57.9

Source: United Nations (1989b: 238)

There was an especially sharp increase in this proportion for people aged 65 and over. In Great Britain the proportion of elderly females living alone rose from 30 per cent to 45 per cent (Wall 1988: Table 4). The increase in one-person households has been attributed to a shift towards more independent life-styles, the improved health and financial situation of the elderly, the fact that few European households now have live-in domestic services, and the unsuitability of most urban housing for more than a one-generation family (Karl Schwarz reported in van de Kaa 1987: 33).

Van de Kaa (1987: 32–5) reviews studies of the distribution of single-parent households and the living arrangements of young people. The proportion of single-parent families among all households has been increasing. A study of six western European countries found the highest proportion (5 per cent) in the Netherlands and the lowest in England and Wales (3 per cent). A study of eastern European countries found a proportion of 13 per cent in Hungary.

There are considerable differences between countries in the living arrangements of 20–24-year-olds. Data for six countries in 1982 showed that the proportion of men still living with their parents was highest in Ireland (62 per cent) and lowest in Denmark (26 per cent). For women, the figures were 57 and 11 per cent. Most of the men and women who had left home were living with a partner.

International migration

Half the countries in the European region have at least a quarter of a million foreign-born persons (United Nations 1988a: 238). These countries include Belgium, where 8.9 per cent of the population were foreign-born in 1981, France with 11.1 per cent in 1982, the Federal Republic of Germany with 7.4 per cent in 1983 and the United Kingdom with 6.3 per cent in 1981.

Le Bras (1991) had roughly estimated the demographic impact of immigration on some European countries over the 40 years following the Second World War. This showed that the impact on total population growth had been considerable – 15 per cent in the Federal Repubic of Germany and between 5 and 10 per cent in France, Belgium and Sweden. However, the rejuvenating effect was modest. The populations had become younger, but only by 0.8 of a year in Belgium, 0.7 of a year in Sweden and 0.4 of a year in Germany and France.

Interpreting the fertility decline

While research on the fertility behaviour of industrial society had produced a number of empirical generalisations, relating fertility to social class and other variables, there was still no well-established general theory that could be invoked to explain the fertility decline of the 1960s, or the rise of the 1950s. Inevitably the magnitude of the decline and its implications for the age structure of European populations gave a new impetus to attempts to find explanations for such phenomena.

There is a general assumption that, when deciding whether or when to produce a child, people in industrial societies typically take into account the expected effects of doing so on projected life-style. The effects will depend on the characteristics of the life-style and the costs of maintaining it, on the parents' income and other resources, and on the expected effects of a child on both costs and (if the earning capacity of a parent would be affected) income. It is assumed that parents weigh the importance to themselves and to their preferred life-style of having a child or another child against any consequences that would be experienced as constraints on life-style.

High living standards and the cost of maintaining them make parenthood in the West expensive. As well as the direct costs, there are the costs, especially for women, of forgoing valued alternatives to parenthood. In these circumstances, fertility level is likely to depend on society's success in maintaining the commitment of its members to a core value system that makes family-building important to people despite its costs. According to the explanations offered by most analysts, it is precisely this battle that society has been losing.

Lesthaeghe (1983) believes the root cause is 'secular individualism'. As recent evidence of its influence, he cites the growing prevalence of cohabitation outside marriage, voluntary childlessness, nonconformist sexual conduct, abortion and euthanasia. Using multi-variate analyses of regional data for three European countries, he demonstrates a close relationship, lasting over a period of at least a century, between decline in marital fertility, falls in indicators (such as church attendance) of the influence of traditional religious ideas, and increases in such indicators of structural modernisation as the proportion of the population employed in industry.

Preston is another contributor to the doctrine that most of the fertility decline is explained by a loosening of normative controls. In the case of Americans, he says, they became 'more inclined to justify their behaviour in terms of its consequences for personal development, and less inclined to justify it on grounds of fulfilling or adhering to valued social roles'. As a result of publicity given to world population growth, responsible parenthood came to mean reducing family size to a level lower than it otherwise would have been. Sustained economic growth increased the expense of children and expanded opportunities in ways that made people increasingly restive 'under the yoke of responsible parenthood and monogamous marriage'. In short, when normative controls became inconvenient, they were abandoned (Preston 1986).

Davis (1986) suggests that there is an incompatibility, or tension between the family on the one hand and the industrial economy on the other. The normative controls required for the maintenance of family life break down, he says, when people live in large cities, strive for social mobility, work in an impersonal environment, receive income as individuals rather than as family members, and acquire formal education in schools beyond parental control. Under these conditions, family norms are violated with impunity, and conformity is labelled 'old-fashioned' or 'conservative'. It is these characteristics of modernity that encourage trends towards later marriage, reproduction outside marriage, high divorce rates and the extensive participation of women in the labour force. According to Davis, these four trends go far towards explaining the below-replacement fertility of industrial nations.

A number of authors refer to evidence collected by surveys of beliefs and values to support the notion of a shift to nonconformist behaviour. A useful source of comparative data on the subject is a set of national surveys of cultural values conducted in European countries in 1981. They were conducted under the sponsorship of a charitable foundation, the European Value Systems Study Group. In each country the respondents were a nationally representative sample of some 1,200 adults aged 18 and over.

Several of the questions asked in the survey were capable of revealing something about the extent and character of commitment to the family. For example, respondents were asked whether they thought it was the parents' duty to do their best for their children, even at the expense of their own well-being. Presumably a positive answer would be one indicator of the endorsement of norms that stressed commitment to the family, while a negative answer would

Table 4.6 **Rank-order relationships (Spearman's rho) between total fertility rate and aggregate responses to selected questions from the International Values Study (1981) for twelve European countries, respondents aged 18–44 only**

	1	2	3	4	5	6	7	8
1 Total fertility rate, 1981								
2 Parents' duty	.89†							
3 Children's duty	.73†	.63*						
4 Incompatibility divorce	−.66*	−.65*	−.27					
5 National pride	.62*	.35	.40	−.39				
6 Importance of God	.39	.23	.65*	−.06	.66*			
7 Marriage outdated	.06	.16	.24	.16	.36	−.08		
8 Political orientation	.20	.12	−.07	−.44	.32	.08	−.87†	
9 Income satisfaction	−.29	−.25	−.46	−.26	−.02	−.10	−.57	.58*

Notes:
* p < .05
† p < .01

1 Total fertility rate, 1981
2 Parents' duty: % endorsing view that it is parents' duty to do their best for their children, even at the expense of their own well-being
3 Children's duty: % endorsing view that, regardless of parents' qualities and faults, one must always love and respect them
4 Incompatibility/divorce: % endorsing view that 'when personalities don't match' is sufficient reason for divorce
5 National pride: mean scale of response to questions: 'How proud are you to be . . . nationality?' (Scale: very proud = 4; quite proud = 3; not very proud = 2; not at all proud = 1)
6 Importance of God: mean scale value of response to question: 'How important is God in your life?' (1 = not at all; 10 = very)
7 Marriage outdated: % tending to agree marriage is an outdated institution
8 Political orientation: mean scale value of reported position on scale from 1 = Left to 10 = Right.
9 Income satisfaction: mean scale value of response to question: 'How satisfied are you with the financial situation of your household?' (1 = dissatisfied; 10 = satisfied)

Source: Computed from survey data supplied by Social Surveys (Gallup Poll)

suggest more pragmatic ideas. For the twelve countries, the national percentage responding positively was highly correlated (a rank order correlation of 0.9) with the total fertility rate. A postive response was given by two-thirds or more of respondents in the age range 18–44 years in five of the twelve European countries for which data were available. In contrast, less than 50 per cent responded positively in the three countries with the lowest fertility: the Netherlands, Denmark, and the Federal Republic of Germany. Similar results were obtained with responses to a question asking whether, regardless of parents' qualities and faults, one must always love and respect them and to a question asking whether children were important for a successful marriage. Table 4.6 is a correlation matrix showing the strength of association, as measured by the rank order correlation coefficient (Spearman's rho), among national aggregate responses to selected questions and the total fertility rate.

The prevalance of a sense of moral obligation to family members is an index of the extent to which the members of a society are committed to its core cultural values. It was suggested earlier that, in the conditions of modern Europe, fertility level also will depend on a society's success in maintaining the commitment of its members to its core values – values that make family-building important to people despite its costs. The observed associations between fertility level and responses to the questions on obligation to the family support this interpretation. It is also supported by the evidence shown in Table 4.6 of links between fertility level, response to questions on obligations to family and response to a question on national pride, which may be regarded as a measure of social integration. As well as being correlated with fertility level and the familism measures, national pride was also correlated with response to a question on 'the importance of God in your life'. In other words, countries with a high mean score for national pride also tended to have a high score for the importance of God. Sociologists may see in this some support for Durkheim's view of the religious character of the link between individual and society (Durkheim 1915).

Most commentators assume that trends to nonconformist sexual conduct (such as cohabitation as an alternative to marriage) and the fertility decline are manifestations of the same growth of pragmatism in the sphere of personal conduct. Analyses of data from the Values survey suggest that this interpretation needs amendment. For example, one question asked whether respondents agreed that marriage was an outdated institution. National response was not correlated with fertility level in the twelve European countries or with the familism measures, nor with the measure of social integration, but was correlated, negatively, with a measure of rightward political orientation. Similar results were obtained for responses to questions about the justifiability of extra-marital affairs and sex under the legal age. Apparently ideas about forms of partnership can vary independently of ideas about reproductive behaviour. If this were not so, some of the demographic evidence might be difficult to explain – for example, the relatively high fertility of Sweden given the popularity of cohabitation there.

Another correlate of rightward political orientation was response to the question: 'How satisfied are you with the financial situation of your household?' Again, aggregate response was uncorrelated with national fertility level or with response to questions on family sentiments.

The findings of the Values survey for individual countries suggested that in most countries family commitment was widespread in 1981, despite the fact that their fertility levels were below replacement level. However, the commitment may have been declining and may decline further. An important feature of the evidence produced by the Values survey is the marked effect of age on responses. An analysis by age group showed that the younger the cohort, the lower the national pride, the greater the leftward political orientation, the less the importance of God and the less the inclination to say that parents had a duty to do their best for their children. No doubt some of the age differences were due to the effects of age itself, but it seems that some were also due to differences in values between younger and older cohorts that were likely to persist.

Some countries appeared to be more successful than others in maintaining their value systems. For example, the inter-generational differences were smaller in Britain than they were in the Netherlands: elsewhere Values data have been combined with other evidence to suggest that Britain has relatively conservative attitudes towards reproduction (Simons 1986a). However, in general, age-group differences suggested a progressive shift away from an ideology that stressed obligation to family and society. The Values survey has recently been repeated, so that it should soon be possible to determine the extent to which the earlier age-group differences have persisted as the cohorts have aged.

Details of the findings summarised above, and of the theory used to interpret them, have been reported elsewhere (Simons 1986b; Simons 1982). Complementary findings and further theorising, based on individual-level analyses of the Values survey and other surveys have been presented in papers by Lesthaeghe and Meekers (1986) and Lesthaeghe and Surkyn (1988).

Not surprisingly, given the expense of child-bearing in the west, it has often been suggested that the explanation of fertility decline lies in the economics of reproduction. In particular it is commonly supposed that the opportunity for women to engage in paid employment is a disincentive to childbearing, and that rises in female employment were a major reason for fertility decline. In fact, the available evidence offers rather little support for this view. Höhn (1983) demonstrates that it is not supported by evidence on trends in women's employment in the fourteen member states of the Council of Europe. British studies have shown that female employment was rising during the 1950s and 1960s when fertility was also high and rising, and that improvements in women's employment opportunities were no more than a partial explanation of fertility decline (Joshi 1989: 174–5; 1990: 122–3).

Social consequences of population ageing

A society supports its elderly population from its current output and income. As shown in Table 4.5, the elderly dependency ratio (the population aged 65 and over as a percentage of the population aged

15–64) is expected to increase from 20 in 1990 to 31.7 in 2025. This implies (assuming no other relevant changes) an increase of about 50 per cent in the per capita cost of supporting the elderly. Because the proportion of the elderly who reach advanced ages will also increase, there will be a real increase in the burden on health and social services.

In a review of these effects, Weaver (1986) reports that, between 1960 and 1980, social security pension payments as a percentage of gross domestic product increased sharply. They doubled in the United Kingdom, Austria and Belgium, and tripled in Switzerland, Sweden and the Netherlands. This was not due to population ageing alone, but also to the fact that provisions were made more generous. The economic events of the 1970s created serious problems for the payment systems: reserves were wiped out in the attempt to meet escalating benefit payments in the face of an eroding tax base. In response, virtually every country increased taxes.

According to Weaver, the buldge in retirements in the next century will mean insolvency for social security systems around the world. On the other hand, population ageing also implies some savings in the costs of supporting children, because there will be fewer of them. According to some analysts, these savings may at least partly offset the rise in the costs of the elderly. And the elderly might themselves encourage this to happen. An increase in their number increases their voting strength, and this may lead to an improvement in the state's contribution to their well-being, at the expense of its contribution to schooling and other resources for children (Coale 1986).

An international symposium on population was convened by the United Nations in 1987. Its report was not pessimistic about the dependency burden. It was agreed that the share of total income going to the elderly was likely to increase, but the report argued that the absolute levels of after-tax income per worker would continue to rise as a result of increased productivity and a reduced burden of youth dependency. The funding of pensions would be a problem but not an insoluble one. The reduced burden of child care in an ageing population could help families to pay higher contribution rates. Eliminating compulsory retirement and raising the age of pension eligibility from 60 to 65 years could substantially reduce the expenditures of pension schemes, by 50 per cent in some cases (United Nations 1988b).

Evidently, much will depend on the capacity of countries to improve the productivity of the ageing labour force. The United Nations symposium mentioned above was sanguine about the prospects of doing so. To prevent the knowledge and skills of an ageing labour force becoming obsolete, opportunity and incentives for retraining could be provided. It was suggested that population ageing might actually increase per-capita income by permitting a greater labour-force participation of women, and by increasing the per-capita availability of capital. For a useful discussion of the relationships between demographic change, economic growth and social welfare, see Ermisch and Joshi (1987).

Policy implications

Pronatalist policy

Given the adverse consequences of low fertility, it is not surprising that governments in several countries have tried to persuade their populations to produce more children. According to responses to a United Nations survey in 1986, nine European countries thought their rates of population growth were too low: Bulgaria, the German Democratic Republic, Hungary, Romania, Greece, France, the German Federal Republic, Liechtenstein and Monaco. With the exception of the Federal Republic of Germany, all these countries had instituted policies aimed at encouraging higher fertility (United Nations 1988a: 34–5). The majority of European countries regarded their growth rate as satisfactory, but five reported having made attempts to maintain the current rates.

Those countries which considered their rates of growth too low wished them to be equal to or slightly higher than the level necessary to ensure population replacement. The measures taken to achieve this aim have ranged from child allowances to housing loans and the right to paid leave from work. Such measures are often included in family policy even in countries which do not have an explicit aim of increasing fertility. Where this is the aim, the measures taken are more likely to be tuned to specific demographic events. For example, in some countries women receive a special allowance on the birth of a third child.

It is difficult to assess the effectiveness of pronatalist policy because fertility is being affected by so many other influences at the same time. According to Klinger (1987: 420) the measures taken affect attitudes to fertility for very short periods only. Most analysts appear to believe that new or increased incentives to produce a child have at most a temporary effect on the timing of births rather than on the size of the completed family (McIntosh 1986: 323). However, some successes have been reported. Calot and Hecht (1978) estimate that approximately 10 per cent of French fertility in the late 1940s and 1950s could be attributed to the effects of family policy. Hoem (1990) attributes the relatively high and increasing fertility of Sweden to social policies that have 'consistently tried to facilitate women's entry into the labor market and their continued attachment to it at minimal cost to childbearing and childrearing'. Klinger (1987) reviews evidence of the effects of pronatalist policy in several countries.

Demeny (1986: 354) believes that measures could be devised that would be much more effective than those that have been tried to date. One of his suggestions is to allow parents to benefit directly in old age from having raised children, by allocating part of individuals' social security contributions to their living but retired parents.

International migration

Major labour migrations to western Europe occurred during the 1960s and early 1970s, but ended in the mid-1970s when the recruitment of foreign workers ceased and strong immigration controls were imposed. Subsequently, most new arrivals were family members (especially wives and children) of immigrants who had settled permanently. It has been suggested that restrictive policies may soon need to be reversed, so that immigration could be used to compensate for fertility decline and rejuvenate Europe's population. The feasibility of doing so has been the subject of recent studies.

Wattelar and Roumans (1991) estimated the migratory flows that would be required to offset population ageing. They found that a policy of using migrants to top up the population of working age, to make up for shortfalls, could keep the elderly dependency ratio (which they defined as the ratio of those aged 20–64 years to those aged 65 years and over) at an acceptable level of 3 to 1. However, such a policy would require annual quotas of immigrants well above those to which countries are accustomed.

In 1985 the European Population Committee of the Council of Europe set up a special committee of demographers from eight member states to consider immigration policy and other issues arising from the differences in population growth rates between Europe and the Third World.

The conclusions adopted by the Committee reject the idea that immigration could be even a partial remedy for Europe's population problem. In fact the Committee recommended that Europe make a sustained effort to promote development in countries lying south and east of the Mediterranean, as a means of eliminating the conditions that encourage people in these countries to want to come to Europe. Another recommendation was that Europe respond more generously than in the past to requests for help with attempts to curb rapid population growth in these countries and in the countries of sub-Saharan Africa. The committee believed it was a delusion to suppose that immigration could compensate for the consequences of low fertility, and thought that, instead, European countries should adopt pronatalist social policies.

Conclusion

Despite the decline in fertility, it is premature to suppose that Europe faces demographic extinction. In recent years fertility in most countries has either been relatively stable or has actually increased. The fact that fertility rose after the long decline that came to an end in the 1930s, and boomed between the mid-1950s and mid-1960s, indicates the regenerative capacities of European societies. It has been suggested (Simons 1986b) that these earlier upswings were a response to familist tendencies generated by 1930s anomie and enhanced by the experience of the Second World War. It could similarly be speculated that the recent upturns were a response to the anomie created by the social upheavals of recent decades, and are therefore unlikely to be transient. Nevertheless, there is no reason to expect, in the foreseeable future, an upswing in Europe's fertility substantial enough to reverse the ageing process. The ageing of their populations will pose complex problems for European society, and will make heavy demands on their resources and resourcefulness.

References

Brass, W. (1989) 'Is Britain facing the twilight of parenthood?', in H. Joshi (ed.) *The changing population of Britain*, Oxford: Blackwell

Calot, G. and Blayo, C. (1982) 'Recent course of fertility in Western Europe', *Population Studies*, 36 (3) 349–72.

——and Hecht, J. (1978) 'The control of fertility trends', in *Population Decline in Europe*. New York: St Martin's Press, 178–96.

Coale, A. (1986) 'Demographic effects of below-replacement fertility and their social implications', in K. Davis, M. Bernstam and R. Ricardo-Campbell, (eds) Below-replacement Fertility in Industrial Societies – Causes, Consequences, Policies, *Population and Development Review*, Supplement to Vol. 12, 1986, New York: Population Council: 203–16.

Council of Europe (1990) *Recent Demographic Development in the Member States of the Council of Europe*, 1989 ed, Strasbourg: Council of Europe.

Davis, K. (1986) Low fertility in evolutionary perspective, in K. Davis, M. Bernstam and R. Ricardo-Campbell (eds) Below-replacement Fertility in Industrial Societies – Causes, Consequences, Policies, *Population and Development Review*, Supplement to Vol. 12, 1986, New York: Population Council: 335–58.

Demeny, P. (1986) 'Pronatalist policies in low-fertility countries: patterns, performance, and prospects', in K. Davis, M. Bernstam and R. Ricardo-Campbell (eds) Below-replacement Fertility in Industrial Societies – Causes, Consequences, Policies, *Population and Development Review*, Supplement to Vol. 12, 1986, New York: Population Council: 335–58.

Durkheim, E (1915) *The Elementary Forms of the Religious Life*, London: Allen & Unwin, (first published in French, 1912).

Ermisch, J. and Joshi, H. (1987) 'Demographic change, economic growth and social welfare', in *Proceedings of Plenary Sessions of European Population Conference, Finland, June 11–16 1987*, Helsinki: Central Statistical Office of Finland: 329–86.

Eurostat (1990) *Demographic Statistics 1990*, Luxembourg: European Community.

Hoem, J. M. (1990) 'Social policy and recent fertility change in Sweden', *Population and Development Review*, 16 (4): 735–48.

Höhn, C. (1983) 'Participation in economic activity and the changing role of women', in *Proceedings of the European Population Conference 1982*, Strasbourg: Council of Europe, 129–47.

Höpflinger, F. (1985) 'Changing marriage behaviour: some European comparisons', *Genus*, XLI (3–4): 41–63.

Joshi, H. (1989) 'The changing form of women's economic dependency', in H. Joshi (ed.) *The Changing Population of Britain*, Oxford: Blackwell.

——(1990) 'Changing roles of women in the British labour market and the family', in P. Deane (ed.) *Frontiers of Economic Research*, Proceedings of Section F (Economics) of the British Association for the Advancement of Science, Oxford, 1988, London: Macmillan.

Klinger, A. (1987) 'Policy response and effects', in *Proceedings of Plenary Sessions of Population Conference, Finland, June 11–16, 1987*, Helsinki. Central Statistical Office of Finland: 387–432.

Le Bras, H. (1991) 'Demographic impact of post-war migration in selected OECD countries', in *Migration – the Demographic Aspects*, Paris: OECD: 15–27

Lesthaeghe, R. (1983) 'A century of demographic and cultural change in Western Europe: an exploration of underlying dimensions', *Population and Development Review*, 9 (3): 411–35.

——and Meekers, D. (1986) 'Value changes and the dimensions of familism in the European Community', *European Journal of Population* (1986) (2): 225–68

——and Surkyn, J. (1988) 'Cultural dynamics and economic theories of fertility change', *Population and Development Review*, 14 (1): 1–45.

McIntosh, C. A. (1986) 'Recent pronatalist policies in Western Europe', in K. Davis, M. Bernstam and R. Ricardo-Campbell (eds) Below-replacement Fertility in Industrial Societies – Causes, Consequences, Policies, *Population and Development Review*, Supplement to Vol. 12, 1986, New York, Population Council: 318–34.

Monnier, A. (1990) 'La Conjuncture démographique: l'Europe et les pays dévelopés d'outre-mer', *Population*, 45 (4–5): 924–36.

Preston, R. (1986) 'The decline of fertility in non-European industrialized countries', in K. Davis, M. Bernstam, R. Ricardo-Campbell (eds) Below-replacement Fertility in Industrial Societies – Causes, Consequences, Policies, *Population and Development Review*, Supplement to Vol. 12, 1986, New York, Population Council: 176–95.

Sardon, J–P. (1986) 'Évolution de la nuptialité et de la divortialité en Europe depuis la fin des années 1960', *Population*, 41 (3): 463–82.

——(1990) *Cohort Fertility in Member States of the Council of Europe*. Strasbourg: Council of Europe.

Simons, J. (1982) 'Reproductive behaviour as religious practice', in C. Höhn and R. MacKensen (eds) *Determinants of Fertility Trends: Theories Re-examined. Proceedings of a seminar held by the International Union for the Scientific Study of Population, Bad Homburg, April 1980*, Liège: Ordina: 131–45.

——(1986a) 'How conservative are British attitudes to reproduction?' *Quarterly Journal of Social Affairs*, 2 (1): 41–54.

——(1986b) 'Culture, economy and reproduction in contemporary Europe', in D. Coleman and R. Schofield (eds) *The State of Population Theory*, Oxford: Blackwell: 256–78.

United Nations (1988a) *World Population Trends and Policies, 1987 Monitoring Report*, New York: United Nations.

——(1988b) *Economic and Social Implications of Population Ageing: Proceedings of an International Symposium on Population Structure and Development, Tokyo, September 1987*, New York: United Nations.

——(1989a) *World Population at the Turn of the Century*, Population Studies No. 111, New York: United Nations.

——(1989b) *World Population Prospects 1988*, Population Studies No. 106, New York: United Nations.

Valkonen, T. (1987) 'Social inequality in the face of death', in *Proceedings of Plenary Sessions of European Population Conference, Finland, June 11–16 1987*, Helsinki: Central Statistical Office of Finland: 201–61.

Van de Kaa, D. (1987) 'Europe's second demographic transition', *Population Bulletin* 42 (1), Washington, DC: Population Reference Bureau.

Wall, R. (1988) 'Leaving home and living alone: an historical perspective', *Discussion Paper No. 211*, London: Centre for Economic Policy Research.

Wattelar, C. and Roumans, G, (1991) 'Simulations of demographic objectives and migration', in *Migration – the Demographic Aspects*, Paris: OECD 57–67.

Weaver, C. L. (1986) 'Social security in ageing societies', in K. Davis, M. Bernstam and R. Ricardo-Campbell (eds) Below-replacement Fertility in Industrial Societies – Causes, Consequences, Policies, *Population and Development Review*, Supplement to vol. 12, 1986, New York, Population Council: 273–94.

CHAPTER 5

Gender and Europe: cultural and structural impediments to change

ANGELA GLASNER

European women outnumber European men: 51.9 per cent of the population is female, a ratio that is relatively constant across the member states of the European Community.[1] However, although they constitute a majority and despite an abundance of national and international legislation to prevent discrimination against them, throughout Europe they remain a disadvantaged group, and gender continues to be a major structural dimension in European societies. This chapter is about exploring and understanding these gender differences, and it will discuss the extent to which women across Europe share experiences, for despite different cultures and traditions, there is evidence of a widespread commonality of disadvantage in their position both across Europe and beyond.

The potential scope of a chapter such as this is immense, and a full consideration would undoubtedly encompass a discussion of gender socialisation, and societal and work-base politics[2]. This chapter is, however, more focused and, after briefly reviewing the role played by the European Commission in attempting to establish commonality of practice across large parts of Europe, it looks at the activities of women themselves through the development of feminism during the last three decades. In evaluating the impact of European Community policy and feminism, the chapter then focuses on abortion and child care as exemplars of the constraints which impinge upon women's private lives, and upon employment as an illustration of the public arena of women's experiences.

There is a long history to gender differences and an equally long history to women's attempts to address the differences. Across the western world, although not entirely throughout Europe, women's organisations from the nineteenth century campaigned for the abolition of laws that discriminated against women and for the introduction of those which would facilitate the emancipation of women. By the second quarter of the twentieth century, it was largely believed that women had achieved emancipation and that equality was no longer an issue:[3] However, during the 1950s and 1960s, issues of equality slowly began to re-emerge with the recognition that, despite a higher involvement in employment outside the home and apparent equality in access to education, women were still significantly disadvantaged.

The late 1960s and early 1970s saw the emergence of what has been described as the Second Wave of Feminism. This period also saw the emergence of Europe as a new economic, and subsequently political and social, force. Joni Lovenduski (1988) suggests that with the emergence of feminism in the late 1960s and early 1970s, women began to influence policy processes and outcomes again, as their predecessors had in the mid-nineteenth century during the First Wave of Feminism. For Buckley and Anderson (1988) there was a 'happy co-incidence' in the establishment of the European Community and the growth of the Second Wave of Feminism,[4] and this raises the question of how far the European Community has reduced discrimination against women and increased the commonality of experience across Europe.

The role of the European Community in promoting equal opportunities

Within the Treaty of Rome, signed in 1957 and implemented with respect to France, Germany, Italy, Belgium, the Netherlands and Luxembourg in 1967, Article 119 specifically addressed women's equal rights in employment.[5] By the early 1980s, with the full membership of twelve partner nations and following the implementation of the Social Charter in 1975, equality of opportunity had become the focus of explicit attention, and in 1982 the first Equal Opportunites Action Programme was launched. The Action Programme recognised that equal pay was only the starting point for a campaign whose ultimate aim was the realisation of full participation in society for women.[6] The programme was designed to strengthen and extend existing individual rights through legislation, but also to change habits and traditions by means of positive action. On the legal front, it required member states to take action to monitor equal opportunities implementation; provide legal redress with respect to equal treatment; review protective legislation, social security entitlement, and taxation; extend equal opportunities as embedded in Article 119 to self-employed women and those working in other protected sectors such as agriculture; and extend parental leave entitlement and abolish discrimination against pregnant women in employment.

It was thus recognised in the first Action Programme that stereotyped attitudes to the roles and responsibilities of both women and men persisted and had been accentuated by the economic crises which had spread throughout Europe in the 1970s and 1980s, and that the question of equality could not be addressed solely through economic and labour force-directed policies. The programme therefore sought also to facilitate the development of positive action budgets for training career enhancement, and to promote desegregation of employment.

In assessing the success of the first programme in 1986, the Commission concluded that although progress had been made, much remained to be done. A new Action Programme[7] was designed to consolidate existing rights under Community law,[8] to follow up and develop the action launched under the earlier initiative, to engage in a broader consciousness-raising campaign, and to develop and intensify support for specific actions, particularly in relation to women's employment. In May 1991, a third medium-term Community Action Programme, this time entitled 'Equal Opportunities for Women and Men' was adopted. In the context of the climate which is now changing and will alter definitively with the completion of the internal market in 1992, the new programme spanning 1991–95 and published in *WoE34* (1991) aims to develop new initiatives directed at women in the vocational training and employment area and to achieve a better integration and more comprehensive strategy for action across the community. It has a three-pronged focus: the implementation and development of the law; the integration of women into the labour market; and improving the state of women in society. The last of these objectives is interesting in that for the first time the importance of measures to promote the participation of women in the decision-making process in economic and social life is recognised, and along with the involvement of women in media and the presentation of positive images of women is a specific target. Given the Community's original constitution it is perhaps not surprising that in the third initiative the lack of visible progress forces attention to broader social and cultural areas of community life.

The concern with equal opportunities and gender-related issues was not unique to the European Community. Randall (1987) notes the important role played by the United Nations after the Second World War in proclaiming 1975 International Women's Year and the following ten years the Decade for Women. The ten-year World Plan which launched the decade pinpointed the three critical areas for women as achieving equality with men, integration into national economic life and development programmes, and recognition of women's contribution to world peace.[9] The end of the decade saw the publication of a document containing 'Forward Looking Strategies for the Advancement of Women'. Despite the non-binding nature of the document, the decade was undoubtedly important in generating a better and more informed understanding of women's position in the world, and in raising women's consciousness and governmental awareness of women's issues, including those associated with employment, the family and sexuality.

Is there a European feminist movement?

The international equality movements which developed in the 1970s and '80s can on the one hand be seen as an outcome of the enlightenment of the individual nation states, and, perhaps, a rational response to the labour-market pressures of advanced capitalism. On the other hand, it would be absurd to ignore the impact of the feminist movement over more than 100 years in raising consciousness of women's issues across the world. The movement is more certainly not a simple phenomenon to understand, and indeed we can question the extent to which is it a single movement as such. Many writers[10] identify clear distinctions, and some would argue divisions, within feminism both nationally and internationally,[11] and it is certainly the case that, despite some areas of clear consensus over the past 100 years, feminists of the world have been concerned with different issues, have espoused different agendas, and embraced different strategies.

The First Wave of European Feminism, which spanned the period from the mid-nineteenth to the first quarter of the twentieth century, had a varied but pervasive impact across Europe. Its legacy was not only the emancipation of women but subsequently in certain countries a series of policy changes, with new measures in health, education and welfare policy in the 1940s and 1950s. It was upon this stage that the Second Wave arose in the 1970s, a renaissance, Lovenduski (1986) suggests, that began during the 1960s in a number of countries and which was by the 1970s a truly international movement. Under the umbrella of women's liberation, a great variety of new women's organisations came into existence alongside older, more established organisations. In Britain, as indeed in Scandinavia, that old wave had never been truly extinguished but has been replaced by what Banks (1981) calls 'welfare feminism' when, in addition to established feminist causes, many women were active in the peace movement and others in the birth-control movement. A variety of factors, the commemoration of fifty years of suffrage, the growth of militancy amongst working-class women,[12] and the rise of the student Left associated with revitalised Marxist parties of the 1960s, combined with growing militancy over the persisting inequalities of pay to provide the stimulus to the British and other European Second Wave Feminist movements.

In Britain, marches were held on International Women's Day in March 1971, by which time four basic demands had emerged as the central British women's liberation platform: equal pay; equal opportunities in education and work; free contraception and abortion on demand; and free 24-hour nurseries. By 1978, three further demands were added: financial and legal independence; a woman's right to determine her own sexuality; and freedom from intimidation and the use of violence or sexual coercion.[13] From these demands came a variety of activities and, Lovenduski suggests, four distinct campaigns. Child care was the earliest but least successful of all the demands, with provision actually declining after the mid-1970s whereas the Women's Aid movement, most visibly realised with the setting up by Erin Pizzey of the first refuge for battered wives in Chiswick in 1972, has been an enduring phenomenon backed by the establishment in 1975 of a National Women's Aid Federation. The third demand, for abortion, was launched through the establishment of the National Abortion Campaign in 1975, aimed at defending the 1967 Abortion Act. Finally, there were various women against violence campaigns, realised in the opening of the first rape crisis centre in London in 1976.

Randall suggests that by the end of the 1970s, radical feminists were in the ascendency in Britain and they had set the agenda for the movement. Indeed, by the end of the decade, the issues of rape and marital violence were popularly endorsed and reflected in numerous discussion articles in the popular press and women's magazines. It was during the 1980s, however, that two further issues came to the fore. In 1978, the Organisation of Women of African and Asian Descent was founded, and increasingly throughout the 1980s black women of Afro-Caribbean and Asian descent have challenged the introspection of the white majority of the British women's movement and their conscious and unconscious xenophobia. Second, the growth of the peace movement, centring on the Greenham Peace Campaign from 1982, has challenged the traditional concerns of radical and socialist feminism and, with the involvement of women such as Pat Arrowsmith, has provided an alternative media image of the feminist woman. In the 1980s, the growing vocalisation of gay women's and men's groups, both allied to and dissociated from the radical feminist movement, gave a higher media profile to lesbian issues and to the question of women's determination of sexuality.

Second Wave Feminist movements of some kind now exist throughout Europe, although, as Randall notes, political liberalism and repression have resulted in some waxing and waning in Spain and Greece. In Germany, Second Wave Feminism crystallised early in the 1960s, providing some impetus for the British movement. A campaign to liberalise abortion was launched there in 1970, and by 1975 a more liberal abortion law had been enacted. Randall suggests that the German movement had a particularly significant impact on changing women's expectations which in turn led to significant modifications in the recruitment criteria and policies of the main political parties by the 1980s. The movement also had a particularly active 'wages for housework' campaign, but since the late 1970s and throughout the 1980s, green issues, both environmental and life-style-focused, have been an important influence in the women's movement, with the growth of the Green Party providing, according to Lovenduski, a change in the political environment which presented new opportunities to the German women's movement.

In France, as in Germany, the student uprising of 1968 provided the stimulus for women's liberation, although the Mouvement de la Libération des Femmes was not formally recognised by the media until 1970, largely because of its highly fragmented nature.[14] Abortion was an early issue for French feminists, with the establishment of a specific movement in 1973 which spread rapidly and was responsible for organising illegal abortions and for aiding the liberalisation of abortion law in 1973. Rather than providing a united platform for French feminism, however, this success appears to have provided a source for division. Duchen(1986) suggests that this is because abortion raised potentially contentious questions concerning the nature of motherhood and femininity. For Lovenduski (1986) it is the absence of any subsequent mobilising issue following abortion, and the lack of any sign of a ground-swell of feminist opinion which account for the pattern of feminism in France, despite a visible, public, feminist presence as illustrated by the existence of feminist bookshops and meeting places, and a news source and information agency.

In contrast with France, Italian feminism has been vibrant and, against the combined back-cloth of Roman Catholicism and left-wing, Marxist politics, has achieved much. Again the student movement of the late 1960s provided an impetus for the women's movement, and two groups formed early.[15] The majority of the movement, however, has been composed of small, informal local groups with mainly consciousness-raising goals.[16] Despite this, three issues in particular seem to have provided a uniting platform for Italian feminism: divorce; workplace status; and abortion. Lovenduski suggests that this happened because the methods of consciousness-raising and the small group structure, often reflected in feminist collectives in ultra-left and trade-union organisations, served the Italian women's movement well because as feminism gained strength, political parties on the left attempted to incorporate it by paying more attention to women's issues. At the end of the abortion campaign, many writers suggest that the Italian movement changed from focusing on issues of rights to those of life-style.[17] The legislative focus has, however, been upon altering the law on rape.

Dutch, Danish and Norwegian feminism, like British feminism, have had strong links with the US movement, but their unique features are largely the product of indigenous factors. In Holland, the precursor to the new women's movement was the establishment of the *Man-Vrouw-Maalschappij* (the Men-Women Society), founded by professional men and women and regarded by Lovenduski as the equivalent to the reformist National Organisation of Women in the United States. However, the movement really took off with the formation of *Dolle Mina* in 1970. Originally including men, *Dolle Mina* developed demands for sexual freedom, free abortion and contraception. However, the lack of a leadership structure and the absence of a theoretical underpinning undermined the probity of the movement, and feminism in Holland has tended to be dispersed in a variety of women's organisations, especially in the political parties and trade unions, and in specific sectors of society such as education and the social services.

In Scandinavia, Dahlerup and Gulli (1985) suggests that women's liberation movements have been strongest in Denmark and Norway. The New Feminists in Norway and the Redstockings in Denmark both began in 1970, both with focus on consciousness-raising activities and diffused, decentralised organisational structures. As in Holland, existing women's groups had remained active following the culmination of the First Wave, and had actively fought for married women's rights. This meant that the decentralised structures which have characterised the Second Wave have been able to work effectively on specific issues, and have mobilised working-class women, established women's studies courses, self-help refuges and rape crisis support, abortion rights and women's meeting places.

Swedish feminism has had a different history from that of other European movements, which Lovenduski attributes to the collectivist culture of the country and to its political context. Although there have been rights groups of various kinds, there has been no Second Wave Feminism as such. Most of the political parties in Sweden have strong and active women's groups, and women constitute a third of parliamentarians. The country has a sex equality policy which is often held up as an exemplar of equal opportunities provision, and the long period of uninterrupted social democratic rule facilitated the continued discussion and recognition of women's rights issues at the collective rather than the individual level.

Rather different political contexts – initially authoritarianism and subsequently the demands of new democratic constitutions – circumscribed feminism in Spain, Portugal and Greece. Lovenduski suggests that women's emancipation in Spain and Portugal has been impeded by Catholicism, combined with the difficulties of advancing sectional women's issues in the context of extremes of poverty and low levels of industrial development. In Greece, the Democratic Women's Movement was founded in 1974 with a platform which included the promotion of equal opportunities, the liberation of women as individuals and associated legal reform. It later became concerned with the official treatment of rape victims and has always proceeded along traditional rights group lines, working to reform legislation. Following the collapse of the old politico-military regime, there was a massive increase in the number of women's organisations, but an autonomous movement is still, in many senses, in the embryonic stages.

Feminism in Europe thus exhibits a wide variety of forms and has a broad agenda of issues and concerns. The political context has clearly been important in determining the specific form and indeed in prescribing or proscribing feminism altogether. In Italy, Holland, Denmark and Norway the Second Wave has been strongly influenced by left-wing politics and has been predominantly led by middle-class women. In France the movement has been largely contained within the academic community, and in Germany it has been significantly diluted by conservatism. Lovenduski suggests that in the case of Italy, Britain, Holland, Denmark and Norway, the campaigns for women's liberation have been enhanced by alliances with other groups and with traditional women's organisations, which has in turn led to more broadly based movements and to a unity of interest across class barriers. Elsewhere, she suggests, the restricted success of feminist movements can be accounted for by the fact that initiatives for much change came from other sources and in some cases – for example, Sweden – actually pre-dated the Second Wave movements. This meant that there was no uniting issue or theme to pull together the various strands of feminism. Randall similarly doubts the existence of a distinctively international or even European movement, but she is more ready to assert the universality with which women's consciousness has been raised, and the importance of the international information networks which now abound.

At the policy level, however, there has been some uniformity of achievement, and the dissimilarities of the constituent European movements can be stressed at the expense of a true appraisal of achievements. Throughout Europe enfranchised women are, in secular law, free to divorce, and abortion has been legalised in most of the European Community. In most of Europe there are self-help and support organisations catering for raped and battered women, and legislation has been enacted to inhibit discrimination in education and employment. There have been common platforms, but there have also been differences.

Abortion

Abortion is a useful mechanism for understanding the extent of Europeanisation and the way in which women's lives have changed over the last thirty years. It illustrates well the link between the changing socio-political culture and women's liberation *and* the limitations of policy. As it clearly shows, national and supra-national cultural values are pervasive forces shaping women's experiences. Joyce Outshoorn (1988) notes that western European states, with the exception of Belgium, Ireland, Portugal and Greece, reformed the law on abortion in the 1960s and 1970s, yet this does not mean that abortion is uniformly available throughout Europe, and in some parts it has been fiercely resisted. A study of abortion law reform in western nations by Field (1979) has concluded that the major obstacle to change is the existence of a strong Roman Catholic church and a predominantly Catholic population, although even a small Catholic presence appears to exert strong pressure.

As Outshoorn notes, abortion law can take many forms, and the extent of variation in Europe is shown in Table 5.1 below. Outshoorn

Table 5.1   **Abortion in Europe in 1988**

	Number of abortions 1981	1986	Date of intial reform	Type of abortion law
Belgium	–	–	–	
Denmark	42.9	37.1	1970	on demand
France	22.4	21.4	1975	term
Germany	14.0	13.8	1976	mixed
Greece	–	–	1986	term
Ireland	–	–	–	
Italy	36.1	34.0	1978	term
Luxembourg	–	–	1979	mixed
Netherlands	11.0	9.7	1973	indication
Portugal	–	–	pending	
Spain	–	–	1985	indication
UK	19.6	24.6	1967	indication

Notes:
Abortions are defined as a percentage of live births

Source: The data for 1981 are drawn from *Women of Europe, Supplement 14* (1984) and *Women of Europe Supplement 30* (1989). The rest of the table is drawn from Outshoorn (1988) and supplemented by information from *Women of Europe, Supplement 27* (1988)

suggests that three main types of abortion law can be distinguished,[18] but as the table shows, the nature of the law does not appear directly to influence the number of abortions actually carried out. Across Europe as a proportion of live births, the abortion rate is declining, and we may better understand this pattern if we consider policy implementation rather than the nature of the legislation *per se*. In Britain, for example, the availability of abortion depends greatly upon the regional location, and is still influenced by medical attitudes and public expenditure. As Outshoorn notes, sometimes the intentions of the law are not strongly against a woman's right to choose, but the non-cooperation of hospitals and medical personnel and the costs of abortion itself mean that women's rights and choice are heavily curtailed. Conversely, where the law has been very restrictive – as, for example, in Ireland and in Italy until the late 1970s – women's access to abortion has been significantly mediated by class factors such as income and ability to travel.

That the issue of abortion is highly contested and controversial is illustrated by the way it contributed to the fall of the Dutch government in 1977, and similarly helped to bring down governments in Italy, West Germany and Belgium.[19] Curiously and contrary to this usual pattern, abortion has been a largely non-party-political issue in Britain. Since 1952, all abortion Bills have been either Private Member's Bills or introduced under the 'Ten Minute Rule', and the Bill which succesfully introduced abortion law reform in 1967 was introduced by a Liberal parliamentarian aided by extra reading time provided by a supportive Labour government.

Legislation alone is not sufficient to secure women's rights to self-determination in pregnancy. Two other factors are of importance: first, the implementation of law; and second, throughout much of Europe, the extent to which there is organised opposition and resistance to abortion. In Britain, Steel's 1967 Act provoked the formation of the Society for the Protection of the Unborn Child (SPUC), and later LIFE, and there have been repeated attempts to introduce restrictive amendments to the law stimulated by the active campaigning of both groups. Perhaps more important in terms of women's access to abortion than reformist attempts at legislation are the policies and practices which govern its administration. Randall (1987) notes that the introduction in Britain in 1982 of new forms to certify the need for abortion, the availability of beds, and the length of waiting lists for consultant appointments all act as effective restrictions on both the form of abortion available, and its extent.

Feminists have argued that access to abortion is a critical right because women's lives are hugely affected by the birth of their children: for radical feminists, abortion symbolises women's sexual and reproductive self-determination, and for others their rights to individual freedom of choice and effective participation in the work-place and other spheres of public life. In summarising the decade to 1988, Janine Mossuz-Lavau (1988) suggests that European women are not equally armed to exercise their rights in deciding when they want to have children, although the past ten years have been marked by what she describes as a true concern for women's rights to physical and sexual self-determination, a concern which has been linked to considerable evolution over the last three decades in the nature and form of the family.[20]

The family

There can be little doubt that social and demographic forces are bringing changes to the structure of European families and communities, and the impact of these changes are widespread: government pension and welfare schemes, health-care provision and education systems all experience consequential pressures.[21] What are these changes, how can they be understood and what consequences do they have for women's lives?[22]

A series of studies carried out by the European Community's Commission[23] since 1975 have shown some shift towards the concept of a complete equality of husbands' and wives' roles, but very little real change. Although the concept of complete equality of marital roles has gained some ground, it is still a minority view held by only four in ten of Europeans. The contrasting view that the woman's

Table 5.2   **The dependent population in Europe**

	1980 actual (%)	1990 projected (%)
Belgium	52.4	49.2
Denmark	54.5	47.3
France	56.8	51.8
Germany	50.4	44.0
Greece	56.1	48.3
Ireland	70.0	63.5
Italy	54.9	46.1
Luxembourg	47.8	47.3
Netherlands	51.1	44.5
Portugal	58.6	52.1
Spain	58.1	52.5
UK	56.2	51.9

Source: OECD, *Ageing Populations* (1988)

place is in the home is still strong, accounting for approximately a quarter of all attitudes, and approximately three in ten believe that the wife should have a less absorbing job and take on more of the housework than her husband. Comparative data suggest that the United Kingdom and Denmark are the most advanced countries in terms of attitudes, and Germany and Luxembourg the least advanced.

If attitudes alone were sufficient, then we should expect to find that objective measures of women's opportunities demonstrated greater advances in those countries where greatest liberalism prevailed. However, whilst attitudes are undoubtedly important in shaping women's lives, equally important in a climate in which women are still assumed to have the dominant, if not exclusive, responsibility for domestic roles are practical policies on child care and support for the elderly and infirm.

In Europe, the young and elderly account for the major proportion of social expenditure. Across Europe, as shown in Table 5.2 above, there is a significant variation in the dependency ratio – that is, the proportion of young and elderly to working-aged people – with the highest ratio in Ireland and the lowest in the Netherlands. Whereas the data suggest that the dependency ratio is declining, OECD projections envisage a substantial increase for nearly all countries as the proportion of elderly in the population increases as the postwar bulge of Europe passes into retirement and out of the working population. In Greece, Ireland, Portugal and Spain, the proportion is not expected to rise significantly until after 2020, but especially large increases are envisaged in Denmark, Germany, Italy and the Netherlands, and by the mid-twenty-first century, the OECD average dependency ratio is expected to be 65.7. Lower birth rates mean that the dependent population is increasingly elderly: in 1980 approximately one-third of Europe's dependants were elderly; by 2050, the elderly will constitute over half of all dependants. If the current pattern of care for the elderly persists, then the burden falling on European women looks set to increase hugely unless there are significant policy initiatives and associated changes in expectations.

The elderly do not constitute the sole familial and community burden for women; children, in particular the child pre-school, are for many women a significant factor. This burden is assumed differentially by the women of Europe, in part because of different cultural traditions, but also because of different national state policies. If attitudes alone were sufficient to determine women's choices and life chances, then with the greater liberalism apparent from the European Commission's studies we should expect that women in Britain and Denmark would experience greater workplace participation and more shared responsibility for child care than elsewhere. However, as Oakley (1974) notes, whereas modern industrial society has created opportunities for equality, it has carried over the ideology of women's innate difference from men, and their domesticity. The role of wife and mother, with very few exceptions, is incompatible with an occupational role and does not allow the individual woman to realise the dominant goal set by our culture. The main mechanisms which ensure this incompatibility are the provision of paid maternity leave and child care, which also affect women's participation in other activities and their well-being, whether they are employed outside the home or not.

In reviewing the provision of child care and maternity benefits in Europe in 1990, Peter Moss (1990) notes that between 1985 and 1988 employment rates for mothers increased in all European Community countries although it remains below 40 per cent, and of those who do work, a third are employed part-time. Britain is the only European country which does not have full, universal maternity rights for employed women; its eligibility conditions exclude a large number of women, and even where leave is granted, as shown in Tables 5.3 and 5.4, it is amongst the lowest entitlement in Europe. In most countries, the full period of leave is covered by earnings-related payments, normally between 70 and 100 per cent, but in Britain only six weeks' leave is covered by earnings-related pay, and most of the twenty-nine weeks of post-natal leave is unpaid. Britain lags in the provision of parental leave as well, which is offered in seven other countries, and paid for in the majority of cases.

Even after the birth of the child, parents in Britain fare less well with a poverty of child-care provision that is only partially remedied by an earlier than average start to the process of full-time education. Unlike in Belgium, France, Luxembourg and Portugal, there is no tax relief for child-care costs, nor for domestic help, as in Germany. The Netherlands has ended its system of tax relief and instead has directed the moneys saved to an increased provision of publicly funded services, and Belgium, France, Luxembourg and Portugal also have policies of increasing publicly funded services. In Spain, tax

Table 5.3   **Maternity leave provision in Europe**

	Post-natal maternity leave period (weeks)	*Payment*
Belgium	8–14 (some may be taken before or after the birth	100% for max. 4 wks then 60% (+20% for low earners
Denmark	14	90%, up to a max. level
France	10 (+8 for 3rd child;+2 for multiple births)	90% earnings
Germany	8 (+4 for premature/multiple births)	100% earnings
Greece	16 (may be taken before or after birth)	100% earnings
Ireland	4–10 (some may be taken before or after birth)	70% tax free
Italy	12	80% earnings
Luxembourg	8 (12, multiple births)	100% earnings
Netherlands	10–12	100% earnings
Portugal	12–18 (6 weeks can be taken before or after birth)	100% earnings
Spain	10–16 (6 weeks can be taken before or after birth)	75% earnings
UK	29 (not technically leave)	90% for 6 weeks; flat rate for 12 weeks; rest unpaid

Source: Adapted from data presented in 'Childcare in the European Communities 1985–1990', *Women of Europe Supplement 31*, Aug. 1990; and Jacqui Lewis, 'Breaking through the creche barrier', *Management Today*, Feb. 1989, pp. 104–6

relief is due to be introduced in 1991, and in Italy, although parents pay for publicly-funded services for under 3-year-olds, local authorities subsidise the costs to the level of two-thirds or more. By comparison, in Britain there are only publicly-funded places for about

Table 5.4   **Parental leave provision in Europe**

	Period (months)	*Payment*
Belgium	None, but scheme for career interruption	
Denmark	2.5	90%, up to a max. level
France	33 (i.e. until the child is 3 years old)	Nil, unless 3 or more children
Germany	18	Flat rate until child 6 months, then earnings-related
Greece	3	Unpaid
Ireland	None	
Italy	6	30% earnings
Luxembourg	None	
Netherlands	Details of new scheme not available	
Portugal	24	Unpaid
Spain	12, plus employees may take 3 yrs' break from work	Unpaid
UK	None	

Source: Adapted from data presented in 'Childcare in the European Communities 1985–1990', *Women of Europe Supplement 31*, Aug. 1990, and Jacqui Lewis, 'Breaking through the creche barrier', *Management Today*, Feb. 1989, pp. 104–6

Table 5.5   **Pre-school child care in Europe**

	Up to 2 years	3–5 years	6–10 years
Belgium	20–25% children	95%+ children & some out-of-hours care	Primary school & considerable out-of-hours care
Denmark	44% children	87% children	Primary school (aged 7+) 3–5 hours per day & some out-of-hours care
France	20–25% children	95% children & out-of-hours care	Primary school & out-of-hours care
Germany	3% children	60% children	Primary school & 3% in out-of-hours care
Greece	4% children	65–70% children	Primary school
Ireland	2% children	55% children	Primary school
Italy	5% children	88% children & some out-of-hours care	Primary school & limited out of hours care
Luxembourg	2% children	55–60% children	Primary school & 1% in out-of-hours care
Netherlands	1–2% nurseries 8% in part-time play centres	50% in early primary school + 25% in p/t play centres	Primary school & limited out-of-hours care
Portugal	6% children	35% children	Primary school & 6% in out-of-hours care
Spain	Information not available	66% children mostly 4–5 yrs	Primary school no out-of-hours care
UK	2% children	19% children in p/t (2.5 hrs a day); 19% on pre-primary (6–6.5 hours)	Primary school & 1% out-of-hours care

Source: Adapted from data presented in 'Childcare in the European Communities 1985–1990', *Women of Europe Supplement 31*, Aug. 1990; and Jacqui Lewis 'Breaking through the creche barrier', *Management Today*, Feb. 1989, pp. 104–6

2 per cent of children aged under 3, mostly in mixed-age day-care centres which are provided mainly by local authorities for children who are severely disadvantaged or at risk. They are not designed to cater for working mothers, and the vast majority of under 3-year-olds are in private care, with the costs unsubsidised.

As Table 5.5 suggests, there is enormous variation in the overall level of provision in child care across the age ranges. Denmark has undoubtedly the most well-developed and comprehensive system, but it is closely matched by that found in France and Belgium, and for children older than 3, by Germany and Italy. At the other end of the spectrum are Britain, Ireland and, to a lesser extent, the Netherlands, where in all cases there is negligible provision for under-3s, and little extra-school provision for those over 3. Moss suggests that most countries provide, or are in the process of providing, two to three years of pre-primary schooling or kindergartens to the majority of their children. In Denmark, France, Italy and Belgium, over 80 per cent of children, and in Spain, Greece and Germany, 60–80 per cent of children experience such care. In Britain, Ireland and the Netherlands, pre-primary schooling is limited or not provided at all, and instead children are admitted relatively early to primary school or they attend playgroups. The latter offer a very short period of provision, on average five or six hours a week, and in Britain and Ireland they are not publicly funded but reliant on parental support, both physical and financial. Not only is the extent of provision variable, but its rate of growth varies significantly. Between 1985 and 1988/89, publicly-provided services increased by more than 10 per cent in Denmark, France, Luxembourg and Portugal, and the attrition in the support for tax relief in the Netherlands meant that from 1989 a massive increase in public-service expenditure was facilitated. In Britain, Belgium, Italy, Ireland and Greece the rate of growth has been significantly slower, and in some cases non-existent.

Official data on privately-funded services are harder to come by and less reliable. The most significant private carers are relatives, and they, often grandmothers, provide more care for children under 3 than any other type of service. In Britain there has been a growth in private nurseries, occasionally funded by employers, and the period since the mid-1980s has also seen an increase in attempts to regulate the provision of private child care. In 1988 registered family day carers provided places for approximately 5 per cent of children under 5. Whilst the number of children being cared for in their own homes is difficult to ascertain, it probably does not exceed 2 per cent. For the vast majority of women who wish or need to work, the typical child carer for their children is a relative, likely to be the children's grandmother, and the burden of care is likely to inhibit effective participation in the labour market.

As Moss notes, child care is an issue of the labour force, of family policy and of women's welfare. It is also an issue for employers, as Lewis notes. She suggests that there are two major barriers which inhibit the effective incorporation of women into the labour market: first, the lack of suitable child-care facilities combined with an inflexibility of working arrangements in the majority of employing organisations, whether private or public sector organisations; and second, the lack of provision leads to the 'child-bearing career break', and to its conscious and unconscious invocation when a woman seeks a job and/or promotion. Child care is thus irrevocably tied in with employment, and employment opportunities are irrevocably tied in with life-style opportunities. Child care is therefore at the heart of equal opportunities for many women in Europe, not the least, British women.

Employment

European Community policy has been directed explicitly at equal opportunities at work. The principle of equal pay for equal work was established in Article 119 of the Treaty of Rome, and reinforced by subsequent Directives aimed not only at ensuring equal pay for men and women, but also equal treatment with respect to access to employment, training, promotion, working conditions, and matters of social security such as pension rights. In this environment it might be reasonably expected that the greatest strides forward in terms of gender equality would have been achieved at the workplace. However, the evidence suggests that, although some steps forward have been taken, there is still considerable differentiation between men and women at work.

The number of women who work has steadily increased over the past two decades. In 1970 less than 29 per cent of European women worked, but by 1980 this had risen to 30 per cent, and in 1986 nearly one-third were working. However, as the data in Figure 5.1[24] show, the participation rate varies considerably from one country to another. In 1970 both Britain and Denmark had participation rates in excess of 30 per cent and both remained at the top of the league in terms of the proportion of women who worked in 1986, with almost 40 per cent of British and 51 per cent of Danish women working. At the other end of the spectrum are Ireland and Spain, where less than 22 per cent of women work. Throughout the last two decades there has been a surge of women into the labour market, and this is reflected in a relative growth of employment for women even during the recession, since when employment growth has slowed down. The pattern is, however, nationally different, and amongst the several factors which account for this the most important are marital status, child care, and whether women work full-time or part-time.

As Figure 5.2 shows,[25] both Denmark (65.9 per cent) and Britain (53.4 per cent), together with France (50.7 per cent) and Portugal (48.2 per cent), have relatively high participation rates for married women, as they do for widowed and divorced women. Elsewhere in Europe, the participation rate for women drops once they marry, and only 20.4 per cent of all married European women work. In the majority of countries, the proportion of women in the labour force is higher for those without children than for those with, the exception being Belgium, Denmark, Greece, France and Portugal. Except in Denmark, the likelihood of a women working decreases as the number of children under 10 increases, although the impact of children is less if the women works part-time.[26]

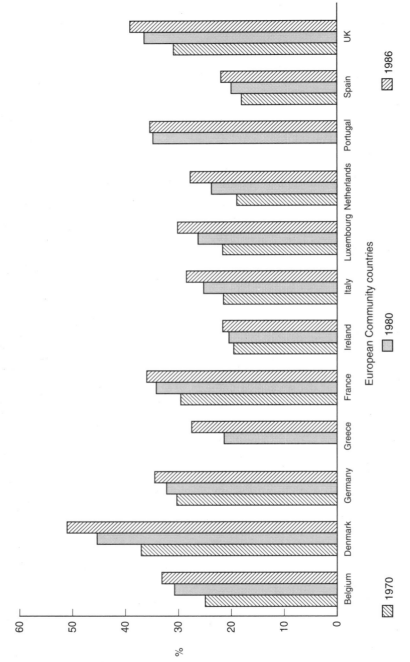

Figure 5.1 **Participation rate for European women 1970–1986**

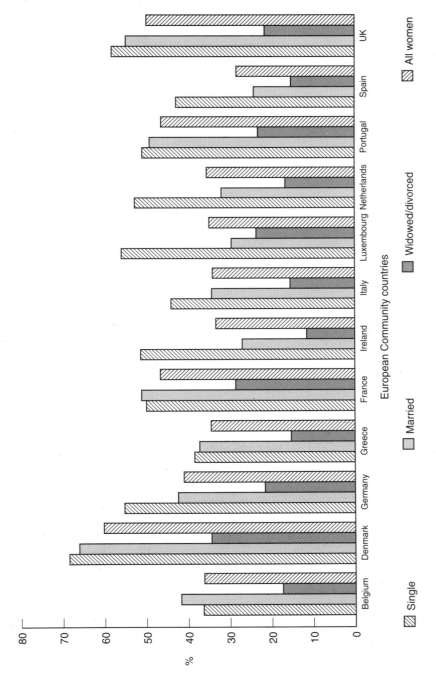

Figure 5.2 **Participation rate by marital status, 1986**

Women are much more likely to work part-time than men, and married women more likely to be part-time than their single counterparts, as is shown by Figure 5.3;[27] overall only 18 per cent of unmarried women work part-time compared to 36 per cent of married women. Once again, Britain and Denmark have significantly higher than average rates, but it is not clear from the data alone whether this is an outcome of national tradition or labour regulations, although in the case of Britain, the overall higher rates of part-time work for all women and for men suggests that there is a higher use of part-time employment than elsewhere in Europe. This may be a reflection of the growing pattern of flexibility in work, with a proliferation of casual, marginal and part-time work, including job-sharing. It is also the case that part-time work is concentrated in specific occupational sectors. For women in Italy, Greece, Portugal and Ireland it is in agriculture, whereas elsewhere in Europe, it is predominantly in the service sector. Little part-time work occurs in industry, and the concentration of part-time working in the agricultural and service sectors tends to enhance job segregation and inequality at work since these sectors are commonly more poorly paid than industry.

Job segregation occurs where men or women are concentrated in different jobs, and across Europe gender segregation can be found both within the broad sectors of economic activity and between occupations within each sector. The majority of Europe's employed women, nearly three-quarters, work in the service sector rather than in either agriculture or industry, as Figure 5.4[28] shows, and they form an increasing proportion of all workers in that sector, accounting for 47 per cent of all service-sector employees. However, women do not occupy the same jobs as men, even when working within the same sector, and within each occupation, women tend to cluster in the jobs and grades at the lower end of the spectrum, where they experience lower pay and poorer working conditions.

Catherine Hakim (1979) suggests that segregation can be both vertical and horizontal. By horizontal segregation she refers to the separation of men and women into different types of occupation, so that men and women are found in different jobs. Vertical segregation refers to the tendency to find men in higher-grade occupations and women in lower-grade occupations, or vice versa. Segregation blurs into discrimination when the consequences of the segregation are inevitably uni-directional and disadvantageous. An OECD study in 1985[29] found that segregation continued to exist at a high level across all OECD countries. In particular, the study found that the degree of segregation varied directly with the level of participation; those countries with the highest participation rate, such as the United Kingdom, tended also to have the greatest degrees of occupational segregation. It also found that segregation by industrial sector was less than segregation by broad occupational grouping, a reflection of the fact that women tend to be concentrated in a small range of

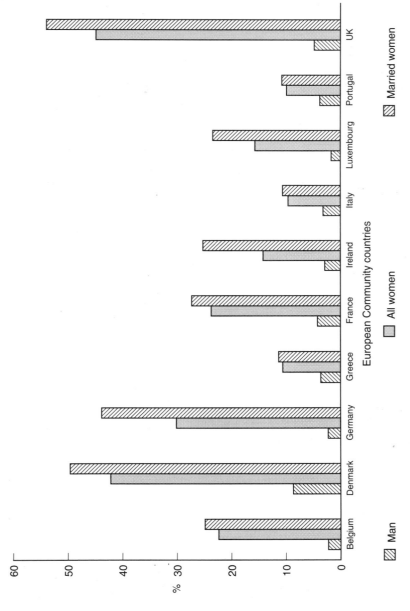

Figure 5.3 **Part-time working by men and women, 1986**

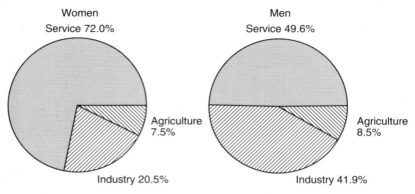

Figure 5.4   **Women and men at work in 1986, economic activity by sector**

occupations within different industries. However, economic restructuring, and in particular the growth of the service sector and a
diminution in the size of the manufacturing sector has tended, rather
than reducing the aggregate level, to increase the extent to which
segregation by industrial sector occurs.

There is a wealth of national data[30] documenting the nature and
extent of gender segregation at work, but there are many difficulties
in assessing the relative level of gender segregation in a comparative
context, not the least of which is the lack of uniformity of measures
and the variation in the structure of national economies. Moreover,
as Beechey (1989) points out, women's participation in the formal
economy masks many variations in actual experience and pattern;
simply put, similar patterns of participation may obscure widely
different experiences, as (for example) is the case in Britain and
France, where similar rates are comprised in Britain of a high level of
part-time and interrupted career employment, and in France of
continuity and a work pattern not greatly dissimilar to that of male
workers. Dex and Shaw (1986) have concluded from their comparative study of British and American workers that the higher level of
upward occupational mobility of American women is in large part a
consequence of their greater tendency to work full-time rather than
part-time, although it may also be a function of the legislative context
in that Britain was been slower to introduce equal pay and sex
discrimination legislation. Crompton and Sanderson (1990) suggest
that Italy illustrates clearly that, although the early development of a
policy on equal pay can have an important influence on women's
employment opportunities, it is moderated by the cultural context.
The active pursuit of equal pay for women since the 1960s has led to
a greater protection of Italian women workers, but a low participation
rate and the rapid growth of the informal sector, including home-
working, and small firms.

As Figure 5.4 has shown, there is clear evidence of differential participation in the three industrial sectors, and when we look within the sectors, we find that this segregation persists. In manufacturing, women are largely absent in the energy and water, engineering and petrochemical firms, whilst in the service sector where they dominate overall, they are relatively under-represented in transport and communications and heavily present in the distributive trades and services, included banking, insurance and finance. Even in those sectors and jobs where women predominate, there is evidence of persisting vertical segregation.

Jean Bocock (1991) presents data on teaching in selected European countries and as Figure 5.5[31] shows, within what is overall a significantly female occupation, women are concentrated in the lower echelons, and under-represented in the management grades. There is variation in the pattern across the ten countries chosen, with Portugal atypically showing almost equal representation of women in management and basic-grade primary teaching, and Greece showing this pattern for both primary and secondary teaching, but overall the percentage of female heads is about half that of basic-grade teachers. At the secondary level, characterised by generally higher status and better remuneration, the difference tends to be even greater, and there is a lower overall proportion of women teachers generally.

This pattern in education holds for many other professions, services and industries, and is an illustration of what Hakim means by vertical segregation. Moreover, the 1985 study of women workers' attitudes found that the proportion of women holding executive or managerial jobs had dropped from 16 per cent in 1980 to 14 per cent in 1985. The 1980 study showed that most women work for male bosses or supervisors (68 per cent), and whilst 24 per cent of women worked in an exclusively female environment where their boss was female, only 4 per cent of women worked in a mixed-gender environment with a female boss. As the study notes, and as Hakim's work highlights, in Britain the incidence of women working in an exclusively female environment is higher than in any other European country. Furthermore, as Hakim suggests, where segregation has been eroded at all in Britain, it is because men are entering jobs which traditionally have been the preserve of women, and not the reverse.

How can this pattern of segregation be accounted for and what are its implications? There is some evidence that historically women have been regarded as constituting a different labour force from men. Several writers[32] have developed and applied the Marxist notion of a reserve army of labour, and suggested that women have constituted a reserve to be drawn into the formal economy when there are labour shortages from traditional sources, as for example at time of war or mass male emigration, and to meet the needs of a changing economy. Because of their domestic role, women are relatively easily discharged from employment when their labour is no longer required.[33] Whereas

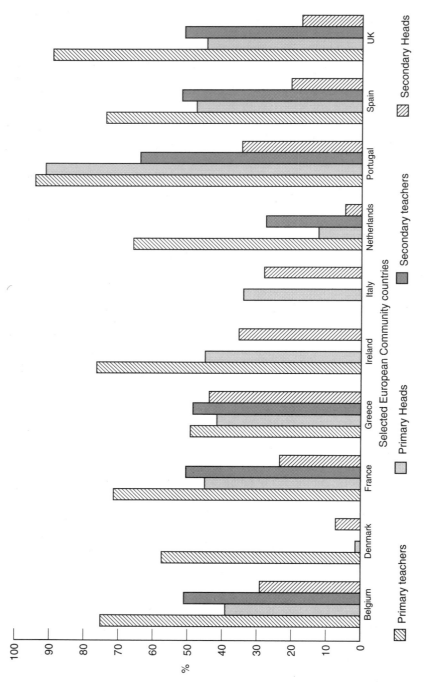

Figure 5.5 **Women in educational management 1985–6. Relative proportions of teachers and head**

in the more established economies of Europe the reserve army thesis of the cyclical use of women's labour to meet the booms and slumps of production is seen as having decreasing relevance, in Portugal it has some currency. Here the rise in women's employment started significantly in 1970 with the introduction of a new industrial policy in the changed political context, and was undoubtedly also influenced by the massive emigration of male labour and the extension of the period of military service. Thus in Portugal it would appear that women have very recently acted as both a cyclical reserve, filling the vacancies created by unavailable male labour, and a secular reserve, meeting the demands of a restructured economy. Despite this, women's concentration there has tended to grow in those industries where they have traditionally predominated, in textiles, clothing and footware, and to have grown at a slower rate in the more advanced sectors of industry, in non-electrical machinery, for example. Even in the service sector where they predominate, women's employment rate grew more slowly than men's. In terms of training programmes, women tend to predominate in traditional women's courses and to be absent, or present in only very low numbers, in mechanics, construction design and so on. There is therefore little evidence that segregation is breaking down, even under the pressure of radical restructuring and high levels of labour shortage.

In general, across Europe, and largely because of the general extension of education to girls and the growth of training programmes directed specifically at women, women have been a particularly useful reserve in meeting the needs of economic restructuring which has characterised European economies during the 1980s and 1990s. The service sector is often cited as a good illustration of this, and indeed women have been increasingly drawn in, but not equally to all areas of work, and in the main to the more marginal and more poorly paid jobs. Overall, even where it does account in part for women's increased labour force participation, the reserve army of labour thesis thus fails to account for the clustering of women at the lower echelons of occupations and within sectors, in the poorer-quality jobs.

It has been suggested that technology and the more flexible work patterns which are emerging throughout the western economies in the 1980s and 1990s will herald new opportunities for equality. Economic restructuring and flexible use of labour are often seen as corollaries and are assumed to have positive implications for women in particular. The growth of the service sector has undoubtedly benefited women, but it has had a greater benefit for men who have increased their relative presence in the sector. Elsewhere, technological change has been associated with new forms of work practice, of which flexibility is but a part. None of the evidence suggests that in any way these new flexible patterns have done anything to redress the established gender imbalances in the labour force. The OECD study of 1985 found that a third of women are fearful that technological advances will lead to redundancy, and less than half of them (43 per cent) feel that they are equipped to meet the challenges of technological change. Women's level of education, types of employment, types of employer and degrees of responsibility are all factors which account for what in many cases are realistic assessments of their futures. In an earlier study, OECD (1976), it was found that because of their disproportionate concentration in the service sector, women were insulated from the harshest effects of the recession, yet, except in the United Kingdom, women are more likely to be unemployed than men, as Figure 5.6 shows.[34] Even in the United Kingdom, where women's employment appears superficially to be protected, Humphries and Rubery (1988) conclude that the adverse economic circumstances and associated government policies have impacted with particular severity upon them, especially the unskilled, minority women and single mothers. Women's availability to work for less than full-time hours is what in Britain has largely shielded them from higher levels of unemployment, together with social security policy that effectively leads to an under-reporting of unemployment by women.

Overall, the evidence suggests that occupational segregation persists in Europe, and that the experiences of women and men workers are different. There is no easy explanation for this common pattern of inequality, nor for the important differences which characterise women's work in the different countries of Europe. There is clearly a relationship between the availability of support for women's work and their ability to do so, but equally clearly, entrenched views about women's roles and their capacity to work influence their experiences. When asked directly, 30 per cent of women indicate that they have been discriminated against on at least one dimension.[35] Promotion is the area of greatest concern, but it is followed closely by pay, and then by training and access to bonuses and other perks. The persistence of these feelings of discrimination in a Europe committed to equal opportunities is disturbing.

Conclusion: a continuing gender divide?

Despite the progress made across Europe in improving the experiences and life chances of European women over the past few decades, gender remains a significant dimension in determining opportunities and experiences. What is clear in looking at the data is that there are important differences in the position of women within Europe, and that specific cultural contexts shape women's prospects. The European Commission's survey of the evolution of opinions and attitudes conducted in 1987[36] concludes that the United Kingdom, together with France, Denmark and the Netherlands, is markedly above the European average with respect to egalitarian ideas concerning the role of men and women in the family, working life and politics.

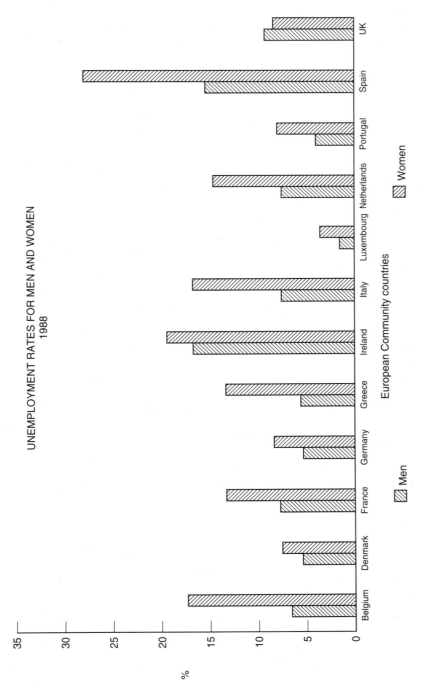

Figure 5.6   Unemployment rates for men and women, 1988

Moreover, Britain has one of the longest of European histories with regard to the formal emancipation of women, markedly ahead of France, Italy, Belgium and the three new democracies. Yet Christine Woesler de Panafieu (1991) describes British women as 'the laggards of Europe', suggesting that they are more obedient to traditional female role expectations. How can these apparently contradictory views be reconciled?

Woesler de Panafieu suggests that under the veneer of egalitarianism in Britain, a rigid middle-class attitude to the ideal of family life, centred on the mother, persists. This, she suggests, affects women's independence in two important ways: work is still mainly considered essentially as an economic necessity, and there are continuing negative connotations associated with the term 'career woman'; and the pivotal focus of the woman's activities is still centred on the home. She suggests that this is because of the apathy of a third of British women, mainly the young; the resistance to change of another third; and the impotence of the final third in transforming the current situation into a positive perspective for the majority of British women. Her analysis, however, neglects to discuss the structural context within which British women live and exercise rights and choices, and it is an understanding of this context that enables apparent inconsistencies in attitude and behaviour to be better understood.

The European Commission survey suggests that Britain shares with France third ranking in the Community for egalitarian ideas, following Denmark and the Netherlands, and all four nations are above or equal to the European average in the importance with which egalitarianism is rated. On these scales, Germany and Luxembourg come at the bottom, and they are particularly rigid with respect to the role of husband and wife within the family. Yet paradoxically the place of women in these societies does not appear to be a serious problem. The Irish are found to be less often in favour of equal roles within the family, but on the other hand they are relatively willing to accept women in politics. In Ireland, whilst the problem of women's place in society is not seen as very great, and is below the European average, the gap between men's and women's views on this question is very great: men minimise the problem whereas women think it very important. In Italy the paradox is even more acute: occupational roles are still believed to be very different for men and women, yet the principle of equality in the family and the role of women in politics are strongly accepted. Here the problem of women's position in society is judged more important than anywhere else in Europe. In Belgium there is most resistance to the notion of equality of roles in the family, and in Greece resistance focuses on women's entry and competence to perform specific occupational roles. In Spain and Portugal, while opinion is generally very close to the European average, the role of women in politics is less readily accepted, especially in Portugal, and certain traditional role models, as in Italy, remain very strong.

Attitudes alone do not appear to determine opportunities for women nor to relate directly to the significance of gender as a factor explaining experiences. However, when considered together with the nature of specific institutions and infrastructural support, a clearer picture can be built up. As Jacqui Lewis's discussion of child-care provision suggests, there are marked differences in the extent to which women's working is supported across Europe. On all the measures discussed earlier in this chapter, British women lose out: they have poorer entitlement to maternity benefit, and almost total absence of crèche and child-care facilities prior to the start of formal primary education. They experience weaker protection of their careers, so that for the majority of British women maternity comes to mean not a career break, where continuity is a prospect, but a career rupture. Once in the labour market, British women are therefore more likely to work part-time than their European counterparts, and the structure of British employment ensures that the great divide between the rights and perks of full-time and part-time work remains, further disabling working women.

We have seen that there has been a pattern of active national and European legislation aimed at reducing the extent of gender inequality. Elizabeth Vallance and Elizabeth Davies (1986) question the extent to which the law can change attitudes, and hence experiences. There is ample evidence, not least from the rulings of the Commission on breaches of its conventions, that discrimination and inequality can persist even after the passing of a law. Vallance and Davies suggest that many factors limit the effectiveness of legislation – amongst others, the attitudes of women themselves, the reactions of employers and trade unions, the economic climate, which may inhibit the claiming of existing rights, and the complexity of the law itself. We can add to these factors the implementation of policy which, as we have seen in the case of abortion law reform, can inhibit the effectiveness of the law. Changes in the law should not be undervalued, however. As Vallance and Davies suggest, the law is an expression of policy and intention, and few industrial and business interests are willing to give the impression of being discriminatory, and thus at the least they make genuflections in the direction of equality.

The prospect for women of Europe in the next two decades shows some promise, but there are no grounds for complacency and there remains a role for those active in consciousness-raising in pushing at the boundaries of established practice and in pressing for the effective implementation of policy to protect and enhance the position of women. In discussing whether women members of the European Parliament have made a difference to equality policy in the European Community, Elizabeth Vallance (1988) suggests that their ability to change traditional political priorities and preoccupations seems to be minimal, but their perception of themselves as women with particular experience and concerns does appear to have affected the emphasis of European politics, especially in the area of equality policy. Although the presence of women alone is not a sufficient condition to ensure that women's political interests are taken seriously, it undoubtedly helps since, as Vallance comments, nobody fights other people's battles, and nothing is an issue until it has been shown to be electorally significant.

Sanzone (1984) similarly attributes advances in women's rights to the actions and influence of women in positions of political leadership, and believes that women in roles of executive political leadership will undoubtedly be instrumental in the creation of a more equal society.

For the 1990s, gender remains very visibly a dimension of European society, but a dimension with different facets in the different member states. Overall the conclusion has to be that structural factors are of greater importance than cultural/attitudinal factors. The prospects for change are therefore promising if the European Commission directs change not simply at policy formation but at its implementation and monitoring.

Notes

1 *Women of Europe Supplement 14*, 1984. In each of the member nations of the European Community, excepting Ireland, women constitute a numeric majority. Throughout the text references to the *Women of Europe Supplements* are abbreviated to *WoE(number)*.

2 Good sources for such discussions include Randall (1987), Vallance (1988), Vallance and Davies (1986), Lovenduski (1990), and Lovenduski and Hills (1981), Byrne (1978), and Osbourne *et al.* (1987).

3 The emancipation of women was spread across several decades: Denmark (1915); Germany (1918); Netherlands (1919); Luxembourg (1919); Ireland (1922); United Kingdom (1928); France (1944); Italy (1945); Belgium (1948); Greece (1952); Portugal (1976); and Spain, formally in 1930 but rarely able to use their votes prior to 1977.

4 This is not to suggest that the European Community, rising as it did from the pursuit of military and strategic nationalistic interests which characterised the 1930s and 1940s, was the sole platform for the pursuit of issues of gender inequality, but it has undoubtedly and explicitly addressed the issues, especially those associated with employment.

5 Article 119 states:

Each Member State shall during the first stage ensure and subsequently maintain the application of the principle of equal remuneration for the same work as between male and female workers.

For the purpose of this Article, remuneration shall be taken to mean the ordinary basic or minimum wage or salary and any additional emoluments whatsoever payable directly or indirectly, whether in cash or in kind, by the employer to the worker and arising out of the worker's employment. Equal remuneration without discrimination based on sex means:

(a) that remuneration for the same work at piece rates shall be calculated on the basis of the same unit of measurement;

(b) that remuneration for work at time-rates shall be the same for the same job.
Treaty Establishing the European Economic Community, Rome, 25 March 1957; London: HMSO, 1962, p. 45

6 The first Action Programme is presented in full, with a commentary, in 'Equal Opportunities Action Programme 1982–1985', *Women of Europe, Supplement 9*, 1982.

7 'Equal Opportunities for Women – Medium Term Community Programme 1986–1990' was launched by a Council resolution in 1985, and is summarised together with a commentary in 'Equal Opportunities: 2nd Action Programme 1986–1990', *Women of Europe, Supplement 23*, 1986.

8 Women's rights under Community law are well summarised in *Women of Europe, Supplement 12*, 1983; *Women of Europe, Supplement 19*, 1985; and *Women of Europe, Supplement 25*, 1987 – each of which is entitled 'Community Law and Women'.

9 As Randall notes, a mid-term conference to review progress was held in Copenhagen in 1980, and a final reviewing conference was held in Nairobi in 1985. Many of the delegations attending the latter conference were exclusively male, and few of the participants were centrally informed about women's issues.

10 See for example, Banks (1981), Bouchier (1983), Deckard (1979), and Wilson (1980).

11 Banks (1981) suggests that the British movement, for example, can be separated into three 'faces': equal rights feminism, present also in the United States but particularly strong in Britain; evangelical feminism, concerned with the reform of the 'less fortunate' and espousing an essentially conservative philosophy; and socialist feminism, questioning the forms of marriage, family child care and housework.

12 The famous strike by women machinists at Ford's in Dagenham is a prime example, cited by many, such as Randall (1987).

13 See Coote and Campbell (1982) for a full account of these demands.

14 Randall (1987) suggests that the French term 'groupuscule' indicates well the fragmented nature of the early movement which had three discernible strands: Femmes Revolutionnaires (radical feminists) formed in 1970; Psych et Po (Psychoanalysis and Politique), which concentrated on psychocultural mechanisms for women's oppression; and socialist feminists, as exemplified by the Cercle Dimitriev, founded in 1972. Lovenduski (1986) adds to the trio a fourth group representing reform or rights interests, and exemplified by the Choisir Party of Gisèle Halimi.

15 These were the Movimento di Liberazione della Donna, concerned with educational opportunity, divorce, abortion and non-sexist education; and Lotta Feminista, concerned with the campaign for wages for housework.

16 This was a natural outcome of the agenda which emerged from the dissatisfaction of many women with the organisational politics of the student groups of the 1960s. Lovenduski (1986) suggests that four dominant agenda items emerged from this context: autonomy from established organisations and ideologies; separatism from men, thus facilitating a realisation of women's culture and history; new small organisational structures (piccoli gruppi) without hierarchy; and consciousness-raising to develop an understanding of women's lives.

17 Colombo (1981), Ergas (1982) and Eckmann (1978) are all cited by Lovenduski as mentioning this change in focus.

18 Outshoorn (1988) labels the first the 'grounds' or indication type. Here,

she suggests, abortion is legal if certain criteria are met, such as a grave danger to the health of the women (England), or if certain procedural rules are observed (the Netherlands). Second, there is what she calls the 'term' type, where abortion is legal if performed before a certain time limit in the duration of the pregnancy, such as ten or twelve weeks (France and Italy). Finally there is the 'mixed' type, where indications are combined with given terms or procedural rules, as is found in the Federal Republic of Germany.

19 Vicky Randall (1987) provides a detailed discussion of abortion rights and reform in the policy context detailing how this happened. Janine Mossuz-Lavau (1988) provides a more succinct account in her discussion of women's private lives, but equally shows the strong political context of abortion law reform.

20 She comments:

> Long symbolized by a married couple accompanied by their two or three children, the family now takes on various shapes, including unmarried couples with children and single parents (usually women, more seldom men) with their children. There are more and more children born out of wedlock. . . . The number of single-parent families is also increasing. These changes, combined with the demands of women seeking legal guarantees of equality with their spouses or companions on the one hand and government concern over falling birth rates on the other, led to the adoption in many countries of new measures adapted to these new families.
>
> (1988:13)

21 Some of the consequences are well discussed in 'The graying of Europe: as the population ages, social pressures build', *Business Week*, 6 Feb. 1989: 12–16.

22 The discussion in this section focuses upon aspects of child care, but equally important to a full understanding of the impact of the changing structure of the family upon women's and men's lives and experiences in Europe are issues associated with the care of the elderly. Hall (1977), Walker (1989), Hunt (1978) and Leonard and Speakman (1986) are but some of the useful sources for a discussion of these issues.

23 See 'Women and men of Europe in 1978', *Women of Europe Supplement 3* (1978), 'Women and men of Europe in 1983' *Women of Europe Supplement 16* (1983), and 'Men and women of Europe in 1987', *Women of Europe Supplement 26* (1987).

24 The figure is created from data presented in 'Women in graphics', *Women of Europe Supplement 30*, Dec. 1989, and drawn from EUROSTAT data.

25 Data drawn again from 'Women in graphics', *Women of Europe Supplement 30*, Dec. 1989.

26 Data are presented in the Commission of the European Communities *Employment in Europe*, Office for Official Publications of the European Communities, Luxembourg, 1989. In most countries having a third child causes the chance of being employed to fall to about the same extent as having a second child. In Belgium, Denmark and France, however, a third child has a much greater impact; in France, for example, a woman with two children is only three-quarters less likely to work than a woman with one child, whereas a woman with three children has an employment rate of only 34 per cent of that of a single-child parent.

27 Data drawn from 'Women in graphics', *Women of Europe Supplement 30*, Dec. 1989, which was based on data from EUROSTAT, *Labour Force Survey*, 1986. Neither the Netherlands nor Spain provided data on part-time

working and hence are not included. Further information can also be found in 'European women in paid employment: their perception of discrimination at work', *Women of Europe Supplement 20*, 1985, and Commission of the European Communities, *Employment in Europe 1989*, Office for Official Publications of the European Communities, Luxembourg, 1989.

28 Data taken from the EUROSTAT *Labour Force Survey*, 1986.

29 OECD, *The Integration of Women in the Economy*, Paris, OECD, 1985. The study was an up-date of earlier research – OECD, *Women and Employment*, OECD, Paris, 1980 – which was a first attempt by the OECD to measure international differences in occupational segregation by gender using indexes of segregation.

30 For example, see the discussion of German women at work in Shaffer (1981); the chapters on Italy, Germany and Sweden in particular in Jenson *et al.* (1988); the special supplement on women in Spain, *Women of Europe Supplement 8* (1981) and the supplement on women in Portugal, *Women of Europe Supplement 11* (1982) for the Iberian peninsula; and for Britain, Hakim (1979) and Walby (1988).

31 The data are drawn from OECD and Eurydice, and relate to 1985/86. The following data were not available: percentage of female primary and secondary teachers in Italy, and the percentage of female secondary teachers in Denmark and Ireland. Missing data on Portugal were drawn from Commission on the Status of Women, *Status of Women*, Prime Minister's Office, Lisbon, 1988. Please note that Eurydice is the education information network in the European Community established in 1980. Experiments began in 1988 with computerised information exchanges. A list of documents prepared by the Central Unit of Eurydice is available from 17 rue Archimede, Bte 17, 1040 Brussels.

32 See, for example Braverman (1974), Beechey (1978), Bruegel (1979) and Simeral (1978).

33 Simeral makes an important distinction between the functions served by a reserve army of labour (RAL). She suggests that first capitalism depends upon a surplus population or RAL to supply its growing spheres. This reserve is formed over time by technological change and transformations in the structure of the economy. There is a need therefore for what she terms the 'secular' reserve. Second, there is the cyclical role for a RAL, to absorb the unemployed and to 'take up the slack' during economic crises and hold down wages during periods of economic growth and prosperity. This reserve she terms the 'cyclical' reserve.

The ease with which women are discharged back into the home is, of course, a function also of the cultural values of a specific country. Where the state is perceived as having a high level of responsibility for child care and formalised state provision of education and welfare more generally, and where traditional gender-segregated roles have been somewhat eroded, the ability to discharge women easily back into the home is undermined.

34 Data are taken from 'Women in graphics', *Women of Europe Supplement 30*, 1989.

35 See the 1980 survey of working women's attitudes, summarised in 'European women in paid employment', *Women of Europe Supplement 20*, 1981.

36 'Men and women of Europe in 1987', *Women of Europe Supplement 26*, 1987.

References

Banks, O. (1981) *Faces of Feminism: a Study of Feminism as a Social Movement*, London: Martin Robertson.

Baxter, S. and Lansing, M. (1980) *Women and Politics: the Invisible Majority*, Michigan, University of Michigan.

Beechey, V. (1978) 'Women and Production: a critical analysis of some sociological theories of women's work', A. Kuhn and A. Wolpe (eds) *Feminism and Materialism*, London, Routledge and Kegan Paul.

Beechey, V. (1989) 'Women's employment in France and Britain: some problems of comparison', *Work Employment and Society*, 3 (3).

Bocock, J. (1991) 'Equal opportunities in a cold climate', *NATFHE Journal*, Feb.

Bouchier, D. (1983) *The Feminist Challenge: the Movement for Women's Liberation in Britain and the USA*, London: Macmillan.

Bouillaquet-Bernard, P., Gauvin-Ayel, A. and Oulin, J.-L. (1981) *Femmes au Travail: Prospérité et Crise*, Paris: Economica.

Braverman, H. (1974) *Labor and Monopoly Capital*, New York, Monthly Review Press.

Brueghel, I. (1979) 'Women as a reserve army of labour: a note on recent British experience', *Feminist Review 3* pp. 12–33.

Buckley, M. and Anderson, M. (eds) (1988) *Women, Equality and Europe*, London: Macmillan.

Business Week, (6 Feb. 1989) 'The graying of Europe: as the population ages, social pressures build'.

Butler, D. and Stokes, D. (1974) *Political Change in Britain*, London: Macmillan.

Byrne, E. M. (1978) *Equality of Education and Training for Girls (10–18 Years)*, Education Series No. 9, Brussesl. Commission of the European Communities.

Colombo, D. (1981) 'The Italian feminist movement', in *Women's Studies International Quarterly*, 4 (4).

Commission of the European Communities (1981a) '*Equal Opportunities: Action Programme 1982–1985*', *Women of Europe Supplement*, Brussels.

——(1981b) 'Women at work in the European Community: 50 questions, 50 answers', *Women of Europe Supplement 7*, Brussels.

——(1981c) 'Women in Spain', *Women of Europe Supplement 8*, Brussels.

——(1982a) 'Women in statistics', *Women of Europe Supplement 19*, Brussels.

——(1982b) 'Women in Portugal', *Women of Europe Supplement 11*, Brussels.

——(1983) 'Community law and women', *Women of Europe Supplement 12*, Brussels.

——(1984a) 'Women in statistics', *Women of Europe Supplement 14*, Brussels.

——(1984b) 'Women at work in the European Communities', *Women of Europe Supplement 15*, Brussels.

——(1984c) 'Women and men of Europe in 1983', *Women of Europe Supplement 16*, Brussels.

——(1985a) 'Community law and women', *Women of Europe Supplement 19*, Brussels.

——(1985b) 'Equal Opportunities: 2nd Action Programme 1986–1990', *Women of Europe Supplement 23*, Brussels.

——(1986) 'Community law and women', *Women of Europe Supplement 25*, Brussels.

——(1988) 'Women of Europe: 10 years', *Women of Europe Supplement 27*, Brussels.

——(1989a) *Employment in Europe*, Directorate General, Employment, Industrial Relations and Social Affairs, Office for Official Publications of the European Communities, Luxembourg: COM(89)399 final.

——(1989b) 'Women in graphics', *Women of Europe Supplement 30*, Brussels.

——(1990) 'Child care in the European Communities 1985–1990', *Women of Europe Supplement 31*, Brussels.

——(1991a) 'Equal opportunities for women and men: the third medium-term Community Action Programme 1991–1995', *Women of Europe Supplement 34*, Brussels.

Commission on the Status of Women (1988) *Portugal: Status of Women*, Lisbon: Prime Minister's Office.

Coote, A. and Campbell, B. (1982) *Sweet Freedom: the Struggle for Women's Liberation*, Oxford: Blackwell.

Crompton, R. and Sanderson, K. (1990) *Gendered Jobs and Social Change*, London: Unwin Hyman

Dahlerup, D. and Gulli, B. (1983) 'The impact of the Women's liberation movement in public policy in Denmark and Norway', paper prepared for the European Consortium for Political Research (ECPR), Freiburg, March.

Deckard, B. (1979) *The Women's Movement: Political, Socio-economic and Psychological Issues*, New York: Harper & Row.

Devaud, M. S. (1968) 'Political participation of western European women', *Annals of the American Academy of Political and Social Science*, 375.

Dex, S. and Shaw, L. B. (1986) *British and American Women at Work*, London: Macmillan.

Duchen, C. (1986) *Feminism in France: from May '68 to Mitterrand*, London: Routledge & Kegan Paul.

Eckmann, E. (1978) 'The new conception of the politics of the modern feminist movement: with special reference to the new Italian feminist movement', Paper presented for the Joint Sessions of the ECPR Workshops, Grenoble: 6–12 April.

Economist (26 March 1990) 'Minding Europe's children'.

Education Guardian Supplement (4 Dec. 1990) 'Sans frontières'.

——(26 March 1991) 'Half the world'.

Elson, D. and Pearson, R. (1989) *Women's Employment in Multinationals in Europe*, London: Macmillan.

Epstein, T. Scarlett, Gehan, K., Gerzen, A.-M. and Sass, J. (1986) *Women, Work and Family in Britain and Germany*, London: Croom Helm.

Ergas, Y. (1982) '1968–79 – Feminism and the Italian party system: women's politics in a decade of turmoil', *Comparative Politics*, 14.

European Trade Union Institute (1987) *Women and Trade Unions in Western Europe*, Brussels: ETUI.

——(1989) *Positive Action for Women in Western Europe*, Brussels: ETUI.

Feldberg, R. and Glenn, E. N. (1984) 'Male and female: job versus gender models in the sociology of work', in J. Siltanen and M. Stanworth (eds) *Women and the Public Sphere*, London: Hutchinson.

Field, M. J. (1979) 'Determinants of abortion policy in the developed nations', *Policy Studies Journal*, 7.

Hakim, C. (1979) *Occupational Segregation*, London: Department of Employment.

Hall, P. (1977) *Europe 2000*, London: Duckworth.

Hamnett, C., McDowell, L. and Sarre, P. (1989) *The Changing Social Structure*, London: Sage.

Hernes, H. M. and Hanninen-Salmelin, E. (1985) 'Women in the corporate system', in Haavio-Mannila *et al.* (eds) *Unfinished Democracy: Women in Nordic Politics*, Oxford: Pergamon.

Humphries, J. and Rubery, J. (1988) 'Recession and exploitation: British women in a changing workplace 1979–85', in J. Jenson *et al.* (eds) *Feminization of the Labour Force: Paradoxes and Promises*, Cambridge: Polity Press.

Hunt, A. (1978) *The Elderly at Home*, London: HMSO.

——(1988) 'The effects of caring for the elderly and infirm on women's employment', in A. Hunt (ed.) *Women and Paid Work*, London: Macmillan.

Jenson, J., Hagen, E. and Reddy, C. (1988) *Feminization of the Labour Force: Paradoxes and Promises*, Cambridge: Polity Press.

Leonard, D. and Speakman, M. A. (1986) 'Women in the family: companions or caretakers', in V. Beechey and E. Whitelegg (eds) *Women in Britain Today*, Milton Keynes: Open University Press.

Lewis, J. (1990) 'Breaking the creche barrier', *Management Today*, Feb.

Lovenduski, J. (1986) *Women and European Politics: Contemporary Feminism and Public Policy*, London: Wheatsheaf.

——(1988) 'The women's movement and public policy in western Europe: theory, strategy, practice and politics', in M. Buckley and M. Anderson (eds) *Women, Equality and Europe*, London: Macmillan.

——(1990) 'Feminism and West European politics: an overview', in D. W. Unwin and W. E. Paterson *Politics in Western Europe Today*, London: Longman.

——and Hills, J. (eds) (1981) *The Politics of the Second Electorate: Women and Public Participation*, London: Routledge & Kegan Paul.

McDowell, L. (1989) 'Gender divisions', in C. Hamnett, L. McDowell and P. Sarre (eds) *The Changing Social Structure*, London: Sage.

Mayo, M. (ed.) (1977) *Women in the Community*, London: Routledge & Kegan Paul.

Moss, P. (1990) *Women of Europe Supplement 31*, Brussels.

Mossuz-Lavau, J. (1988) *Women of Europe Supplement 27*, Brussels.

Norris, P. (1987) *Politics and Sexual Equality*, London: Wheatsheaf.

Oakley, A (1974) *Housewife*, London: Allen Lane.

Organisation for Economic Cooperation and Development (1976) *The 1974–1975 Recession and the Employment of Women*, Paris: OECD.

——(1988) *Ageing Populations: the Social Policy Implications*, Paris: OECD.

Osbourne, R. D., Cormack, R. J. and Miller, R. L. (1987) *Education and Policy in Northern Ireland*, Policy Research Institute, Belfast: Queen's University.

Outshoorn, J. (1988) 'Abortion law reform: a woman's right to choose?' in M. Buckley and M. Anderson (eds) *Women, Equality and Europe*, London: Macmillan.

Phillips, A. (1991) 'Pregnant pause', *Guardian*, 9 April.

Phizacklea, A. (1987) 'Minority women and economic restructuring: the case of Britain and Germany', *Work, Employment and Society*, 1 (3).

Purcell, K. (1984) 'Militancy and acquiescence among women workers', in J.

Siltanen and M. Stanworth (eds) *Women and the Public Sphere*, London: Hutchinson.

Randall, V. (1987), *Women and Politics: an International Perspective*, 2nd edn, London: Macmillan.

Sanzone, D. S. (1984) 'Women in positions of political leadership in Britain, France and West Germany', in J. Siltanen and M. Stanworth *Women and the Public Sphere*, London: Hutchinson.

Shaffer, H. G. (1981) *Women in the Two Germanies: a Comparative study of a Socialist and a Non-socialist Society*, New York: Pergamon.

Siltanen, J. and Stanworth, M. (eds) (1984) *Women and the Public Sphere*, London: Hutchinson.

Simeral, M. (1978) 'Women and the reserve army of labour', *The Insurgent Sociologist*, 8:2, 3.

Ungerson, C. (1985) *Women and Social Policy: a Reader*, London: Macmillan.

Urwin, D. W. and Paterson, W. E. (1990) *Politics in Western Europe Today: Perspectives, Policies and Problems*, London: Longman.

Vallance, E. (1988) 'Do women make a difference? The impact of women MEPs on Community Equality policy', in M. Buckley and M. Anderson *Women, Equality and Europe*, London: Macmillan.

Vallance, E. and Davies, E. (1986) *Women of Europe: women MEPs and Equality Policy*, Cambridge: Cambridge University Press.

Walby, S. (1988) *Gender Segregation at Work*, Milton Keynes: Open University Press.

Walker, A (1989) 'The consequences of an aging population for the social security system', *Contemporary European Affairs*, 2 (1).

Wilson, E. (1980) *Only Half-way to Paradise: Women in Post-War Britain 1945–1968*, London: Tavistock.

Woesler de Panafieu, C. (1991) 'British Women: the laggards of Europe. *RSA Journal*, 139 (5417) (April), Royal Society of Arts.

CHAPTER 6

Race and ethnicity in Europe

JOHN REX

Arguably the most important problem in the political sociology of Europe today is that of the relationship which develops between the various nation states and the immigrant communities which have settled within their boundaries. Indigenous class struggles within the various European countries had, by the 1970s, led to the establishment in all cases of some sort of political consensus around the ideas of the welfare state, a mixed economy with public and private sectors, the establishment of mechanisms for collective bargaining by trade unions and employers, planning for full employment and the provision of basic services in such spheres as housing, health, education and personal and family social welfare. Moreover, although this consensus came under attack in the eighties with more emphasis upon privatisation, a reduction in trade-union power, the tolerance of higher levels of unemployment, and generally greater reliance on the free market, this did not mean a return to class struggle, and what emerged were societies based upon the notion of a 'social market' with an incorporated working class. During the period between 1945 and 1970, however, economic expansion led to the settlement of some 16 million immigrants. Such immigrants were recruited to fill the jobs which indigenous workers were unwilling to do, and, though they joined trade unions, were often inadequately protected by those unions and the state (see Castles and Kosack 1973; Piore 1974). Some immigrant leaders claimed that they indeed constituted the new European proletariat.

The statistics of immigration to the various European Community countries are somewhat difficult to interpret. The best comprehensive source is to be found in the *Demographic Statistics* published by Eurostat (1990). These give the numbers of the foreign residents in the various countries, and are shown in Table 6.1.

What this table does clearly show is that Germany, France, the United Kingdom, Belgium and the Netherlands have been the largest importers of labour, while Denmark, Greece, Ireland, Italy, Portugal and Spain have had relatively small inflows. If, moreover, one looks at emigration from the European countries to other countries within the community, as shown in the breakdown of the EC migrant figures by country, it is clear that there are considerable outflows from Greece, Ireland, Italy, Spain and Portugal. The most significant groups of these EC migrants are 508,656 Italian and 274,793 Greek

Table 6.1 **EC and Non-EC migrants in EC countries**

Country of Residence	EC migrants	Non-EC migrants
Belgium	536,836	321,814
Denmark	26,875	109,302
France	1,577,900	2,102,200
Germany (Federal Rep.)	1,275,858	3,213,247
Greece	107,781	108,860
Ireland	66,400	17,100
Italy	89,844	206,012
Netherlands	156,901	434,946
Portugal	25,296	69,157
Spain	193,312	140,424
United Kingdom	766,000	1,019,000

Source: *Demographic Statistics*, Eurostat (1990)

migrants in Germany, 764,860 Portuguese, 333,740 Italian and 321,440 Spanish migrants in France, 532,000 Irish in the United Kingdom, and 250,209 Italians in Belgium.

From outside the European community, the principal sources of migration listed are Yugoslavia, Turkey and the Maghrebian countries. Germany has 1,523,678 Turks and 579,073 Yugoslavs; France has 1,416,440 Maghrebians (including 795,920 Algerians), and 123,540 Turks; the United Kingdom has a total of 1,091,000 foreign residents from non EC countries, of whom 120,000 were from non-EC European countries, 95,000 from Africa and 804,000 from other countries; Belgium has 128,566 Moroccans and 78,433 Turks and the Netherlands 167,325 Turks and 130,094 Moroccans. Italy, traditionally a country of emigration, now has 206,012 foreign residents from non-EC countries, suggesting that it is now also becoming a country of immigration.

One should note that the figures given here are for resident foreigners; namely, those who have a citizenship other than that of their land of settlement. They do not include those who have acquired citizenship in the country of settlement or who had it on arrival. These foreign-*born* residents who are not listed as foreign residents include all those who have been naturalised in any of the EC countries, most of the 2.2 million New Commonwealth immigrants in the United Kingdom, Indonesians and Surinamese in the Netherlands and immigrants from France's overseas departments such as Guadeloupe and Martinique.

In the case of the United Kingdom the 1.41 million New Commonwealth immigrants included, in 1981, 272,000 from the Caribbean, 412,000 from India, 177,000 from Pakistan, 47,000 from Bangladesh, 133,000 from East Africa (mostly East African Asians), 80,000 from the Far East and 91,000 from the Mediterranean (mainly from Cyprus). In the 1981 census the number of those living in a household with a New Commonwealth head was recorded in order to obtain a rough approximation of the numbers of New Commonwealth immigrants and their British-born children. The total number was 2.2 million, of whom 546,000 were from the Caribbean, 674,000 from India, 295,000 from Pakistan, 65,000 from Bangladesh, 181,000 from East Africa, 120,000 from the Far East and 170,000 from the Mediterranean. A question was included on claimed ethnicity in the 1991 census in order to discover the numbers in these various ethnic communities, including those of the third and fourth generation (Commission for Racial Equality 1985).

Official figures equivalent to these are not available for other European countries, although the publication *Immigrant Policy*, a Report to the Government by the Netherlands Scientific Council for Government Policy (1990) gives estimates of the numbers of those from 'non-indigenous groups with Netherlands citizenship'. The total number of these is 327,000, of whom 194,000 are from Surinam, 66,000 from Aruba and the Antilles, 40,000 who are Moluccans and 23,000 Chinese. In the case of the other European countries, the fact that relatively few of those from certain groups have sought naturalisation does, of course, mean that the statistics for the numbers of foreign citizens does give some indication of the size of minority communities. This is particularly true of the Turks in Germany, France and Belgium as well as in the Netherlands, and it is probably also true of the Moroccan minority in Belgium. The number of Maghrebians or the number from Guadeloupe and Martinique in France, however, is not deducible from the numbers having citizenship in those countries. Many Algerians who settled in France before independence had French citizenship, and many have been naturalised, while, so far as Guadeloupe and Martinique are concerned, immigrants from these territories are simply counted as French. There are no reliable estimates of the numbers of Maghrebians, West Indians or Africans in France, although the number of Maghrebians and their children is variously estimated at between 3 and 4 million.

Problems and policies

The problems of race and ethnic relations with which we are here concerned arise in the major countries of settlement, and each has its own distinctive profile. The primary pre-occupation of Germany has been with its Turkish population, that of France with its Maghrebians, that of the United Kingdom with its black and Asian immigrants, that of Belgium with its Moroccans and that of the Netherlands with its Turks and Moroccans as well as with Surinamese and Indonesians. This is not to say that Portuguese and Spanish immigrants in France, Italians, Yugoslavs and Greeks in Germany, the Irish in the United Kingdom and Italians in Belgium have not faced problems, but, given their cultural similarity to the peoples of their host societies, they have been and are likely to continue to be assimilated within three generations, with the internal EC migrants assimilating most readily of all. Significantly, too, the question of race and colour has not emerged as strongly in France as it has in Britain, immigrants from the overseas departments being seen as black Frenchmen.

Although most of the migrants discussed above have been labour migrants, a small number of those from non-EC countries are refugees from the Middle East, from Africa and Asia, and from the communist countries. The collapse of communist regimes in 1990 will also add large numbers of east Europeans who are no longer likely to be refugees but may well become labour migrants. West Germany now also faces an inflow of East Germans following German unification. Problems arising from labour migration might well, therefore, be pushed into the background as the traditional countries of immigrant labour face new problems of dealing with refugees and east Europeans.

British policy for dealing with its immigrants was discussed and dealt with in a way quite different from other European countries. Although well over half of those born overseas were white, discussion of 'immigrants' was commonly focused on those who were thought of as 'black'; that is, those from the Caribbean and those coming directly or indirectly from the Indian subcontinent. The collection of separate statistics of those coming from the New Commonwealth seems to have been designed to achieve this without making overt reference to race or colour. Moreover, the ethnic question in the 1991 census offers a choice between 'white', 'black (West Indian, African or other)' or 'Asian (Indian, Pakistani or Bangladeshi)'.

Before 1962 all Commonwealth immigrants whether from the old and largely white Commonwealth or from the new and largely black Commonwealth could settle freely in Britain. In 1962, however, controls were introduced. At first these applied equally to those from the old and new Commonwealth, but, when the Act was amended in 1971 so-called 'patrials' (those with parents or grandparents who had lived in Britain) were given few rights of settlement, whereas even more severe restrictions were applied to 'non-patrials'.

Such distinctions were coupled with special policies of integration for the non-patrials, and a series of bodies culminating in the Commission for Racial Equality in 1976 were set up to combat 'racial' discrimination. These were based upon American models for dealing with the problems of black Americans, but were thought of as dealing not merely with the problems of West Indians, whose condition to some extent paralleled that of American blacks, but also with the immigrants of Asian origin, who outnumbered the West Indians in a proportion of 11 to 5. The Commission had powers to help individual complainants who claimed they had suffered racial discrimination, and to carry out its own investigations of organisations against whom there was a prima-facie case of discrimination whether the discrimination was of a direct or indirect sort. The Commission was also empowered to do promotional work to promote good 'race relations', and the Act called upon local councils to set up their own machinery for promoting equality of opportunity and good race relations.

The purpose of rehearsing these developments in Britain here is not, however, simply to describe the British situation, but rather to draw attention to the fact that British practice was not replicated in continental Europe. Some of those working in the race relations field have suggested that Britain should lead the way and offer a model to European countries for setting up machinery to overcome racism and racial discrimination. What this ignores, however, is the fact that European countries do not necessarily conceive of their immigration problems in terms of race and colour at all.

Discussion of the problems of immigrants and ethnic minorities in terms of race was discredited in most of western Europe by the experience of Nazism. The very use of the term 'race' has, in fact, been to a large extent taboo, and there is a fear of a revival of racism which is often focused on the question of anti-Semitism. This is particularly true in Germany, where there is very considerable majority opposition to neo-Nazi movements, while in France colour-consciousness has never played the same role in political thinking that it has in Britain.

French thinking about immigrants and ethnic minorities is based upon central political ideas deriving from the French Revolution. All citizens, it is thought, should be entitled to the full rights of citizenship regardless of race and of national, ethnic or religious origin. The state is thought of as being secular, and, crucially, educational policy is based upon the notion of the '*école laïque*'. Involved in this is a relative absence of colour consciousness of the British sort together with a fear that alien and immigrant cultures will undermine French political ideals. The major tensions in French society, so far as immigrants are concerned, tend to be ethnic and cultural rather than racial. It focuses especially on the fear of Islam and of what is referred to as 'Muslim fundamentalism', and the most pressing problem of ethnic relations in France today concerns the way in which the native majority and the secular state on the one hand and immigrant Muslim communities on the other come to terms with each other.

In Germany the situation is quite different. Its central political ideals involve not the sort of universalist political and republican conception of citizenship to be found in France, but rather an exclusive ideal of an ethnic group or '*Volk*'. Thus the constitution of the Federal Republic provided automatic citizenship for a spouse or descendant of persons who were settled in the German Reich on 31 December 1937, as well as refugees or deportees with German '*Volkszugehörigkeit*' (ethnicity), and this category has been extended to take in a wide range of ethnic Germans from the east, including, for instance, Germans who had settled in Romania between the twelfth and seventeenth centuries (Wilpert 1990). Non-Germans can, of course, also acquire citizenship by naturalisation, but the guest-worker ideology and policy insists that Germany is not a country of immigration, and that, unless they do become naturalised, the guest-workers and their families may be workers and residents, but not citizens. The combination of the ethnic nationalist and the guest-worker ideologies therefore makes for a kind of racism or, perhaps one should say, ethnicism, more sharp than in any other European country.

Policy in the Netherlands was directed to dealing with two major problems. One was the assimilation of various groups from the Dutch colonies; the other dealing with migrants from outside the former Dutch Empire. Prior to both of these problems, moreover, was the fact that the Netherlands had already developed on pluralistic lines to accommodate the religious division of Dutch society. Relatively progressive policies were adopted towards those coming from the former colonies, the more so because they included many Dutch or half-Dutch immigrants from Indonesia. But, so far as Turks and others coming from outside were concerned, the first reaction was to treat them as guest-workers. Eventually, however, it was recognised to an extent which was not possible in Germany that what was needed was a policy for the integration of immigrants of both kinds. The government became concerned to promote equality of opportunity for immigrants, even though it did not set up elaborate institutional machinery to this end as in Britain. Yet at the same time it did not adopt the sort of assimilationist position to be found in France and, in accordance with Dutch tradition, was prepared to give recognition to minority cultures in a multi-cultural society.

Belgian experience was affected by the fact that Belgium is the most pluralist society in Europe. The country is divided in terms of language, religion and politics, and government depends upon a balance between the linguistic groups, the different religions and differing class-based parties (Deprez 1989). The main early source of immigration was Italy, and the various indigenous political and cultural groups sought to assimilate the newcomers to themselves. Much more difficult is the assimilation of Moroccan immigrants. They have remained in relatively poor jobs and poor housing conditions, and their religion keeps them from assimilating to the predominant groups.

Finally, one should note the case of Italy. Italy was, until recently, primarily a country of emigration, a sending rather than a receiving society. At the same time, however, the Italian borders were excep-tionally open, and the 1980s saw the arrival of many legal and illegal immigrants from eastern Europe as well as Africa and Asia. For the first time in 1989, Italy was becoming concerned both about the threat of large-scale immigration and about the dangers of the growth of racism and the resurgence of fascism. A new government edict in

1989 gave an amnesty to existing illegal immigrants and sought to promote their social rights without actually according them citizenship. It remains to be seen how Italian policy towards its immigrants will develop. Recently there have been spontaneous outbursts of racism and racist attacks against blacks, and racism has found some political expression. At the same time, however, there is concern in the political parties and the unions to promote the interests and the rights of immigrant workers.

Multi-culturalism

One particular feature of the British situation has been the gradual acceptance of the notion that Britain has become a 'multi-cultural society'. This was not the first reaction to the coming of West Indian and Asian immigrants. In 1964 the Commonwealth Immigrants Advisory Council stated that 'a national [educational] system cannot be expected to perpetuate the different values of minority groups'. In 1968, however, the Home Secretary, Roy Jenkins, defined integration as 'not a flattening process of uniformity, but cultural diversity coupled with equal opportunity in an atmosphere of mutual tolerance'. It is to be doubted whether all of those who accepted the idea of a multi-cultural society really based the idea on this definition. For many it meant simply an acceptance of the fact that there was a large immigrant population whose appearance, language, religion and customs were different from those of the British. Some also saw such diverse peoples and cultures as inferior, but eventually the Swann Committee, which was appointed to investigate the problems of ethnic minority children in schools (Department of Education and Science 1985) concluded that all children should have their education enriched by learning about ethnic minority culture and that the practice of the schools and the content of the school syllabus should be anti-racist.

The actual problems facing West Indian and Asian children, however, differed from one another. West Indian children, although differing in race and colour from their English peers, spoke English as their home language and had a cultural background which was largely British. None the less, there was a considerable body of evidence to suggest that they were not doing well at school (Rex and Tomlinson 1979). Children from Asian homes, on the other hand, spoke different languages at home and came from different cultural and religious backgrounds, and Indian children at least were doing as well as their English peers (Department of Education and Science 1981). West Indian parents and teachers claimed that their children's relative failure was due to racism both in the school and in the wider society. Asians, on the other hand, had linguistic problems, and some, primarily Muslims, were concerned that the schools might undermine their religion and culture.

Because the education system in England is a highly decentralised one, the actual developments which occurred varied from one local area to another, but there was considerable development of multi-cultural policies in many local authority areas and most teachers were expected to develop their teaching in a multi-cultural way as well as being aware themselves and making their pupils aware of the dangers of racism.

Such developments as these have not occurred in France. The French educational system is both highly centralised and secular. It might well include as part of its Civics teaching the inculcation of democratic, egalitarian and anti-racist values, but it could have no place for the perpetuation of minority cultures and religions. It is no way surprising that Muslim girls at a French school with a black French headmaster should have been sent home merely for wearing the scarf which was a normal part of Algerian Muslim dress. This contrasts quite sharply with the British situation, in which some local authorities have accepted religious instruction in minority religions in schools, the provision of *halal* meat in school meals, the right of Muslim girls to opt out of physical education and swimming lessons and the maintenance of some single-sex schools out of deference to the views of Asian parents.

The education of Turkish children in Germany has been considerably affected by the guest-worker system. Not merely are these children concentrated in the poorer schools, but there is also uncertainty on the part of the schools and of parents as to whether their children would not be best served by trying to achieve the sort of education which would help them on return to Turkey, rather than that which equipped them for competing in German society. No doubt this position is changing as more and more Turkish families become committed to remaining in Germany, but there is little doubt that so long as the parents are simply regarded as temporary workers there will be little in the way of educational development which will give Turkish children equality of opportunity and still less for the development of any sort of multi-culturalism in the schools. Any development of the latter sort would also run counter to the ethnic nationalist ideology which we have discussed above.

The European country most open to the idea of multi-culturalism, other than Britian, is the Netherlands. Even there, however, the report *Immigrant Policy*, written as recently as 1990, envisages only that 'education in own language and culture henceforth be provided outside the regular curriculum but within the school' (Netherlands Scientific Council for Government Policy 1990). Clearly there is some acceptance here of the obligation of the schools themselves to provide for education in minority cultures rather than simply leaving it to voluntary effort by the parents and the community, but any such education is clearly to be kept 'outside the regular curriculum'. This contrasts with the recommendation of the British Swann Committee that all children should receive education in minority cultures as part of the curriculum, although it should be noted that the Swann Committee also suggests that the teaching of minority mother-tongue languages should actually occur outside the school.

It would seem, then, that the various European countries are far from being committed to multi-cultural education or to the idea of the multi-cultural society. The more normal response is either to base education on a shared culture in the public domain or simply the maintenance of traditional nationalist cultures. Even in Britain, moreover, it is to be doubted whether the notion of 'cultural diversity' coupled with 'equality of opportunity' is being realised. What actually occurs in many schools may involve no more than a token recognition of minority cultures.

Looking beyond the schools to the wider issues involved, it must be said that all European countries fall short of realising the two ideals of promoting both multi-culturalism and equal opportunity for ethnic minorities. French critics of British policy sometimes accuse the British of actually achieving the 'ghettoisation' of minorities under the guise of multi-culturalism, and rightly so, because, too often, diverse cultures are accepted only on unequal terms. On the other hand, British social scientists, looking at French practice, see the pressure towards giving the same rights of social citizenship to all, as actually being based upon an assimilationist philosophy which allows no space for cultural diversity. In the German case, moreover, given the commitment to both German ethnic nationalism and to the notion of guest-workers, neither equal opportunity nor multi-culturalism are likely to be attained.

Ghettoisation also occurs, in actuality, in all countries. One only has to look at British inner cities to see a process whereby most members of ethnic minority communities are increasingly isolated from their British born fellow-citizens as 'white flight' from the inner areas increases. But similar developments occur in other European cities. In France the ethnic minorities are often concentrated, not in the inner city, it is true, but in cheaply built suburban estates, while in Germany Turkish quarters emerge where apartments are available to immigrants. Such processes of segregation may in part be due to the choice of the ethnic minorities who need to be near their own mosques and temples, their own shops and their cultural centres. But they are also due to the constraints imposed by discrimination both in the private housing market and in publicly-provided housing. No serious attempt has been made in any country to ensure that, while ethnic communities are encouraged to develop their communal facilities, they also have equal access to the better types of housing. Ghettoisation of the minorities is therefore likely to remain as a feature of western European cities for several generations.

A similar process of ghettoisation occurred in the field of employment when immigrants originally arrived to fill jobs unwanted by indigenous workers, and little was achieved by way of training or education on the job for these workers, so that they often remained in an industrial ghetto. When unemployment increased in the eighties, moreover, immigrants bore more than their fair share, and trade unions were more inclined in these circumstances to defend the interests of indigenous workers. In Britain the position of the children of black workers was particularly acute, since they were neither acceptable in the jobs which their parents had done, nor, because of discrimination, in the jobs for which they were qualified. Not surprisingly, Britain led the way in the occurrence of urban riots as the young black unemployed came into conflict with the police, but recently there have been similar developments in France.

Refugees and EC controls

Worst placed of all in all the European countries are refugees, who have been given leave to remain while awaiting the outcome of their applications for asylum, and unknown numbers of illegal immigrants. While technological developments made large-scale legal labour-immigration unnecessary and undesirable and led to the immigration stop in the early seventies, and capital moved to labour in the Third World rather than importing it, there was still a need, even in the new technological conditions, for casual unskilled labour in restaurants, in domestic service, in agriculture and in some unpleasant manufacturing jobs, and this need was largely filled from this new illegal and semi-legal population (Heisler and Heisler 1986). In Britain, Sivanandan has recently pointed out that 'hotel and catering workers, the contract cleaners in hospitals, airports and so on, the security guards in the private security firms, petrol pump attendants, domestics, fast-food assistants, hospital auxiliaries and porters and . . . many others come increasingly from Colombia, Chile, Turkey, Sudan, Sri Lanka, Eritrea, Iran'. He says that these workers 'with no rights to housing or to medical care, and under the constant threat of deportation . . . are forced to accept wages and conditions which no indigenous worker, black or white, would accept' (Sivanandan 1990: 156). The numbers of workers in these categories are probably greater in the continental European countries and are also to be found there in other industries (as in Italy where they play a larger part as itinerant agricultural workers). Thus, if guest-workers are seen as a kind of relatively rightless 'underclass' compared with established immigrant workers, this new category of workers would appear to form a kind of underclass beneath the underclass (Layton-Henry 1990).

In the preparation for 1992, the EC countries have sought to maximise the rights to EC citizens migrating from one EC country to another, while at the same time restricting the rights of non-EC migrants. This means that amongst those already settled, a distinction will exist between mobile migrants, who, because they have acquired citizenship, can move from one country to another, and non-mobile migrants like the guest-workers, who will not be entitled to move in this way. The implementation of such distinctions, moreover, will mean that minorities who are visible by virtue of their skin colour or culture will, at best, be called upon to provide documentary evidence of their status, and, at worst, will be subject to harassment by the police and other authorities.

So far as new refugees and migrants are concerned, the position will be even more difficult. Already groups of civil servants from the EC countries have been meeting to discuss the harmonisation of their policies at the borders, taking in as well as the questions of immigration and the rights of refugees to asylum, the question of drug traffic and terrorism. One group consisting of representatives of France, Germany and the Netherlands (with the later adherence of Italy) has met at Schengen to consider the creation of a common external border for those countries, while an all-EC group meeting at Trevi has dealt with the problems of the EC countries as a whole (Minority Rights Group 1990). From what is already known of the findings of these groups, it seems likely that immigration and refugee policy will be harmonised at the level of the greatest possible restriction, an outcome which is the more inevitable when it is noted that immigration and refugee questions are being discussed in the same fora as the questions of the drug traffic and terrorism. Although there are lobbies in all countries concerned with defending the rights of immigrants and refugees, the overall ideology which at present informs policy-making is that of 'Fortress Europe', with the strongest possible defences against outsiders.

A new environing element in this situation has been created by the collapse of communist regimes in eastern Europe and indeed, the Soviet Union itself. The likelihood is that within the next ten years millions of east Europeans will seek to move to the greater prosperity of the west. In the immediate euphoria surrounding the end of the Cold War, migrants and refugees from this quarter will enjoy a certain prestige, and there will be pressure for their admission, and, even though this euphoria will abate as cheap east European labour comes to compete with that of western Europe, it seems likely that such labour will be more acceptable than that coming from the Third World, or even from Turkey. Already in West Germany, ethnic Germans from the east may readily acquire German citizenship, while Turkish and other guest-workers remain relatively rightless, and it is likely that in other countries, east Europeans who are thought of as being 'like us' will be regarded as being like the ethnic Germans, while existing guest-workers, refugees waiting for asylum, and illegals of all sorts will form a relatively rightless underclass.

It is clear that, even though there remains a fear of immigration as such in Europe, during a period of economic recession, the declining birth rate in west Europe, coupled with future economic expansion, will mean that there will inevitably be a considerable new immigration in the nineties. The countries which have a demographic surplus and which can potentially meet this need are in east Europe, Africa and Asia, though any one of them could meet the whole need. It is conceivable that immigration policies could be based on actual economic needs, regardless of nationality and race, but the likelihood is that the consciousness of kind of the west Europeans will lead them to opt for their fellow-Europeans from the east. The fact that these east Europeans are white could well mean the emergence of a new type of European colour racism, which, as well as closing the boundaries to Africans and Asians, could rebound on Europe's existing black and Asian populations.

In these circumstances it is likely that those immigrants and their children who are relatively rightless will organise themselves along ethnic lines across European boundaries, and there is some evidence that this is happening. Such transnational organisation is a source of considerable concern in some European countries, particularly in France, but at the level of the European Commission steps were already being taken in 1990 to set up a consultative mechanism for such organisations. Although the theory behind this development is that, because non-EC migrants are not represented in the European Parliament, their interests should be taken care of through a consultative mechanism, it is interesting to notice that the Commission has included British black and Asian organisations in their consultation even though they represent EC citizens. This reflects the fact that black British and Asian workers share *de facto* the political and economic position of the non-EC migrants in Europe; but, in any case, it is clear that the Commission recognises that it has to deal with classes of immigrants who are not represented through normal political channels (Gordon 1989; Hammar 1985).

All in all, the new European society which is likely to come into being will include a politically stratified system of groups. The majority will be citizens of the EC countries entitled to mobility between these countries and having representation in the European Parliament. Included in this group, however, there will be some like British blacks and Asians, who, despite their citizenship, may be confused with non-EC migrants, and *de facto* fail to enjoy the same rights and freedoms as other EC citizens. There will also be immigrants and refugees from east Europe, who, although not enjoying full citizenship at first, may be recognised by virtue of their shared skin colour and culture, as being especially entitled to rights and as having an easy path to naturalisation. There will still be many contract labourers and guest-workers who will be, as Hammar (1990) has put it, 'denizens' rather than citizens, and who will not enjoy the rights of citizens. And, finally, there will be a residue of refugees and illegals, whose presence is tolerated so long as they are in employment, but who can readily be deported and dispensed with. Given such distinctions of political, legal and social status, these different groups of European inhabitants will have differing access to employment and social rights and will in effect be distinct classes. In a Marxist interpretation, the existence of such classes might be seen as a necessary consequence of the needs of European capitalism (see, for example, Sivanandan 1990: ch. 9). In other interpretations, their emergence may be seen as an historic accident, but one which none the less provides the environment within which the capitalist economic development of Europe is likely to occur.

At least at the level of rhetoric, however, the new Europe is unlikely to accept this picture of a politically and economically stratified society within 'Fortress Europe' as a fair and final definition of itself. Thus it may be expected, that, entrenched though the guest-worker ideology may be in some countries and the ideology of racism in others, there will be some pressure to alleviate the position both of guest-workers and of those who suffer racial and ethnic discrimination. There will also be pressure to harmonise future immigration and refugee policy on a non-racist basis. It would be wrong, however, to imagine that rhetoric in these areas actually describes the structural reality of Europe.

Conclusion

In more general terms, European countries and the EC as a whole will need to, and probably will, develop policies to promote equality of opportunity and to prevent racial and ethnic discrimination on the one hand, and to deal with cultural diversity on the other. At the moment the debate about these issues has, however, hardly begun; different countries have different ideologies and different institutions; harmonisation of policy will be by no means easy, and the likelihood is that the first steps towards harmonisation will be at the level of the lowest common denominator; that is to say, at the level which does least to protect inferior groups.

So far as equality of opportunity and the prevention of racism is concerned, what is most likely to occur is a rhetorical denunciation of 'racism' as in the European Parliament's *Declaration against Racism and Xenophobia*, without any serious attempt to require the setting up of institutions to prevent discrimination and overcome racial and ethnic disadvantage. In this matter, Britain, having established elaborate institutions on an American model, might be thought of as leading the way. In many European countries, however, it will be argued that such machinery has been developed in Britain precisely because colour-racism is endemic there to an extent that it is not in other countries. It remains to be seen, though, whether these other countries will move beyond the level of rhetoric and develop appropriate forms of enforcement to prevent racial and ethnic discrimination. Clearly, without effective enforcement machinery of this kind (and it should be noted that as the most recent studies of the Policy Studies Institute show (Brown 1984) – even the elaborate institutional machinery established in Britain has been far from fully effective), any move towards multi-culturalism, taken on its own, will mean only ghettoisation at best and apartheid at worst. None the less, the issue of multi-culturalism or assimilation to a unitary culture is one which has to be faced.

It is not to be expected that most European societies will wish to become pluralistic in the way which Belgian society, and in a lesser way, Dutch society is. Belgian society is pluralistic because of the relative equality of power of two linguistic groups, and the so-called 'pillarisation' of the Netherlands arose to meet the needs of two religious communities. What is possible, however, is that, while maintaining a unitary political culture in the public sphere, these societies might develop policies for the tolerance of minority cultures in the private and communal sphere.

A real obstacle to the emergence of this kind of limited multi-culturalism, however, lies in the ethnic nationalism of majority groups, as represented most clearly in the German case. It is one thing to proclaim a culture based on political values of liberty, equality and fraternity, as the French do, or to recognise the existence of common social rights, as has been suggested by T. H. Marshall (1950) in Britain, since all groups can be invited to share in such a culture, while preserving their own communal cultures. It is quite another to proclaim a culture based on ethnic nationalism, from which minorities are by definition excluded.

Even if a national political culture rests upon political values which all groups can share, however, the problem remains as to how far private communal cultures should be, or are likely to be, maintained. In this matter, the French tend to be the most assimilationist, the Dutch and the British the most inclined towards multi-culturalism. Probably, in the long run, the dogmas and ideologies surrounding these notions may be modified in practice, with assimilationists recognising that there has to be some at least temporary recognition of minority cultures in the private sphere and the multi-culturalists recognising that the problem which they face may become less urgent over several generations. Possibly, the major problem which may arise is about the place of Islam in European society, since there are now, probably, some 6 million Muslims in Europe and Islam is unlikely to disappear, but even here dialogue is beginning about the place which Islam claims and can be accorded in European society.

Thus there are many problems which still have to be resolved relating to the position of immigrant ethnic minorities in Europe. They concern both the question of equality of opportunity and of cultural coexistence. They may, indeed be the major problems of the political sociology of Europe in the nineties.

References

Brown, C. (1984) *Black and White in Britain: the Third PSI Survey*, London: Heinemann.

Castles, S. and Kosack, G. (1973) *Immigrant Workers and Class Structure in Western Europe*, Oxford: Oxford University Press.

Commission for Racial Equality (1985) *Ethnic Minorities in Britain*, London: Commission for Racial Equality.

Department of Education and Science (1981) *Committee of Enquiry into the Education of Children from Ethnic Minority Groups: Interim Report: West Indian Children in our Schools*, Cmnd 8272, London: HMSO.

——(1985) *Education for All: Report of the Committee of Enquiry into the Education of Children from Ethnic Minority Groups*, vol. 2 (Chairman, Lord Swann), Cmnd 9453, London: HMSO.

Deprez, K. (ed.) (1989) *Language and Intergroup Relations in Flanders*, Dordrecht: Foris Publications.

Eurostat (1990) *Demographic Statistics*, Brussels.

Gordon, P. (1989) *Fortress Europe: the Meaning of 1992*, London: Runnymede Trust.

Hammar, T. (ed.) (1985) *European Immigration Policy*, Cambridge: Cambridge University Press.

——(1990) *Democracy and the Nation State*, Research in Ethnic Relations Series, Centre for Research in Ethnic Relations, University of Warwick, London: Gower.

Heisler, M. and Heisler, B. (1986) 'From foreign workers to settlers: transnational migration and the emergence of new minorities', *Annals of the American Academy of Political and Social Science*, 485.

Layton-Henry, Z. (ed.) (1990) *The Political Rights of Migrant Workers in Western Europe*, London: Sage.

Marshall, T. H. (1950) *Citizenship and Social Class*, Cambridge: Cambridge University Press.

Minority Rights Group (1990) *Refugees in Europe*, London: Minority Rights Group.

Netherlands Scientific Council for Government Policy (1990) *Immigrant Policy*, The Hague: Netherlands Scientific Council for Government Policy.

Piore, M. (1974) *Birds of Passage: Migrant Labour and Industrial Society*, Cambridge: Cambridge University Press.

Rex, J. and Tomlinson, S. (1979) *Colonial Immigrants in a British City*, London: Routledge & Kegan Paul.

Sivanandan, A. (1990) *Communities of Resistance: Writings on Black Struggles for Socialism*, London: Verso.

Wilpert, C. (1990) 'Racism – the blind spot of migration research in the Federal Republic of Germany', Unpublished paper delivered to the Congress on Racism and Migration in Europe, Hamburg.

PART TWO

Responding Social Institutions

CHAPTER 7

A crazy quilt: education, training and social change in Europe

LYNNE CHISHOLM

At first glance, institutional and policy arrangements for education and training across Europe are bewilderingly diverse. These complex patterns win some coherence if we regard European societies as responding to sets of common problems with a range of different solutions, which themselves are structured by divergent forms of social and cultural organisation and relationships (Jallade 1989:103). In other words, we need to identify unifying features which can anchor variations in educational and training policies, provision and participation within wider debates about social change in advanced economies.

However, not all EC member states are at similar stages of economic development and prosperity. The educational and training problems faced by Greece and Portugal as opposed to the FRG[1] and France are not entirely common, just as the consequences of post-1992 economic and social integration will differ for the EC's peripheries and its centre. Portugal, for example, established the legislative basis for a modern educational system only in 1986, the year it joined the EC. Six years of compulsory elementary education had been intro- duced in 1968, but had not been fully implemented almost two decades later. Of the working population 72 per cent currently have six years or less schooling behind them (Tavares Emídio 1988:196). The modernisation initiative focused especially upon the role of education in assisting economic development, and, within this, the professionalisation of the teaching force was viewed as a key factor.

Portugal . . . suddenly finds itself setting off in pursuit of other European countries in an attempt to make up for lost time. . . .The country must eliminate the endemic delays in development compared with other European partners. Secondary education is therefore of major importance in national plans.

(1988:195)

A further complicating dimension has been added by the demise of the eastern European state socialist polities and the destabilisation of their economies. It is no longer at all clear where the ultimate boundaries of the EC will be placed, nor do we know what medium- term effects the 'opening up' of eastern Europe as a whole will have upon the movement towards European political unity.

We do know that eastern European societies also developed particular kinds of solutions in relation to education and training (for examples, see Adamski and Grootings 1989). So it is not surprising to find that both the legitimacy and the sheer operational efficiency of education and training policy and practice in the former GDR lurched into severe crisis across the 1989/90 school year as the country's polity and economy actually collapsed. Curriculum structure and content were rejected by pupils and parents alike and many teachers lost both their professional credibility and their sense of purpose. Large numbers of higher education students found themselves working towards qualifications which suddenly lost any 'cash-in' value, not in the first instance due to the sharply rising unemployment rates but more particularly because their studies were predicated upon a differently constituted occupational and labour-market structure.

Dramatic shifts in demand have also taken place in occupations and specialisms that western Europeans would immediately 'recognise' (as opposed to those that simply do not exist here). Popular demand (rationally or otherwise) has rejected Russian as the first and compulsory modern foreign language in the GDR school curriculum, with the result that large numbers of teachers must be retained to teach western European languages, especially English, for which demand has soared.

As a final example, school-work transitions in western Europe in the 1980s were essentially a problem of the mismatch between young people's aspirations/expectations/qualifications and their employment opportunities. But the problem in eastern Europe was one of under-employment: young people all found, or were allocated to, training courses and jobs, but these did not necessarily match their aspirations, their qualifications or their potential (Adamski, Grootings and Mahler 1989: 26). In autumn 1990, many East German school-leavers found themselves with no immediate prospects for training and employment when firms, in severe financial difficulties and with uncertain futures themselves, were unable to take on apprentices, including those to whom they may have offered a place up to two years before leaving school.

It is important here to appreciate just how much of a personal and social catastrophe this constitutes within the context of German society and culture. Effectively, an established social contract regarded as fundamental to generational and education – economy relations had been broken, more or less without warning. In that young people had grown up in a society where no one was required to compete for training and jobs in the same way that this routinely occurs in the west, such confrontations with 'reality' inevitably proeduce extreme disappointment, disorientation and anger. This does not mean that young people (or adults) in the east are 'unrealistic' or somehow 'lacking' in competence – on the contrary. But their skills and resourcefulness had been turned to a different kind of social formation, and now the 'rules' have suddenly changed.

This chapter considers education and training in a sociological context across the EC as it presently exists. Nevertheless, I have begun by making some reference to eastern Europe, and particularly the former GDR, for several reasons. First, it is as well to bear in mind that events in the east will have implications for the west, although we still lack a great deal of the information we need to offer a sensible analysis of the consequences. Second, with the unification of Germany, the EC has acquired an ex-nation-state which over a period of four decades had developed a distinctive identity at all levels of society and polity. In many ways, the old boundaries will remain in place for some considerable time to come, creating a German economy and culture marked by internal divisions, perhaps matched in intensity (if not nature) within the EC only by the divisions between southern and northern Italy. Third, and most pertinently, both the differing conditions of life and the pace of transformation in eastern Europe throw up illuminating examples of the interactions between education/training and social/economic change, as we have seen above.

In the discussion which follows, the key underlying concepts are those of transitions and critical turning points (see Chisholm 1990). The term 'transitions' emphasises processes of moving between social locations. So, for example, young people are in the process of moving between childhood and adulthood, and their progress through education, training and into employment is one of the central and socially legitimated means by which they do so. 'Critical turning points' direct our attention both to the institutional arrangements and to the decisions which privilege and enact different kinds of routes through to adult life. Youth transitions are therefore highly socially structured experiences. Education and training policy, provision and practice, whatever forms these may take in particular countries, contribute very significantly to that structuring. At the same time, the conditions of young people's lives – and it is young people who continue to remain the primary target and recipients of education and training – are shifting, too, as part of wider patterns of social change in Europe.

In the next section of this chapter we shall look at some of these changing conditions for youth transitions. The third section describes some of the diversity amongst solutions to partially common problems, by comparing how different EC member states organise their education/training systems. The final section then considers some of the issues educationalists and policy-makers will need to address as we approach 1992: the development of common policy principles, rethinking the academic/vocational split, and the implications of cultural, economic and social diversity across the Community for educational opportunities and outcomes.

Youth as a changing 'social condition': transitions to adult life

Many researchers currently argue that the youth phase has become longer in duration, is now dominated by schooling rather than employment, and that the phases of transition to adulthood no longer necessarily follow the established sequencing of the past. In other words, youth transitions are subject to a certain 'destandardisation' (Krüger 1990). This is accompanied not only by expanded opportunities for choice and formulation of one's own 'life plan', but equally by an intensification of associated risks of failure to make the transition 'successfully' in both personal and social terms. These ideas are widely accepted amongst sociologists of education and of youth, especially those working in north-western continental Europe, who of course in the first instance interpret patterns in their own societies.

In Britain, these ideas have been less widely discussed, but have also been viewed more critically. This is partly because for the majority of young Britons the transition to adult and (non-)working life still occurs rather earlier on and under different conditions than in comparable European economies (see here Jones and Wallace 1990). But the key question is that of internal differentiations: young people are not a homogeneous group in any country, but are rather specifically located – historically, regionally, socially and culturally. It is the structured specificities of youth transitions by class, gender, ethnicity/race *and* European region of origin that should centrally inform our analyses (Brown and Chisholm 1991; Chisholm 1990; Chisholm and du Bois-Reymond, forthcoming).[2]

Notwithstanding these provisos, between the 1950s and the 1980s the patterns of young people's lives have changed remarkably, especially so in northern and north-western Europe. We can usefully take the FRG as a particularly marked example (SHELL-Studien 1985; OECD 1986; Statistisches Bundesamt 1985). Over this period, the minimum school-leaving age was raised from 14 to 16 years, and the age at which vocational training is typically completed rose from 18 to 20 years. Concomitantly, young people's labour-force participation rates dropped. The percentages of 15–20-year-olds who were employed halved: from 85 to 46 per cent in the case of boys, and from 76 to 39 per cent for girls. The age at which young people reported having had their first experience of sexual intercourse dropped from 18 to 16 years. Young people now leave the parental home somewhat earlier, at around 20 rather than around 21–22 years old. The average age at marriage dropped from about 28 to 26 for men, from about 25 to 24 for women. National figures for 'markers' such as these differ in various ways, but the essential trends are consistent across countries. Theoretical interpretations of these trends also differ, of course. Since the late 1970s, the difficulties of school-to-work transitions at 16-plus have dominated research and policy concern in the United Kingdom. British writers have thus talked theoretically in terms of broken or fragmented transitions rather than in terms of a destandardisation of youth biographies, as West German youth researchers have done. In the FRG, high rates of youth unemployment also drew research and policy concern, but youth research as a whole retained a broader remit.

Adulthood is still socially defined as being economically independent and setting up one's own household/family (although we may be approaching a redefinition of adulthood, too). It clearly now takes longer to reach that status, and much of the time is spent learning rather than gainfully doing. The high rates of youth unemployment from the mid-seventies through to the mid-eighties accelerated this shift, producing both increased competitiveness and instrumentalism as well as anxiety and resignation amongst young people attempting to achieve successful school-work transitions. The extension and the fragmentation of the youth phase have also 'muddled up' the order in which various milestones are passed. The earliest example was that of student cohabitation, another might be (the return of) 'marriage on the dole,' and a third could be having a credit card guaranteed on one's parents' account.

On the other hand, there are very significant differences between European countries in the extent to which these kinds of changes have taken place, how they have taken place, and the cultural contexts in which they have taken place. The OECD's (1984) comparative study of education and training shows that in Italy the minimum school-leaving age remains set at 14, but in 1981 47 per cent of 17-year-olds were still at school full-time (and another 23 per cent in full-time vocational training). In the United Kingdom, young people may not leave school until 16, yet in 1981 only 30 per cent of 17-year-olds were still in full-time education (whereas 31 per cent were employed, and 17 per cent unemployed). In France, university students normally take their first degree at 21, whereas in the FRG they are at least 23 years old before they do so. However, with the exception of Spain and the United Kingdom (but see below), between 67 and 96 per cent of 17-year-olds (and 52 to 81 per cent of 18-year-olds) in all European OECD countries were in some form of education and training by the mid-eighties (OECD 1986). In a nutshell, we might say that in northern and north-western Europe, significant proportions of all those under 20 are still in some form of education and training; in southern and south-western Europe most of those aged 17 plus are no longer being educated or trained.

The picture for Britain has changed markedly across the eighties, however, with the introduction of the Youth Training Scheme (YTS; now YT). This has meant that the majority of school-leavers no longer enter employment directly, but rather pass through a variety of two-step transitions into the labour force (Bynner 1990: 5). DES (1987) figures show that by 1986 fewer than half of 16–18-year-olds in England and Wales were available for employment. At the close of the decade, 70 per cent of this age group were in some form of part-time or full-time education/training (DES 1989). Similarly, the Youth Cohort Study's (YCS) findings suggest that around two-thirds of those reaching the age of 16 in the mid-eighties did not cease education or training of some kind until they were at least 17 years old (LMQR 1990). The latest YCS cohort data (from those leaving school in 1988) indicate that almost half decided to stay on in full-time education, in contrast with two-fifths of those in each of the first three cohorts studied (in 1985–87). However, the proportion of those opting for YTS dropped from about 30 to 25 per cent, and a slightly higher proportion (one in six as opposed to one in five) went straight into employment. Improved examination results following the introduction of the GCSE, a demographically induced improvement in the youth labour market, and the withdrawal of benefit to the young unemployed may all have contributed to these trends (LMQR 1991). Gray and Sime (1990: 39) thus conclude from YCS data that the key transitions decision point of 16-plus no longer holds. The point of decision over routes into adult and working life has been delayed now that the majority stay at school, go to college or enter youth training, until 17-plus.

The UK situation in these respects is of particular interest to us for two reasons. First, it shows that the argument for a lengthening of the youth phase through the extension of education and training also applies here, though the process of change has been differently timed in comparison with, for example, the Netherlands, Denmark or the FRG. Second, it raises the question of the meaningful interpretation not only of comparative education/training statistics but also of policy-orientated documents. Definitions of what constitutes education/training and of what counts as participation as such vary between countries, which makes precise comparisons difficult. (For example, in the case of the United Kingdom, DES statistics do not exactly tally with OECD figures.) Where education and training is largely or wholly school-based, participation rates will show different patterns than for countries where employer-led training predominates.

It can be argued both that comparative statistics have traditionally underestimated British participation rates and that the YTS has had the effect of misleadingly pushing up those rates across the eighties. On the policy-making front, there is no question that the British government and the state education/training administration have been under some pressure to increase educational participation rates and the quality of vocational training over the last decade. Set against the majority of EC countries, the United Kingdom compared badly on both measures, however one presented the data. The complexion of internal British politics meant that the need for change was represented in particular ways: specifically, the 'failure' of schools to educate pupils to an acceptable standard, the need to improve training in order to rejuvenate the economy, and so forth (see Jones 1989).

Nevertheless, the pressure was there, and current government-linked policy documents have an interest in demonstrating that the United Kingdom no longer has a workforce of below-average educational and skill level. (Few more distanced commentators would agree, including the CBI; see Finegold *et al.* 1990.) After 1992, the United Kingdom will want to attract as much EC production and service-sector activity as it can to operate from its territory; the balance between cost of wages/overheads and quality of the workforce will be crucial to company decisions and European competitiveness. It is thus easy to see why education and training are critical areas of policy for EC member states.

The national labour forces into which young Europeans must integrate are also differently structured and populated. In the Netherlands, Ireland and the United Kingdom, relatively high proportions of the overall labour force are on temporary contracts; and the United Kingdom has a relatively large number (13 per cent) of part-time workers (Jowell *et al.* 1989: 18). Part-time and temporary employment rates are both indicators of highly polarised and segmented labour markets, in which particular social groups – such as young people – are vulnerable. Levels of part-time employment are very high amongst the under-25s in both Denmark (1987: females: 39 per cent; males: 24 per cent) (CEC 1989a: 74–5). On the whole – and relatively speaking – we might suggest that in recent years young people in France, Denmark, and in particular, the United Kingdom and the Netherlands have faced the most fragmented and difficult transition to adulthood as far as moving from education and training into employment is concerned. At the time of writing, however, it is at the EC peripheries where youth unemployment rates continue at a very high level: in Spain, in southern Italy, in Portugal, in Ireland – and in the former GDR.

The social and economic context in which young people grow up will shape their views on what they must do, what they would ideally like to do, and what they can permit themselves to take advantage of as they negotiate their course through youth transitions. In brief, economic affluence and expansion of educational opportunities produces generations of young people who can be optimistic about their futures and the worlds in which they live. This was the case in many EC countries through to the end of the sixties (although to varying extents and, in some countries, for a shorter period of time altogether). The seventies and eighties, in contrast, have erased that carefree optimism and adventurousness, to leave us the legacy of a youth phase all too frequently marked by social and personal disillusion and pessimism. Young people today must be much more 'careful' about formulating their plans and taking decisions, and they must weight up closely the benefits and risks of particular courses of action.

This will remain the case despite demographic changes and the real or manipulated disappearance of high youth unemployment rates in some EC countries. For employers and policy-makers alike, sharp declines in youth cohort numbers across the coming decade have attracted both relief (in alleviating unemployment rates) and concern (in presaging recruitment shortages). But Spain, for example, has a very different demographic prognosis from Belgium. Its population is rising at a rate well above the EC average and the shifting balance between the young and the old will take a relatively mild form in the coming decades (CSO 1990: 15, 34). Youth unemployment rates in most Spanish regions are extremely high: in 1987 ranging from about 30 per cent of the under-25s in Castile-La Mancha to 63 per cent in País Vasco (Eurostat 1988). The urgency with which Spanish educational reforms have been treated in the past few years is hardly surprising under such circumstances (Carabana 1988).

But even in those EC countries where the demographic shift will have its sharpest effects, including the United Kingdom but most particularly in the FRG, Belgium and parts of northern Italy, the social and economic contextualisation of education and training is not that of the 1960s. One can easily gain the impression that young Europeans are rapidly becoming cosseted rarities – parental and social investment treasures with the world once more at their feet. This ahistoricist interpretation neglects the fact that wider opportunities in education and on the labour market, greater personal autonomy in making life plans and decisions, and a plurality of lifestyle options have become available to relatively large numbers of young people only recently, to different extents, and for a fairly short period of time; namely, from the fifties through to the seventies.

Youth transitions are too important, socially, culturally and economically, to leave them to young people's possibly fleeting and frequently normatively precarious preferences, let alone to chance. On the whole young people have been subject to a great deal of guidance and containment. We might well argue that it has been the forms taken by guidance and containment that have changed, rather than their substance. In other words, social, cultural and economic institutions and processes have but changed the ways in which most young people are encouraged, cajoled and forced to become 'respectable and productive adults'. This is not to say, of course, that some forms of social organisation and patterns of experience are not more preferable than others, but this is a question of value rather than purpose.

The paradox of contemporary youth entails a wider range of opportunities and experiences from which young people are invited and expected to select, combined with a higher risk of failure and a widening gap between those who succeed and those who will not or cannot. The patternings of risks and chances share common features across Europe, but the differentiations between and within EC countries and regions are just as significant. Extreme examples from the lower and upper ends of the youth phase indicate this point on the simplest dimension, that of educational participation. In 1982, over half of Greek 16-year-olds had left full-time education/training altogether, whereas in the Netherlands, only 10 per cent of the same cohort were not at school full-time. In the same year, only 2 per cent of Irish, but 15 per cent of West German 24-year-olds were full-time higher education students (CEC 1986: 99–100), and we have not even considered the very complex patterns of difference that open up once we break down such data by sex, socio-economic background and majority/minority group membership (see here Chapters 2, 5 and 6).

The organisation of educational selection and participation

All European countries face sets of fundamental tensions about the purposes of modern education. Education concerns itself with cultural socialisation, but also with economic sustenance through the provision of appropriately skilled and knowledgeable individuals for the labour market. Education is orientated towards the optimal development of a wide range of individual human potential, but also to selection and allocation into social and economic positions according to the demands of the (dominant) collectivity rather than personal capacities and preferences. Education aims in principle to offer equal access and opportunity to all children, but in practice outcomes reflect the structured inequalities of the wider society. Educational policies and patterns of provision reflect these tensions in one way or another.

Whereas most contemporary educationalists would favour broad-based and open-ended education for all, centred on the concept of a common curriculum (Lawton 1989), specialisation will and must occur at some stage in the process. Young people's capacities, preferences and motivations are diverse, too, quite apart from the considerable influences exerted on the shape of educational options by labour markets. How and when specialisation is introduced into education systems by the provision of different kinds of routes – together with the ways in which these routes are valued and rewarded – are key markers in charting national/regional responses to these various tensions. By the stage of post-compulsory education and training at the latest, specialisation into different routes and levels becomes virtually axiomatic. For this reason, 'a key and perennial question is the extent to which it is possible to develop choice and diversity at this stage whilst keeping to a minimum the well-known negative effects of educational differentiation' (OECD 1989a: 10).

This does not mean that cultural specifics are of little importance: these contribute significantly to the bewildering diversity of educational provision and practice across Europe. So, for example, in considering the prospects for a common school curriculum in post-1992 EC Europe, McLean (1990) contrasts the encyclopaedic and rationalist quality of French curricula with the specialised and human-ist traditions of English schools. Green (1991: 9–10), in applying these ideas to post-compulsory education/training provision and reform, suggests that the universalistic and standardising principles of French educational organisation stand out in sharp relief against the insti-tutionally diversified and pedagogically individualist quality of English post-compulsory provision and practice.

For our purposes we might simply bear in mind some of the axes along which particular countries find their specific educational solu-tions. These axes would certainly include: common and specialised education/training; academic versus vocational knowledge; education-led as opposed to employer-led teaching/learning; school-based rather than workplace-based provision; unilinear access and progression in contrast with modular, interlinking systems of participation and accreditation. Table 7.1 uses some of these distinctions to identify critical turning points in education systems; that is, institutionalised moments at which young people select themselves and are equally selected into (or, more often, out of) particular kinds of transitions routes. These are not, of course, the only kinds of critical moments in the educational shaping of social biographies, but they are important ones. They offer us a skeleton, and thus a starting point, for thinking about how western European transitions systems may develop in the future.

If we then turn our attention to current post-compulsory education and training participation rates, complex patterns begin to emerge. So, for example, Finegold *et al.* (1990) characterise UK education (especially in England and Wales) as an early selection–low partici-pation system. European economies and societies of the future require, however, late selection–high participation educational sys-tems (OECD:1989b). On the one hand, rapid technological and structural change requires more highly qualified workers with poly-valent competences. On the other hand, not only contemporary values but also socio-political stability require a much greater measure of social justice in the distribution of opportunity and rewards.

Looking at Table 7.1, we can immediately see some broad common-alities in the internal structuring of educational provision. Compulsory primary schooling begins between the ages of 5 and 7 in all countries (modally at the age of 6). In those countries where compulsory schooling starts earlier, the first year is similar to the last year of kindergarten in purpose. Where schooling begins later, most children do attend kindergarten by the age of 5. So, for example, whilst primary school begins at 6 in France, state-run *écoles maternelles* provide for part-time crèche and kindergarten classes from the age of 2. One-third of French 2-year-olds attend an *école maternelle*, an exceptionally high proportion in comparative terms (OECD 1989c: 78–9). In the United Kingdom, primary school begins at 5, and 'rising fives' are accepted where capacity permits. Although the proportion

Table 7.1 **Critical turning points in the educational systems of EC member states**

Ages at which . . .	School begins	First branch in system occurs	Compulsory general FT school ends	Compulsory FT/PT voc. ed./tr. ends	Entry to HE	First degree taken
F	6	13	15/13[1]	16	18	21
D	6/7	10/11	15/16	18	19/20	23/24 plus
I	6	14	14[2]	14	19	23
NL	5	13	15	16	18	22
UK	5	11/14[3]	16	16	18	21
B	6	12	16	18	19	20/21
DK	6/7	16/17[4]	16/17	16	[5]	[5]
H	5+	12	14 plus	14 plus	17/18	23
IRL	6	15/16	15	15/16	17/18	21/22
L	6	12	15	15	19/20	[6]
P	6	15	14	14	18	24
E	6	14/16[7]	14/16[7]	14	18	23

Key to abbreviations:

F	France	UK	United Kingdom	IRL	Republic of Ireland
D	FRG	B	Belgium	L	Luxembourg
I	Italy	DK	Denmark	P	Portugal
NL	The Netherlands	H	Greece	E	Spain

Notes:

1 Transfer to shorter vocational courses
2 Completion of first stage of second level (middle schools)
3 At 14 and for the majority: curriculum and examination option-based branching, reinforced by streaming/setting practices which may begin earlier. The effect of the National Curriculum is unclear at present. At 11 for some: bi/tripartite divisions.
4 Compulsory schooling ends at 16, but an additional year at comprehensive school may follow before transfer into the labour market or post-compulsory academic or vocational education/training
5 From 16 no clear correspondence between age and educational level (hence no entry under degree completion, but at least four years' study in the majority of cases). See note 3, p. 143.
6 University studies are pursued in other countries
7 Current educational reforms in Spain see an extension of compulsory education/ training from 14 to 16. Under these proposals, a wide range of options, including vocational subjects, are introduced from age 12, i.e. curriculum-based branching. Until the late eighties, the first branching was institutional, located at the juncture of compulsory schooling with post-compulsory education

Source: OECD (1989b: Annex), supplemented by Carabana (1988) and Tavares Emídio (1988)

of British children attending some form of pre-schooling rises from 25 to 68 per cent between the ages of 3 and 4 (*ibid*.), state provision is very patchy and regional variations in both provision and take-up are marked. In the Netherlands, where compulsory schooling also begins at 5, almost all 4-year-olds attend the non-compulsory first year of *Basisonderwijs* (pre-primary and first-level schooling). In the FRG, the concept of *Schulreife* (individual readiness for school) is applied to determine when a child should begin school. The standard age is 7, but some may start up to a year earlier, others a year later. But by the age of 5, 85 per cent of West German children are at kindergarten on a half-day basis (*ibid.*).[3]

Leaving aside for the moment the matter of cohort participation rates, at the other end of the spectrum we see that young people typically enter higher education between 17 and 19 years of age, although in Denmark the correspondence between age and level has by this time weakened to the point that to give any specific age would be atypical. By definition, this is also the age range at which upper-level secondary schooling ends. (This does not mean that post-compulsory *school*-based routes alone can lead to higher education.) Compulsory secondary schooling ends between the ages of 14 and 16-plus in all countries. However, compulsory vocational education and training for between one and three years beyond then (not necessarily on a full-time basis) currently applies in only four EC member states (France, FRG, the Netherlands and Belgium).

Across the Community, then it is possible for today's young Europeans to experience a minimum of eight and a maximum of twelve years of *compulsory* education/training of some kind. The member states divide quite clearly into three groups. Portugal, Spain and Italy each run an eight-year minimum; Ireland, Greece, Luxembourg and Denmark a nine-year minimum. France, (ten years), the Netherlands, the United Kingdom, the FRG (all eleven years) and Belgium (twelve years) comprise a third group with the lengthiest compulsory systems. All countries in this last group – with the exception of the United Kingdom – include (in principle) a period of mandatory upper-secondary-level vocational education and training for those who do not pursue academic tracks orientated towards higher education.

However, it would be quite inaccurate to assume that a shorter compulsory system necessarily links up with low post-compulsory participation rates. (This is not so in Italy, nor in Denmark, for example.) Neither can we propose that early specialisation (whether by curriculum tracking or institutional branching) is associated with any given post-compulsory participation patterns. The internal structuring of educational systems most definitely positions young people into tracks, options and routes with very different prospects for further/higher education, training and on the labour market. But internal structuring in itself does not exert a dominant influence upon ultimate participation rates. We must look beyond educational systems themselves for the explanations here. Specifically, we would need to examine the state policies that set the 'rules of the game', government and employer funding strategies, and established modes of operation of national labour markets.

Taken together, however, patterns of provision and participation illuminate the options available in considering future arrangements for education and training in the Community as a whole. We now turn to Table 7.2, which summarises participation rates for the 15 to

Table 7.2   Patterns of educational participation for 15–19-year-olds: school pupils/ students enrolled in any type of full-time or part-time education as a proportion of their age group, 1986–87

Age:		15	16	17	18	19
D	all	100	100	99.7	83.9	57.2
	of which part-time	6.2	28.4	48.4	47.8	35.0
B	all	94.6	92.7	86.4	68.3	53.0
	of which part-time	2.4	3.9	4.8	4.9	5.9
DK	all	97.1	89.9	75.4	68.0	52.3
F	all	94.8	87.9	79.7	60.1	46.0
	of which part-time	0.4	8.6	10.3	4.5	1.2
NL	all	99.0	92.9	78.3	60.4	43.2
	of which part-time	–	–	–	–	0.1
H	Full-time only	85.8	75.1	58.7	43.2	28.6[2]
UK	all	99.0	68.9	49.3	32.9	25.5[3]
	of which part-time	–	18.9	16.2	14.5	8.8
IRL	Full-time only	91.2	82.0	64.7	40.8	24.1
E	Full-time only	79.2[1]	62.3	53.1	28.6	15.0

Abbreviations as in Table 7.1

1 1984–85: 70.9%
2 1985–86
3 There is a typographical error in the relevant OECD table; accompanying text indicates 'slightly more than 25%'; 1984/85 rate was 23.2%
Note: No comparable figures available for Portugal, Luxembourg and Italy. OECD (1984: Table II.1, p.45) gives the following figures for Italian 17-year-olds in 1981: 47% at school full-time, a further 23% in full-time vocational training
Source: OECD (1989) *Education in OECD Countries 1986–87*, Paris, Table 4.2: 81; OECD (1986) *Education in OECD Countries 1984–5*, Paris, Table 4.2: 71

19 age group. The countries are ordered by the level of participation at 19, although we need to remember that in some cases, compulsory education or training of some kind continues through to 18-plus (see Table 7.1 above), which clearly affects the profiles of participation rates by age.

Firstly, in three (FRG, Belgium and Denmark) of the nine EC countries for which OECD figures are available, in 1986/87 at least half of 19-year-olds were still in some form of part-time or full-time education/training. This was the case for over two-fifths of French and Dutch 19-year-olds, but only for about a quarter of their British and Irish peers.[4] The FRG and Belgium, as we saw earlier, have the lengthiest compulsory systems; but only in the FRG do part-time routes account for a major slice of 16 to 19 participation rates. It is, of course, part-time routes as a post-compulsory strategy that the United Kingdom has pursued through YTS across the 1980s. As a consequence, overall participation rates rose across the decade, though now it is full-time education/training rather than YT that – at a slower rate – is continuing to drive the rates upwards.

Secondly, however, the patterns of decline in participation between 15 and 19 vary too. Figure 7.1 uses the data in Table 7.2 to chart

136   *Responding Social Institutions*

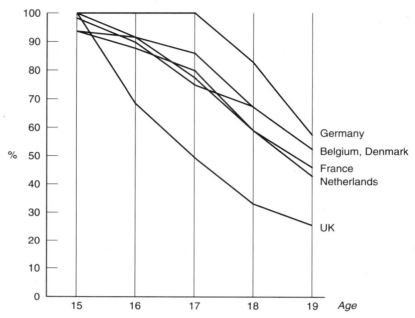

*Figure 7.1   **School pupils enrolled in any type of full-time or part-time education/
training as a proportion of their age cohort, 1986–7***
Source: OECD, *Education in OECD Countries 1986–7*, Paris (1989), Table 4.2,
p.81 (amended)

these patterns for six countries: France, the Netherlands, the United
Kingdom, the FRG, Belgium and Denmark. These are those countries
with the lengthiest compulsory systems, together with Denmark, which
maintains high post-compulsory participation rates through to the age
of 19. This graph shows clearly that, in the FRG and in Belgium,
participation rates decline most sharply after 18. In France and the
Netherlands, participation rates decline fairly steadily from 16 through
to 19, though Dutch rates begin to decline rapidly a little earlier within
this range. The overall decline is less steep altogether in Denmark, and
is concentrated at two points: between 16/17 and 18/19. In the United
Kingdom, participation declines steeply and swiftly from 15/16.

We pointed out earlier that the UK system can be described as one
of early selection–low participation. How might we describe other
countries along the selection/participation dimension? The FRG and
Belgium are examples of early selection–high participation systems;
they also require young people to remain in education/training for the
longest periods of time; relative to other countries, participation rates
drop markedly latest of all and remain highest through to 19. In
comparison, France and the Netherlands both select somewhat later
and retain somewhat lower proportions of young people in education/

training; declining participation rates are noticeable rather earlier on. They both occupy 'middling' positions on each of the features we have considered.

In the United Kingdom, participation rates begin to drop steeply as soon as compulsory schooling ceases at 16. This is also the case, incidentally, for Spain, which we could equally characterise as having an early selection–low participation educational system. Schooling in both countries tracks relatively early: in Spain, this begins with curriculum options from age 12 and proceeds to institutional branching on to academic and vocational routes at 14. In the United Kingdom, some pupils are still selected into a binary system at 11/12, but the majority find themselves in comprehensive schools in which curriculum and examination-based options begin at 14. The National Curriculum will ensure a broader core for all pupils through to 16 than was previously the case, but is unlikely to remove the well-established hierarchies amongst subjects and syllabuses that guide pupils into clearly distinguishable, if 'unofficial' routes.

Denmark, however, approximates most closely to a late selection–high participation system. It achieves high rates of participation through to the age of 19 without extending compulsory education/training beyond 16, and its schooling is fully comprehensive through to the age of 17. Denmark has established a particularly flexible approach to educational participation and process. The link with age is weaker than elsewhere, the commitment to forward-thinking curricula and pedagogies well developed, and the involvement of the community (and the pupils) in the shaping and evaluation of their own schools and schooling is both explicitly planned and actively taken up (see HMI 1989).

Nine out of ten Danish children attend the ten-year *folkeskoler*; less than 1 per cent attend special schools. (The remainder go to generously subsidised private and 'free' schools, established to cater to particular social, political, religious and educational philosophies.) Young people may leave school (into employment and/or training) at 16, after completing Year 9, but just over half stay for the final tenth year. All receive a leaving certificate, which simply records the subjects they have studied and the grades they have achieved in the final three years of their schooling. In principle, pupils may be requested to repeat a year, but in practice very few do so. Teaching groups are fully mixed-ability for the first seven years (that is, to the age of 14). Schools may set into basic and advanced teaching groups for some core curriculum subjects (modern foreign languages, mathematics and science) after this, but a decreasing minority do so. Curriculum options, mainly from Year 9, are confined largely to aesthetic, practical, recreational and vocationally-orientated subjects. After the *folkeskole*, two basic post-compulsory 'youth education' routes are available. Academically oriented tracks at gymnasia lead to general or commercial Higher Examinations; vocational education and training includes both employer-led (such as apprenticeship) and education-led (for instance, certificated FE) options (HMI 1989).

There is something else about Denmark that is especially notable: the high resourcing of its educational system. In 1986 Denmark spent over 7 per cent of its GDP on financing its education system, a higher proportion than in any other OECD country except for Sweden (7.5 per cent) (OECD 1989c: 26–31). Of further interest is that whereas in the United Kingdom, for example, per capita educational expenditure is skewed towards higher education students, in Denmark the priorities are weighted towards pupils in primary and secondary schooling (*ibid.*). With Finegold *et al.* (1990) we might suggest that a late selection–high participation system can most readily address demands both for economic efficiency and for social justice. Education and training in Denmark show us that this is certainly a practicable proposition, but it demands high levels of resources. Some EC countries are unaccustomed to spending so much on education and training; others simply cannot afford to do so. Reducing the resulting inequalities for young Europeans, both as individuals and as social-cultural groups, would require not only a commitment to spend more resources, but also to transfer resources between EC countries and regions. Only in this context would it make sense both to promote common principles and to preserve 'local' diversities in Community education/training policies and practices.

Education/training and 1992: some policy issues

The European Commission sees education and training as a key field for policy formulation and action initiatives in the coming decade. A number of recent documents (CEC 1990a, 1990b, 1990c, 1990d) indicate that the scope of activities here is about to expand, within the context of a holistic EC youth policy. In the past, EC Action Programmes have been directed almost wholly towards vocational training initiatives and, more recently, towards cooperation and exchange in higher education. COMETT, for example, supports transnational university–industry links that promote advanced training for technological change. The EUROTECNET initiative focuses on the impact of technological change for vocational qualifications and training systems in terms of the identification of new skill needs. LINGUA programmes aim to improve the teaching of Community languages. ERASMUS, which funds inter-university curriculum and accreditation cooperation, together with exchanges of university students and staff, has grown very rapidly since its introduction in 1987 (and is now complemented by TEMPUS for east–west links). (See page 142 for official descriptions of programme objectives.)

These various programmes have therefore been of relevance for young adults; that is, those aged between 20 and 24, and it has primarily been advanced/higher education and training students who have benefited. Programmes directed at younger people, both those still at school and those in initial vocational education/training, are now to be expanded accordingly – both to achieve a more equitable balance, and in the recognition that the key to creating an integrated Eruope lies with the young. This means that the funding and the scope of the PETRA programme (which is similar to ERASMUS but for students and young workers aged 16 to 19) will expand. In addition, a revamped and extended youth exchange scheme (called 'Youth for Europe') is to be introduced.

With an eye to 1992 and beyond, three core policy issues have now been identified at Community level. First, vocational education and training remains a key priority, in order both to maintain competitiveness as a Single Market within the global economy, and to develop more internal coherence and balance in a more mobile Community labour market. Here, promoting the transferability of qualifications and competences, which partly rests on including modules of education and training abroad, is of central importance. The rationales for this policy priority are clearly mainly economic; but an integrated Europe has to be more than a market-place – it has to become a people's Europe, both socially and politically.

In this connection, as a second core issue, the promotion of a European (as well as a national/regional) dimension to citizenship and identity takes on a higher policy profile altogether. Hence, schools, curricula, pupils and teachers are bound to receive more Community attention than hitherto. Visits, exchanges and inter-school links will undoubtedly be accompanied by the development of curriculum materials and in-service teacher-training courses. There is, as yet, no suggestion that EC policy initiatives will venture into the politically highly sensitive area of a European-wide policy for the shape of compulsory schooling. For the present, there is an agreement that educational policy will remain wholly in the hands of the member states. In the medium term, however, it is difficult to see how this stance can be maintained, given the involvement of the Commission in vocational education and training policy and programmes. General education and vocational education/training are always interrelated; changes in one sector have effects on the other. So, for example, the introduction of the National Curriculum in the United Kingdom is intended to alter (for the better) young people's knowledge and skill profiles, and this must be taken into account in designing post-compulsory courses (including A-levels). Similarly, if vocational training courses for 16- to 18-year-olds began to include mandatory study modules abroad, British schools would need to ensure that 16-year-olds left school with much better foreign language skills than they do at the moment.

Equally as significant, however, is the fact that the relationship between academic and vocational education itself is beginning to shift towards a much greater degree of integration. The division between academic *knowledge* and vocational *skills* is deeply structured into modern teaching/learning systems. In English this division is mirrored in the very terms 'education' and 'training', traditionally viewed as quite separate activities. We all 'know' – so well that it appears axiomatic – that this distinction between *philosophia* and *technica* is also an intensely hierarchical one. (Unsurprisingly, it is equally a deeply gendered division – see Chisholm 1991.) Curricula gradually separate out into subjects commonly understood as 'theoretical' and 'practical'; examination tracks and selective school systems all branch into the 'academic' and the 'vocational-technical.' Pupils are selected – and select themselves – on to these different routes. Selection processes are mediated primarily through formal attainment, but fundamentally they are social in nature, reproducing existing gender, ethnic/race and class divisions. Those who do well at school choose academic tracks; vocational tracks absorb 'the rest'.

We can find examples of these sorting mechanisms operating everywhere in Europe. The range of French *baccalauréats* (examinations usually taken at 18) offer us but one very clear example. There are three basic types of *bac* qualification, which are usually pursued at specialised *lycées*, and which are prestige-ranked: general, technological, and (since the mid-1980s) professional. The general – that is, academically oriented – category is the most prestigious; but students may follow five internal *séries* or tracks. Within these, track C, specialising in mathematics and physical science, is the most prestigious, sending a high proportion of its holders on to the *grandes écoles*, the most prestigious higher education institutions (Watson 1990).[5]

It is the iniquity and inappropriateness of these kinds of distinctions and their consequences that lead Finegold *et al.* (1990) to propose that a reform of 16 to 19 provision in the United Kingdom should be founded on the principle of their abolition. In other words, all students should study both the academic and the vocational, both the theoretical and the practical. Curricula must be restructured to integrate both elements wherever feasible. Courses should be modular in nature, allowing for incremental progression along a wide range of part-time and full-time routes, all of which lead to a unified, common qualification at 18 or older. This is a grand idea – in both senses of the term – but it is difficult to imagine how such deep-rooted divisions can be overcome well enough to prevent them re-emerging in another form – for example, in differently valued internal tracks.

Jeffcutt (1989) has argued, in contrast, that in Britain the concept of training has now ousted education from its former privileged position as the herald of a new social order: education is narrow, academic and elitist; training is broad, relevant and, above all, a democratising influence. But Jeffcutt suggests that this merely *reverses* the hierarchy and disguises the continuity of inequalities. It might be argued, then, that attempts to 'end the division between education and training' are naïvely idealistic given the tenacity of cultural tradition and the influence of dominant economic interests.

This leads us to a third core policy issue: the unequal distribution of opportunities and life chances across the Community. EC reports and policy documents about young Europeans demonstrate a concern that existing regional and social disparities will deepen after 1992 unless positive action measures are adopted. Education and training are seen as a key mechanism of intervention in this respect. It has to be said that expanding educational opportunities to reduce social disadvantage has been, on past experience in the United Kingdom, a fairly unsuccessful policy measure. There is no doubt that the economic implications of an ageing European population plays an important role in the identification of this third core policy issue. The almost standard refrain about the need to 'tap all talent' has found a new rationale. The aim of promoting inter-cultural tolerance in order to defuse the potential for social conflict might equally be interpreted as a disguised anxiety over the economic and political costs of youth unrest rather than a real concern for social justice. The uprisings of the 1980s, most dramatically but not solely in Britain's inner cities, have not yet vanished from the political memory; the recent return of student riots in France and the continuing instability of much of eastern Europe serve to underline the potential explosiveness of young people's anger.

Where life chances and standards of living are manifestly unequal, where disparities are experienced at close quarters, and where nationalist identities are fostered for a variety of outdated but powerful reasons, legitimate anger can turn to festering, misdirected resentment. In this sense, a commitment to encourage not simply a common European market-place but, more pertinently, a European *social community* in which we all have a genuine stake must be viewed as a positive policy step. Equalising young people's access to education and training, ensuring greater transferability and comparability of qualifications, and promoting teaching/learning environments built on critical respect, cultural celebration and tolerance, are all indisputably part of creating a truly social Europe. But just as education has never been the kill-all or cure-all for economic and social evils at the level of the nation state, neither can we expect it to carry the load of European harmonisation on its shoulders. This is a mistake we have already made, and we should avoid repeating it.

Glossary of programme objectives

LINGUA   The principal objective shall be to promote a quantitative and qualitative improvement in foreign language competence with a view to developing communications skills within the Community.

PETRA

The objective is to ensure, for all young people in the Community who so wish, one, or if possible two or more years' vocational training in addition to their full-time compulsory education.

ERASMUS

The principal objectives are:
- to increase the number of students spending an integrated period of study in another Member State;
- to promote cooperation between universities in all Member States;
- to increase the mobility of teaching staff, thereby improving the quality of the education and training provided.

COMETT

The objective is to reinforce training in, in particular, advanced technology, the development of highly skilled human resources and thereby the competitiveness of European industry.

EUROTECNET

The objective shall be to promote innovation in the fields of basic and also of continuing vocational training with a view to taking account of current and future technological changes and their impact on employment, work and necessary qualifications and skills.

FORCE

The objectives are:
- to encourage greater investment in continuing vocational training and an improved return from it;
- to support innovations in training management, training methods and facilities;
- to promote the strategic planning and design of training measures;
- to contribute to a greater effectiveness of training mechanisms

TEMPUS

The main objectives are:
- to facilitate the coordination of assistance and to contribute to the improvement of training in the countries of Central and Eastern Europe, particularly for university students and teachers, through exchange and mobility.
- to increase opportunities for the teaching and learning of Community languages.

Notes

1 To avoid confusion over what constitutes the FRG, I have adopted the following terminology: the FRG refers to postwar West Germany in its borders through to October 1990; the former GDR refers to postwar East Germany in its borders through to October 1990; German/y refers to (a) the unified state after October 1990, and (b) a set of cultural and social traditions generally applicable to both former states; east/west German/y distinguishes between social institutional arrangements and social-cultural aspects of life of the two former states and their respective citizens. At the time of writing, the accurate title of the united state of Germany remains the FRG (that is, Bundesrepublik Deutschland), since the former GDR exercised its rights under the FRG's constitution to join the West German federal state. The terms 'East' and 'West' are here used as short-hand terms to refer to the NATO and Warsaw Pact countries and their associated states as these existed prior to 1988/89.

2 Comparative statistics are indispensable for constructing a differentiated picture of 'European' youth. But the wider the scope of comparison, the more the finer patterns are obscured. This means, for example, that regional differences within nation states inevitably lose profile, although in fact these are increasingly significant in both economic and socio-political terms. However, the problems of comparison between smaller-scale qualitative studies are arguably even greater than those which arise in comparative statistics, whether national or regional. In any case, the availability and nature of such studies varies enormously between countries. For the purposes of this chapter, we must restrict ourselves to rather simple and inevitably crude comparisons.

3 This alerts us to an important point to consider when interpreting data such as that in Table 7.1. In some countries, pupils' ages at given stages are expected or typical rather than necessarily accurate in all cases. The further one moves through the system, the more likely it will be to find pupils/ students of somewhat different ages in the same year group or stage of schooling.

In the first instance this is due to the practice of repeating a year where achievement has been assessed as below par. This can happen more than once, although where it does so with regularity or frequency, pupils may find themselves transferred to a different type of school or track, perhaps into special education. In the second instance, where pupils/students may transfer between specialist tracks – for example, in moving back and forth between academic and vocational routes – they can find themselves 'losing' a year in the process.

The relevance of these features varies by country, of course, and we do not yet have comprehensive comparative statistics that would allow us to assess their impact accurately. The ages shown in Table 7.1 can be safely taken as minimum ages at each stage; they are for the most part also reliably typical. At the upper ends of the system most participants would be covered by a two-year extension beyond that shown.

4 OECD does not have breakdowns for Italy, Luxembourg and Portugal; EUROSTAT do not produce comparable substitutes in this instance. The note to Table 7.2 uses OECD data from the early 1980s showing that Italy falls at the high participation end of the distribution; an EC survey of young people in the late eighties (CEC 1989b) suggests Luxembourg to be in a

similar position; participation rates in Portugal certainly fall at the lower end of the distribution. The OECD figures for Spain and Greece in Table 7.2 cover full-time students only. In this connection, it is worth noting that Greek participation rates are nevertheless higher than those for the United Kingdom at all ages after 15. The proportion of Spanish 19-year-olds in FT education is similar to that in the United Kingdom. Of further interest is the marked increase in participation rates in France between 1984–85, (at 17: 65.5 per cent; at 18: 52.2 per cent; at 19: 34.9 per cent) and 1986–7, overtaking the Netherlands in rank order for 19-year-olds. This increase can be directly linked to the introduction of the *baccalauréat professionel* from 1985 (see Watson 1990).

5   Watson (1990) explains that in contemporary France, mathematics has replaced Latin as the discipline seen most rigorously to 'train the mind'. The origin of the *grandes écoles* as Napoleonic military academies means that many have strong engineering links – and hence a scientific focus. Not surprisingly, their students come disproportionately from professional/ managerial and elite families.

   Similarly, French girls consistently out-perform boys throughout the educational system, and as a result comprise 56 per cent of all *baccalauréat* entrants. But the more scientific (and especially the more technological) the *bac* track, the fewer the numbers of girls are to be found. In 1988, women students at the *grandes écoles* were between 21 per cent (engineering) and 40 per cent (law and administration) of all those registered (Charles 1991).

References

Adamski, W. and Grootings, P. (eds) (1989) *Youth, Education and Work in Europe*, London: Routledge.
Adamski, W., Grootings, P. and Mahler, F. (1989) 'Transition from school to work: introduction', in W. Adamski and P. Grootings (eds) *Youth, Education and Work in Europe*, London: Routledge, ch. 1.
Brown, P. and Chisholm, L. A. (1991) Nicht so wie manche Eltern für manche Jugendliche: Bemerkungen zum neuen kulturellen Modell', in R. Zoll (ed.) *Ein neues kulturelles Modell? Internationales Symposium*, Opladen: Westdeutscher Verlag.
Bynner, J. (1990) 'Education and training: provision and experience', *British Journal of Education and Work*, 3(2): 5–11.
Carabana, J. (1988) 'Comprehensive educational reforms in Spain: past and present', *European Journal of Education*, 23(3): 213–28.
Central Statistical Office (CSO) (1990) *Social Trends 1990*, London: HMSO.
Charles, F. (1991) 'France', in M. Wilson (ed.) *Girls and Young Women in Education: a European Perspective*, Oxford: Pergamon Press, ch. 4.
Chisholm, L. A. (1990) 'A new lens or a different camera? Youth, youth research and social change in Britain', in L. A. Chisholm, P. Büchner, H. H. Kruger, and P. Brown. (eds) *Childhood, Youth and Social Change*, Brighton: Falmer Press, ch. 4.
——(1991) *Beyond Occupational Choice: a Study of Gendered Transitions*, University of London Institute of Education, London.
——and du Bois-Reymond, M. (in press) Gender, youth transitions and social change, *Sociology*, **26**.

Commission of the European Communities (CEC) (1986) *Social Europe: The Social Dimensions of the Single Market*, Luxembourg: Directorate-General for Employment, Industrial Relations and Social Affairs.

——(1989a) *Employment in Europe*, Luxembourg: Directorate-General for Employment, Industrial Relations and Social Affairs.

——(1989b) *Young Europeans in 1987*, Luxembourg.

——(1990a) *Young People in the European Community*, Memorandum, 15 Oct., COM(90) 469, Brussels.

——(1990b) *The Rationalisation and Coordination of Vocational Training Programmes at Community Level*, Memorandum, 21 Aug., COM (90) 334, Brussels.

——(1990c) *An Action Programme for the Vocational Qualification of Young People and their Preparation for Adult and Working Life*, Proposal 9, Nov., COM(90) 467, Brussels.

——(1990d) *An Action Programme to Promote Youth Exchanges and Mobility in the Community: the Youth for Europe Programme*, Proposal, 22 Nov., COM(90) 470, Brussels.

Department of Education and Science (DES) (1987) 'Educational and economic activity of young people aged 16 to 18 years in England from 1975 to 1986', *Statistical Bulletin*, 1/87, London: Department of Education and Science.

——(1989) 'Educational and economic activity of young people aged 16 to 18 years in England from 1975 to 1989', *Statistical Bulletin*, 9/90, London: Department of Education and Science.

Eurostat (1988) *Regional Statistics*, 12/1988, Luxembourg.

Finegold D., Miliband, D., Raffe, D., Keep, E., Spours, K. and Young, M.F.D. (1990) 'A British "baccalauréat", ending the division between education and training', Education and Training Paper **1**, London, Institute for Public Policy Research.

Gray, J. and Sime, N. (1990) 'Extended routes and delayed transitions amongst 16–19 year olds: national trends and local contexts', *British Journal of Education and Work*, 3(2):13–40.

Green, A. (1991) 'The reform of post-16 education and training and the lessons from Europe', PSEC Working Paper **11**, Post-Sixteen Education Centre, University of London Institute of Education, London.

Her Majesty's Inspectorate (HMI) (1989) *Education in Denmark: Aspects of the Work of the Folkeskole*, Department of Education and Science, London: HMSO.

Jallade, J-P. (1989) 'Recent trends in vocational education and training: an overview', *European Journal of Education*, 24(2):103–25.

Jeffcutt, P. (1989) 'Education and training: beyond the Great Debate', *British Journal of Education and Work*, 2 (2): 51–9.

Jones, G. and Wallace, C. (1990) 'Beyond individualisation', in L. A. Chisholm, P. Büchner, H.-H. Krüger and P. Brown, (eds) *Childhood, Youth and Social Change*, Brighton, Falmer Press, ch. 9.

Jones, K. (1989) *Right Turn*, London: Hutchinson Radius.

Jowell, R., Witherspoon, S. and Brook, L. (eds) (1989) *British Social Attitudes: Special International Report*, Social and Community Planning Research, Sixth Report, London: Gower.

Krüger, H-H. (1990) 'Between standardisation and disintegration: youth in the FRG since 1945', in L. A. Chisholm, P. Büchner, H-H Krüger and P. Brown, (eds) *Childhood, Youth and Social Change*, Brighton, Falmer Press, ch. 7.

Labour Market Quarterly Review (LMQR) (1990) Special feature: 'Youth Cohort study' (May) pp. 13–15.

——(1991) Special feature: 'Youth Cohort study' (Feb.) pp. 8–10.

Lawton, D. (1989) *Education, Culture and the National Curriculum*, London: Hodder & Stoughton.

McLean, M. (1990) *Britain and the Single European Market: Prospects for a Common School Curriculum*, London: Kogan Page.

Organisation for Economic Cooperation and Development (OECD) (1984) *Education and Training after Basic Schooling*, Paris.

——(1986) *Education in OECD Countries 1984–5*, Paris.

——(1989a) *Pathways for Learning: Education and Training from 16 to 19*, Paris.

——(1989b) *Education and the Economy in a Changing Soceity*, Paris.

——(1989c) *Education in OECD countries 1986–7*, Paris.

SHELL-Studien: Jugendwerk des deutschen SHELL (ed.) (1985) *Jugend '85*, 3 vols.

Statistisches Bundesamt (1985) *Jugend 1985*, Bonn.

Tavares Emídio, M. (1988) 'The process of modernisation and secondary education in Portugal', *European Journal of Education*, 23(3):195–202.

Watson, J. (1990) 'The French baccalauréat professionnel', PSEC Working Paper 9, Post-Sixteen Education Centre, University of London Institute of Education, London.

CHAPTER 8

Trade unions in Europe

IAN PROCTER

European trade unionism has long been marked by national diversity in structure, degree of workplace organisation, ideology, and place within industrial and political relations. In this chapter no attempt at a geographically comprehensive review of unionism in western Europe is attempted. Rather, the focus is on Germany, Italy and France. These are the largest societies of continental western Europe but they also represent different historical traditions of unionism. Germany exemplifies a highly legalised, centralised and cooperative form of labour representation, Italy and France the alternative pattern of politically differentiated unionism with a conflictual relationship to employers.

One theme of this chapter is the maintenance of national diversity over the recent past. The period since the mid-1970s has posed considerable problems for unions. The era of postwar economic growth, high employment rates, developing welfare provision and expanding unionisation came quickly to an end. Union movements were faced with rising unemployment, retreats from welfarism and calls for wage restraint despite price inflation and demands from employers for concessions in labour deployment. Yet despite this common set of circumstances, the chapter will show that national variations remain. A second theme is that one reason for this is the relationship between unions and the state. Variation is partly a result of historical origins, but these are renewed through the interaction of unions and the state, a process particularly highlighted in times of national economic crisis such as the recent past. Then the political legitimacy and institutional robustness of unions comes to the fore. Unlike in Britain, no fundamental challenge to the legitimacy of unions has been displayed in these three societies. In Germany the state has largely maintained its distance, whilst in Italy and France the state has been interventionist but in markedly different ways – in Italy seeking to incorporate unions into economic management, in France by legally reshaping the form of worker representation. Finally, the chapter is written for a British audience, schooled in an experience of political exclusion and legal constraint of unionism. The intention is to display how other kinds of unionism fared under conditions of economic change.

In order to avoid overloading the text with a myriad of organisational names, abbreviations are used throughout the chapter and a glossary is provided at the end.

Germany

This section discusses unions in what was West Germany. The reverberations of the reunification of Germany in 1990 will not be discussed in detail as these are currently unclear. However, despite the upheaval of labour migration to the west and the economic liberalisation of the east, it might be ventured that reunification will not materially affect the German system of industrial relations. This is because a united Germany was achieved by the incorporation of the former GDR into the FRG, thus extending the federal legal system to the east. As, in matters of industrial relations, legal institutions are extensive, this should extend what was the federal system to the east. Second, the federal system has been marked by its stability over the economic troughs of the last two decades and thus should be capable of adapting to the politically induced change of reunification.

There are four trade-union confederations in Germany: the DGB (7.7 million members), DBB (0.8), DAG (0.5) and CGB (0.3) (FRG 1986, figures for 1986). As these membership figures show, the DGB is by far the dominant union organisation and will be the focus here. The DGB is a federation of seventeen industrial unions. This small number indicates that each union covers a broad sector. This applies particularly to the largest and most significant, the Metal Workers Union (IGM), which includes workers in steel, machine tools, ship-building, aerospace, electrical and mechanical engineering and car manufacture. IGM, with 2.6 million members, accounted for 34 per cent of DGB membership in 1989 (SLB 1990 (1): 38).

The employers also form a national confederation (BDA) which Furstenberg (1984: 618) estimates includes 80 per cent of all enter-prises. Both the DGB and BDA are essentially supportive organis-ations for their constituent members, providing research, coordination and representation. Although the DGB has historical and ideological links to German Social Democracy (SPD), these are not institutionalised. For example, the DGB always has two members of the Christian Democrats on its nine-person executive (Berghahn and Karston 1987: 35). However, it is the constituent industrial unions and employers' associations in industrial sectors which are the effec-tive units of industrial relations outside the workplace. These relations are regulated by an elaborate code of labour law which defines the scope and procedures of collective bargaining generating legally binding agreements, which include a peace obligation to avoid conflict over the contract's duration. Industrial conflict is also legally con-trolled with mediation mechanisms built in and specific requirements for legal strikes and lock-outs (Weiss 1987; Berghahn and Karston 1987: ch. 3).

Unions are characterised by their centralism, the leading role of full-time officials and the coordination of heterogeneous industries and workplaces into an industrial union. The justification for this is a 'solidaristic wages policy' whereby wages and conditions across regions, industries and firms are regulated by nationally coordinated agreements which do not discriminate between workers in weaker or stronger market positions. These features are illustrated in Streeck's (1984: ch. 2) account of bargaining by the IGM with particular reference to the car industry. The union's national executive, which is dominated by officers, initiates the process several months before the expiry of an agreement, with a statement of issues and demands. These are extensively discussed at lower levels and modifications incorporated, this phase culminating in resolutions from regional pay committees which cover the range of industries and occupations in the sector, their composition carefully regulated by the national executive. The executive has final say in the claim. Bargaining takes place regionally, by teams dominated by officers. Any proposals for industrial action, conciliation or arbitration must be agreed nationally. When the bargain is struck it must cover the 'industry' as a whole, be consistent with other regions and be approved by the national executive.

Legal controls on strikes/lock-outs and the centralised control of bargaining are two reasons for the low level of industrial conflict in Germany, consistently amongst the lowest in the industrialised world. However, adherence to the law and central control are not unproblematic. Rather, they are dependent upon the form of worker representation *within* the workplace, the system of 'codetermination' via Works Councils and worker directors (Neal 1987; Streeck 1984: ch. 3).

Works Councils are legally required in all firms and public organisations with more than five employees. All employees of the firm are entitled to vote in four-yearly elections of a Council to represent the workforce's interests on a wide range of issues. These are formalised as a works agreement, which includes disciplinary procedures, hours of work, holidays, health and safety, pay schemes, bonuses and piece rates, the hiring and dismissal of labour, worker transfer, training, work reorganisation and introduction of new technology. In all of these, employers have to gain the assent of the Council or face legal action. The Council is also responsible for monitoring the legality of the firm with respect to the legal rights of workers and the firm's compliance with agreements entered into with unions. What Councils do not do is negotiate such agreements, nor are they permitted to engage in industrial action. The recourse of Councils is to law; unions maintain the monopoly of the strike weapon.

As legal entities Councils are formally separate from unions which, in many industries, have no organisational presence within the firm. However, in reality, the Council is 'the extended arm of the union movement' (Schregle 1987: 325–6). Unions put up slates of candidates and nominate union officers as candidates. In fact, the great majority of councillors are unionists. Jacobi and Muller-Jentsch estimate that 85 per cent of councillors in the industrial sector are union nominees (1990: 134). As such, union policies are represented within the statutory system of the firm. However, as Councils are independent entities, unions cannot simply impose their policies; they have to be acceptable within this context. The legal independence of Councils thus imposes an important check on the central powers of unions. Councils also enable unions to overcome a perennial problem of solidaristic wage policies – allowing some leeway for better-placed workers to exploit their market position without undermining agreements across an industry. Councils cannot enter negotiation on wages but can influence actual wages by codetermining piece rates and hours (Streeck 1984: 34–6).

The unions' effective monopoly of representation within Works Councils was challenged by amendments to the legislation in 1988 to strengthen the access and rights to minority groups within the firm. For example, the number of supporters required for a councillor nomination was reduced, and Councils' control of their appointments of officers and committees was shifted from simple majority to proportional representation (SLB 1989(1): 29–30). However, unions' experience in using Councils is expected to incorporate these changes and, as Jacobi and Muller-Jentsch point out, given the extensive powers of Works Councils, 'the employers fear losing competent, reliable and predictable bargaining partners' (1990: 140).

The second aspect of codetermination is the presence of worker directors on the supervisory boards of companies which appoint and monitor the firm's management board. The composition of supervisory boards varies according to industrial sector and size of firm. Broadly, in medium-sized companies, workers have one-third representation on the board, whilst in companies with more than 2,000 employees, half the supervisory board are worker directors. They are elected by the workforce but are generally union nominees and often officials not employed by the firm (Berghahn and Karston 1987: ch. 4).

The German system is thus centralised industrial unionism outside the firm and codetermination, in which unions have a substantial *de facto* role, within the workplace. This system remained remarkably stable in the 1980s. This was despite shifts in the political and economic context. The era of Social Democratic hegemony, originating in 1966, ended in 1982 with the election of the Christian Democrats. Although this marked a shift in ideological tone, it amounted to little change in substance in industrial relations. Three legislative changes have been introduced. The 1985 Act on Improvement of Employment Opportunities was intended to loosen worker security by permitting temporary contracts in which the worker was not protected by legal procedures for dismissal (Weiss 1987: 46–8). But it is noticeable how temporary contracts are hedged around by legal safeguards. The limitations of the 1988 amendments to the Works Constitution Acts have been noted. Finally, the government has impeded the unions' use of the strike by restricting unemployment benefit to those laid off as a result of a strike in another area. This was intended to frustrate the effectiveness of the strategy of the 'focal' strike (Furstenberg 1984: 628) deployed by the IGM. Strikes were called in key firms, which quickly led to disruption of production elsewhere. The government intervention means that laid-off workers are not compensated. Although this is an impediment, the success of the IGM's use of the focal strike to move to the thirty-five-hour week (see below) shows it to be still effective.

German employers have joined the movement for greater flexibility in the hours and deployment of labour. Quality circles have been introduced, raising the possibility of an alternative line of communication and representation to the Works Council (Jacobi and Muller-Jentsch 1990: 132–4). But, crucially, such changes go through not around codetermination and thus unions have a degree of control over their implications. Again this will be illustrated below by the thirty-five-hour week.

Unions maintained their numerical strength in the 1980s, at around 42 per cent of the workforce. What is noticeable is that this not only remained stable in the 1980s but has been around that figure for the last thirty years. Although the composition of members has shown shifts to increased white-collar, female and public-sector workers, this is not so extensive as elsewhere (see below) and has not led to structural change in the balance of unions.

These various points can be illustrated by what was the major employment issue of the 1980s: hours of work. Here the leading role of the IGM has been confirmed with concessions won in metal-working, setting the example for others such as public-sector workers (1988) and shop workers (1989) (SLB 1988(1): 214: 1989(3/4): 266). IGM pressure came to a head in 1984 with a series of focal strikes in the car industry (Jacobi and Muller-Jentsch 1990: 144–6). The dispute lasted seven weeks, with over half a million workers on strike or (the majority) locked out. The strike achieved a reduction in hours to 38½. This was followed by further action culminating in the winning of the thirty-five-hour week in 1990 (SLB 1990(2):161–2). To some commentators, however, the hours of work issue marks a crack in the German system, as they rightly point out that the shorter working week has been achieved in return for concessions on the flexibility of hours (Windolf 1989; Schroder 1989; Katz and Sabel 1985). The 1989 agreement, for example, allowed the standard working week to vary between thirty-seven and forty hours, and the 38½ hour average had to be achieved over a two-month period. Furthermore, these practical arrangements were not fixed in the agreement but left to negotiation by Works Councils. Windolf, in particular, argues that 'In the long run, this arrangement may weaken industrial unions and their central-ised bargaining system' (1989: 12).

What this judgement overlooks is that union bargaining in the workplace through the Council system is not new. Streeck (1984) describes how short-time and overtime were key areas of codetermi-nation in the Volkswagen plants in the 1970s. The delegation of detail to Councils is, in his judgement, one way in which the unity of industrial unionism is maintained. Clearly, German unions face problems with structural changes in the labour market and the workplace, but as yet the dual system of industrial unionism and codetermination has proved durable both in institutional continuity and the maintenance of workers' strength.

Italy

Unions in Italy need to be set against the background of the decade after the 'hot autumn' of 1969, a period of very rapid membership expansion, from 28 to 44 per cent of the workforce (Santi 1988: 154). The basis for this was the organisational renewal of 'delegates' councils', which became active media for worker representation in the workplace. A second trend was towards organisational unity. Italy has three main national union confederations, the communist-inclined CGIL, the Christian Democratic CISL and the socialist UIL. In the 1970s this ideological and institutional pluralism seemed to be in decline, with the establishment of the 'Unitary Federation' (Giugni 1984) in 1972. The three confederations worked together and put aside their political allegiances in advancing the common interests of the working class. This does not mean that the unions became apolitical.

The 1970s saw the mobilisation of the union movement not just in negotiation with employers but in the exertion of political influence. Union power, expressed in the willingness to take militant action in the strike or demonstration, achieved considerable gains. Rising living standards were accompanied by some egalitarian redistribution, especially through the *scala mobile*, whereby a proportion of wage increases was indexed to price rises to favour the lower-paid. Exten-sion of the forty-hour week throughout manufacturing, improvements in working conditions and legislative reform of pensions, health care and public housing represented the unions' political accomplishments.

Unions in the 1970s could legitimately claim to represent a wide spectrum of the population through the direct action tradition, which remained alive within the Italian movement (Golden 1988) and through the unity of a grass-roots-based unionism.

These qualities of unity, a democratic base, egalitarianism, political influence and class representation were all called into question in the crisis years from the mid-1970s. Like other economies, Italy's experienced soaring inflation, rising unemployment and widening balance of payments as well as public expenditure deficits. In response to the crisis, the state did not ignore the power and legitimacy of unions but rather incorporated unions. One key aspect of this was the politicisation of collective bargaining by an active state involvement in industrial relations (Negrelli and Santi 1990: 169–73). Tripartite negotiation focused on regulating wages, especially curbing the automatic, price-indexed rises of the *scala mobile*. But they also included state policy on employment and social welfare. State resources were deployed to counter the effects of recession and restructuring. One important example was the Short-Term Earning Compensation Fund (CIG), originally designed as a bridge to help workers in cyclical downturns, in the 1980s deployed to compensate workers made redundant from industries in structural decline. Another example was the extension of early retirement provision to whole industries, as in steel in 1984. The state also intervened actively in conflict mediation, not only in recourse to the Ministry of Labour's conciliation service but the spread of political involvement to other ministries such as Education, State-Controlled Companies, and Industry.

The extent of tripartite 'concertation' in the early 1980s was such that a distinguished analyst of Italian industrial relations suggested that a neo-corporatist future was a distinct option for Italy (Giugni 1984: 613). In fact, a permanent institutional role for Italian unions in state economic management did not materialise (see below).

In terms of absolute numbers, union membership slightly increased in the 1980s. In 1979 unions claimed 8.7 million members, in 1986 8.9 million. But in terms of the proportion of the workforce unionised, membership fell from 44 to 37 per cent (Negrelli and Santi 1990: 188,190). Furthermore, as Santi (1988) points out, there was a significant change in the composition of membership. Italian unions do not only organise employees but also pensioners. The increase in pensioner members was remarkable, their confederation has 2 million members and is one of the largest unions in Europe (SLB 1988(3): 326). But this area of growth substituted for a decline in employee members, a fall of 1¼ million members, 17 per cent of the 1980 membershiship (Santi 1988: 159). This decline was concentrated in agriculture and manufacturing, with a slighter decrease (but not increase) in services. A key feature is the falling proportion of union members who work in large factories – the bastion of union power in the 1970s.

These changes are linked to the restructuring of the Italian economy, the decline in agricultural and manufacturing employment and increase in service jobs. Two features are particularly prominent, the rising number of small businesses and the 'underground economy'. Casual workers, temporary and seasonal workers were estimated to amount to 23 per cent of the regularly employed workforce in 1984 (Negrelli and Santi 1990: 161). Italian unions have failed to recruit in these areas to compensate for loss of membership in agriculture and manufacturing.

As well as this, Kriele (1988) argues that two other factors weakened the union movement. The first was the unintended effects of the very successes of the unions in the 1970s. One such success was the 1975 agreement on the *scala mobile* which provided a standard flat-rate increase to all workers as inflation rose. This had been intentionally redistributive in favour of lower-paid workers but the extent of this and the negative response of the better-paid were not foreseen. A second area of strength had been the increase in union control of labour deployment, in which delegate councils had considerable say in the hiring, allocation, transfer and firing of workers. Although this was of considerable benefit to union members protected by it, it worked to the detriment of others, especially young workers coming into the labour market and those working in the underground economy. Finally, participation by the unions in tripartite negotiations led to a shift in union power to the centre, which then had to police militancy in the delegate councils.

Kriele's second factor relates to the political party affiliations of the three union confederations. Throughout the late 1970s and early 1980s the struggle for party advantage in Italy's ever-changing coalition governments ramified into the unions. Time and again disputes within the unions were interpreted as expressions of their political allegiances. The 1983 tripartite agreement on incomes policy was hailed by CISL as a move to northern European corporatism, which the communists of CGIL rejected. CGIL communists refused to sign the 1984 agreement, a decision the other unions interpreted as the result of the Communist Party's opposition. The Unity Federation was formally dissolved in 1984 and the trend to a unified movement brought to an end.

So by the mid-1980s the trends of the 1970s seemed to have been reversed. The vitality of the delegates' councils appeared to have been suppressed by the shift to centralised participation in tripartite negotiations. Party political competition had brought the move to a unified movement to a halt. The claim of organised labour to represent the interests of the whole working class was undermined by discontent amongst rank-and-file members, the growth of independent unions amongst technicians and professionals (Garonna and Pisani 1986: 160–2), and lack of interest amongst young workers and in the service sector. Steeply rising unemployment and the unions' policing role spiked the strike weapon.

Such a turn-around leads Kriele to refer to the 'crisis' of Italian trade unionism, a crisis not simply of declining organisational strength and power but in the unions' sense of identity and legitimacy as the expression of working-class interest and aspiration (1988: 54). This is perhaps an exaggeration, as Negrelli and Santi put it: 'More than a profound, decisive "turning point",. . . the changes constitute an adaptation to new conditions' (1990: 192). In sustaining such an assessment three points can be made: maintenance of membership, continuity of political credibility and the sustained vitality of plant-level bargaining.

The observations above regarding the declining rate of unionisation and changing composition of unions are significant, but the fact remains that, in absolute terms, Italian unions, unlike many others, maintained their membership in the 1980s. The rise of 'non-active' members also has another side, through the medium of trade-union organisation pensioners have successfully mobilised to protect their pensions (SLB 1988(3): 326).

The trend to neo-corporate tripartisanism came to an end, the 1984 agreement being the last. The experiment was in no way a success from the point of view of organised labour, yet through difficult years the unions maintained a presence and defended the interests of labour. Due to their pressure, a host of measures such as CIG and early retirement schemes eased the cost of restructuring on labour. Although much weakened, Italy still has a measure of wage indexation protecting the lower-paid. In social welfare, although workers have suffered some losses, union pressure also led to gains. Family allowances, for example, had fallen in value by 1984 due to inflation. In reforming the system the state introduced means-testing. In the autumn of 1986 union–government negotiations led to a substantial rise in means-test thresholds (Negrelli and Santi 1990: 171). This indicates that the legitimacy of unions as expressions of broad worker interests has not been fundamentally challenged. Italy has not introduced anti-union legislation to undermine the legal protection of workers and unions in the 'Workers' Statute'. To speak, as Garonna and Pisani (1986) do, of a 'crisis of political unionism' seems to be an exaggeration.

The emphasis on early 1980s centralism tends to obscure the continuing vitality of plant-level bargaining. Although this is not the assertive neo-syndicalism of the early 1970s, the union within the workplace is still a potent force. Employers have demanded greater flexibility of labour time and work organisation but, other than in the small firm and private services, have had to *bargain* for them. Greater flexibility in hours of work has been conceded but in return for a reduction in hours.

Italian unions have changed significantly since the 1970s, but this represents an evolution rather than a change in fundamentals. The trend to centralism emerging in the early 1980s has not led to a neo-corporate system; rather, the unions remain an important and independent lobby on the state. The trend to a single-union movement has dissolved with a return to politically defined pluralism. Yet, in conjunction with an active grass-roots presence, it is arguable that this fosters democratic processes (Regalia 1988). This condition is met, the delegates' councils, the bedrock of 1970s unionism, seem to be firmly in a bargaining relationship with employers.

France

In 1981 the French elected their first left-wing government since the inception of the Fifth Republic in 1958. The Socialist-Communist coalition government quickly introduced a wide range of reforms (Hanley *et al.* 1988), including a comprehensive recasting of labour legislation, collectively known as the Auroux laws. This package of five laws and several government ordinances came into effect in 1982–83 and can serve as the focus for review of French unionism. Their manifest intention was to strengthen unionism and introduce a degree of democracy within the workplace. Their actual effects, in the context of economic recession and industrial restructuring, seem to be very different. But before describing the Auroux laws and their impact, an overview of the character of French unions and industrial relations is necessary.

There are five major union confederations in France. With one exception they are differentiated by their political allegiances rather than their appeal to separate sections of the workforce. Until recently, by far the strongest union was the CGT, with its Marxist-Leninist allegiance. From the 1960s the CFDT became the second most powerful confederation. Politically the CFDT was also Marxist-inspired but with an ideology of workers' control rather than the statist emphasis of the CGT. The FO and CFTC are social democratic in politics, whilst the CGC is a centrist union of managerial, technical and supervisory employees (Goetschy and Rojot 1987).

The leading unions in postwar France have thus had an explicitly class-struggle conception of their role and objectives. This was matched by the stance of French employers, with their reputation for jealousy of managerial prerogatives and a virulent anti-unionism. The 'patronat' formed a powerful federation, CNPF, which Kendall described as 'highly representative, well-staffed, well-equipped, disciplined and above all unified. The unions are outmatched in each respect' (1975: 73). The class-struggle orientations of both unions and employers have been mediated by an elaborate system of legal regulation. The law stipulates the working week, holidays, a job-classification scheme of skill levels, the minimum wage. The law provides mechanisms for arbitration and the designation of unions as 'representative'. Except in small firms, companies are required to form enterprise committees for consultation between management and workers. After the events of 1968, unions were (at last) legally protected in the workplace.

French unionism has historically the lowest level of membership of the developed capitalist societies. In the 1970s it was generally reckoned to be around 20 per cent of the workforce, although precise figures were difficult to establish. Both the low numbers and the lack of precision were a function of the nature of unionism in France. Legal rights had a paradoxical effect on membership. Whilst the right to union membership was legally established, so was its converse; the closed shop was illegal. Until the early 1970s union organisation in the workplace was legally inhibited, but a legal process was established in which unions were 'representative' of the workforce. Rather than this being based upon actual membership, a labour court established union bargaining rights (Forde 1984). Workers thus had little incentive to join unions, especially in the context of anti-union employer practices. Kendall (1975: 83) and Gallie (1978: ch. 11) note the routine victimisation of union members. But the union objective and strategy was never to establish high rates of membership and organisational strength at the workplace. Grass-roots members were expected to be activists, committed to the political ambitions of the union (Smith 1987: chs. 3 and 5).

Gallie's (1978) study of British and French oil refineries brings out the distinctiveness of French unionism compared to British practice. British unions aimed to maximise membership and organisational strength at the workplace in order to negotiate routinely with the employer on day-to-day matters of wages and conditions. French unions put their effort into propaganda in order to raise the consciousness of the workers for a political role. Rather than representing the workforce in negotiation with the employer, French unions sought to mobilise workers in a wider context.

This context was two-fold. Industrial relations negotiations were conducted at an industry or national level, agreeable to employers in their maintainance of control of the workplace, and to unions to maximise their class rather than sectional representation. But on occasion, the objective of French unions of mobilising the working class politically was achieved – in 1936 after the election of the Popular Front, in the years immediately after the war and in the 'events' of 1968. These were periods of mass radicalisation of the French population, and it was at these points in time that the legal rights of workers and unions were advanced. Unions thus sought to serve the interests of workers by political mobilisation rather than bargaining strength in the workplace.

This pattern of legally-regulated class struggle was associated with a high level of unpredictable industrial conflict. The lack of local institutionalised bargaining meant that grievances exploded in wildcat strikes, often to the surprise of the unions (Smith 1987: ch. 5). Union activists were successful in galvanising the workforce, in Gallie's oil refineries there were twenty-four strikes between 1961 and 1971, all of them one-day 'demonstration' strikes in support of a broad slate of objectives. Such politicisation culminated in the national upheavals symbolised by 1968, the nearest any western capitalist society has come to revolution.

The Auroux laws are complex and only their main thrust can be indicated here (a detailed description is given by Glendon 1984). The rights of unions in the workplace were strengthened to give greater protection to members. Employers and unions were required to negotiate annually at the firm level on wages and hours. But other forms of worker representation were also developed. The long-established works committees were granted greater powers to require information from employers, appoint expert assistance and call workforce meetings. Firms of more than fifty employees were required to appoint committees on health, safety and working conditions. Perhaps the most controversial innovation was the introduction of 'expression groups', giving workers the right to express their views collectively on the content and conditions of their work.

The government introduced Auroux in the language of workers' control, which had long been dear to the CFDT and to which the CGT had also inclined in the 1970s. The Auroux Report had declared, 'Citizens in the political sphere, workers must also be citizens in the workplace' (quoted in Smith 1987: 210). But the left-wing influence was by no means the only one. Gallie (1985) points out that during the 1970s large French employers had developed rather different management strategies from the traditional autocracy of the 'patron'. These involved greater efforts to integrate workers in a way parallel to Auroux's emphasis on the worker's rights within the firm. Others note that throughout the 1970s (right-wing) governments were concerned to address the perceived 'chaos' of French industrial relations by encouraging a 'modern' system of institutionalised rights and obligations (Moss 1988a; Eyraud and Tchobanian 1985).

As well as these various motivations, the context of introduction of Auroux should be borne in mind. The Keynesian-inspired response to recession by the left-wing government was reversed from 1983, with a shift to state encouragement of profitability and flexibility in the use of labour. Unemployment rose, and the initiative passed to employers (Segrestin 1990). In this context a pessimistic diagnosis of the effects of Auroux predominates.

Auroux required annual bargaining at firm-level (Amadieu 1988). It did not, however, control for the economic context of bargaining nor provide the organisational basis for it. Moss (1988a and b) thus charts the increase in plant-level agreements but argues that these have been made very much on the employers' terms. Aldir (1989) and Smith (1987) point out that, as well as economic weakness, union organisational strength within the workplace was weakened rather than bolstered by Auroux. The old pattern of legal rights inhibiting the need for *de facto* strength from organisation continued. Smith further develops the ambiguities posed for the traditional union militant. The Auroux reforms were introduced not in the manner of other legal rights, by mass mobilisation, but by legislation following electoral victory. Shop-floor interest was minimal. The militant could not, therefore, count on popular backing in establishing new patterns of workplace relations. Yet the union activists were faced with a plurality of forms of worker representation to administer: works committees, annual bargaining, expression groups, and health and safety committees. All of this amounted to a bureaucratising of the activist's role. This jarred with the essentially political definition of union activity, leaving the militant stranded between his/her political aspirations and role as a cog in a complex bureaucratic mechanism.

The form and purpose of expression groups was left open by the legislation. Despite initial opposition, it appears that it was employers rather than unions who seized the opportunity to shape this innovation. Membership of groups, terms of reference, timing of meetings, control of the agenda and the chair have been determined by management. Personnel staff have been trained in small group management to use the groups in a way parallel to quality circles, so that workers 'control' has been deflected to incorporating the worker into the firm (Borzeix *et al.* 1986; Jenkins 1987).

Auroux has certainly not stimulated union membership, the level of which is still a matter of informed estimate rather than a reliable measure. Segrestin puts the rate at 15 per cent in the mid-1980s (1990: 106). Overall decline has occurred through falls in CGT and CFDT membership and stabilisation of FO and CFTC support. This shift in the balance of confederations is reflected in works-committee elections with the CGT/CFDT losing their overall supremacy to FO/CFTC and non-union candidates (Segrestin 1990: 106). These election figures are often taken as the measure of worker support for unions, and the current trend suggests a shift away from worker allegiance to the political aspirations of the radical unions.

The term 'crisis' has been used to describe many European union movements in the 1980s. It seems most applicable to the French. This is paradoxical in that the French state introduced a comprehensive package of prima-facie pro-union legislation in the 1980s. Yet this legal intervention deflected rather than built upon the strength of French unions. This lay in the unions' role in radicalising and mobilising the working class at local, workplace and national levels (Lash 1984). Auroux has completed a process of incorporating unions into a complex web of legal rights and mechanisms which contradicts this role. As Sellier and Silvestre comment, 'the weakness of unions in France is largely a state-created weakness' (1986: 173), but this is a function of legalisation rather than repression.

Conclusion

In this chapter the workings and recent development of unionism in three major European societies have been examined. In the postwar period these came to exemplify two very different types of labour representation system. In Germany, highly legalised, centralised and cooperative; in Italy and France politicised, pluralistic and conflictual. The evidence of the last two decades shows that these systems are not static but evolving. The economic circumstances of this period have not been propitious, so that the ascent of unions which marked the years up to 1975 has ended. Yet the responses of unions to these economic conditions has varied, and a key factor in this variation has been the complex relationship between unions and the state.

Germany represents the most stable of these three systems. Although highly legalised, the German state has but tinkered with the workings of industrial relations in the recent past. Neither has the DGB attempted to use political influence to achieve its main objective, relying on the solidarity of industrial unionism to bargain with employers to reduce working hours. This situation contrasts with those of Italy and France, yet the contrasts between the two are just as marked. The Italian state attempted to incorporate unions into policy implementation and intervened actively in industrial relations but without legal reform. This phase proved temporary, and Italian unionism has returned to its pluralism, politicisation and grass-roots organisation.

By contrast, in France, despite the socialist pretensions of the government of the Left, unions were not incorporated into state policy implementation. Rather, the state embarked upon a massive reformulation of labour law. Pro-union and pro-worker in rhetoric, the indications are that the Auroux package has seriously and permanently undermined the tradition of French unionism.

The trend to maintenance of national variability in European unionism and the influence of union–state relationships is confirmed by developments in other European societies, to which brief reference can be made. Germany's stability is not generic to all highly institutionalised forms of unionism. In Sweden[1] the leadership of the predominantly private sector, male, manual worker labour organisation has been challenged by unions representing white-collar, public-sector and women workers. The former pattern of bipartisan collective bargaining without state involvement has been broken by the unions' use of statutory means to advance workers' interests, the parallel higher political profile of employers and state attempts to regulate industrial relations. National coordination of bargaining by a solidarity wages policy has weakened, with employer attempts to decentralise and union confusion over egalitarian objectives. Sweden, long the model for social democrats, is itself rapidly evolving.

By contrast, in Belgian unionism,[2] also a highly organised system, the state responded to the economic crisis of the early 1980s by a five-year suspension of the elaborate network of national, industrial and plant-level institutions. From 1986, however, the system was reactivated. Furthermore, the procedure whereby the state can suspend the system has been formalised, with the role of unions in that process legally specified.

Three European societies, Spain, Portugal and Greece, moved from dictatorship to parliamentary democracy in the 1970s, Spain[3] being the most significant here, as the underground union movement played a leading role in the downfall of Francoism. Unions expanded rapidly in the late 1970s, yet the political priority of Spanish society was the consolidation of parliamentary democracy and the unions subordinated themselves to the political objectives of their sister political parties. The late 1980s saw Spain's unions taking a more independent stance and unifying around a much tougher negotiating position. Once again the relationship between unions and the state leads to a distinctive national pattern being established.

The legal definition and political role of unions in the nation state means that unions face considerable problems in responding to their next economic challenge, the liberalisation of capital and labour markets in 1993. This economic shift may be accompanied by some legal and political harmonisation, as embodied in the 'Social Charter'. However, this is unlikely radically to shift the embeddedness of unions in national legal and political systems. On the basis of the union's response to recession, the prediction must be that they will respond to market liberalisation within the legal and political frameworks of their own national societies.

Notes

1 For discussion of the Swedish model and recent developments, see Ahlen (1989), Fulcher (1987), Hammarstrom (1987), Lash (1985), Peterson (1987), Rehn and Viklund (1990) and Svensson (1986).
2 An introduction to Belgium unionism can be found in Albertijn *et al.* (1990), and Fitzmaurice (1983).
3 For further detail on Spain, consult Balfour 1989, Estirill and de la Hoz (1990), Ferner (1987) and Lucio (1989).

Glossary of names

Germany

BDA	Bundesvereinigung Deutscher Arbeitgeberverbande (Confederation of German Employers' Associations)
CGB	Christlicher Gewerkschaftsbund Deutschlands (Confederation of Christian Trade Unions of Germany)
DAG	Deutsche Angestelltengewerkschaft (German Salaried Employees Union)
DBB	Deutscher Beamtenbund (Confederation of German Civil Service Officials)
DGB	Deutscher Gewerkschaftsbund (German Trade Union Federation)
IGM	Industriegewerkschaft Metall (Metal Workers' Union)

162   *Responding Social Institutions*

Italy

CGIL   Confederazione Generale Italiana del Lavoro (General
       Italian Confederation of Labour)
CIG   Cassa Integrazione Guadagni (Short-term Earnings
       Compensation Fund)
CISL   Confederazione Italiana Sindacati Lavoratori (Italian
       Confederation of Workers' Unions)
UIL   Unione Italiana dei Lavoratori (Italian Union of Workers)

France

CFDT   Confédération Française Démocratique du Travail (French
       Democratic Confederation of Labour)
CFTC   Confédération Française des Travailleurs Chrétiens (French
       Confederation of Christian Workers)
CGC   Confédération Générale des Cadres (French Confederation
       of Managerial Staffs
CGT   Confédération Générale du Travail (General Confederation
       of Labour
CNPF   Conseil National du Patronat Français (National Council of
       French Employers)
FO   Force Ouvrière (Workers' Strength)

References

Note: Throughout the chapter reference is made to recent developments as
reported in the International Labour Office's *Social and Labour Bulletin*.
In the text this is abbreviated to SLB, followed by the year of publication,
the issue number and the page; e.g. (SLB 1990 (1): 38).

Ahlen, K. (1989) 'Swedish collective bargaining under pressure: inter-union
rivalry and incomes policies', *British Journal of Industrial Relations*, **27**(3):
330–46.
Albertijn, M., Hancke, B. and Wijgaerts, D. (1990) 'Technology agreements
and industrial relations in Belgium, *New Technology, Work and Employ-
ment*, **5**(1): 18–30.
Aldir, L. (1989) 'The American model, unrealised: a re-evaluation of plant
bargaining in France', *Comparative Labour Law Journal*, **10**(2): 196–213.
Amadieu, J. (1988) 'Employment flexibility, unions and companies in France',
Industrial Relations Journal, **19**(2): 117–23.
Balfour, S. (1989) *Dictatorship, Workers, and the City: Labour in Greater
Barcelona since 1939*, Oxford: Clarendon.
Bamber, G. and Lansbury, R. (1987) *International and Comparative Industrial
Relations*, London: Allen & Unwin.
Berghahn, V. and Karston, D. (1987) *Industrial Relations in West Germany*,
London: Berg.
Borzeix, A., Linhart, D. and Segrestin, D. (1986) 'Direct workers' expression

in France: the voice of management?' *International Journal of Sociology and Social Policy*, **6**(2): 22–9.

Estivill, J. and de la Hoz, J. (1990) 'The complexity of Spanish industrial relations', in G. Baglioni and C. Crouch (eds) *European Trade Unionism: the Challenge of Flexibility*, London: Sage.

Eyraud, F. and Tchobanian, R. (1985) 'The Auroux laws and company level industrial relations in France', *British Journal of Industrial Relations*, **23**(2): 241–59.

Federal Republic of Germany (FRG) (1986) *Employers and Unions*, Bonn: Press and Information Office.

Ferner, A. (1987) 'Industrial relations and the mesopolitics of the public enterprise: the transmission of state objectives in the Spanish national railways', *British Journal of Industrial Relations*, **25**(1): 49–75.

Fitzmaurice, J. (1983) *The Politics of Belgium*, London: Hurst.

Forde, M. (1984) 'Trade union pluralism and labour law in France', *International and Comparative Law Quarterly*, **33**(1): 134–57.

Fulcher, J. (1987) 'Labour movement theory versus corporatism: social democracy in Sweden', *Sociology*, **21**(2): 231–52.

Furstenberg, F. (1984) 'Recent trends in collective bargaining in the Federal Republic of Germany', *International Labour Review*, **123**(5): 615–30.

——(1987) 'The Federal Republic of Germany', in G. Bamber and R. Lansbury (eds) *International and Comparative Industrial Relations*, London, Allen & Unwin, ch. 8, p. 165.

Gallie, D. (1978) *In Search of the New Working Class*, Cambridge: Cambridge University Press.

——(1985) 'Les lois Auroux: the reform of French industrial relations?' in H. Machin and V. Wright *Economic Policy and Policy Making under the Mitterrand Presidency 1981–84*, London: Francis Pinter.

Garonna, P. and Pisani, E. (1986) 'Italian unions in transition: the crisis of political unionism', in R. Edwards, P. Garrona and F. Todtling (eds) *Unions in Crisis and Beyond*, London: Auburn House, ch. 4, p. 114.

Giugni, G. (1984) 'Recent trends in collective bargaining in Italy', *International Labour Review*, **123**(5): 599–614.

Glendon, M. (1984) 'French law reform, 1982–83: the struggle for collective bargaining', *American Journal of Comparative Law*, **32**: 449–91.

Goetschy, J. and Rojot, J. (1987) 'French industrial relations', in G. Bamber and R. Lansbury (eds) *International and Comparative Industrial Relations*, London: Allen & Unwin.

Golden, M. A. (1988) 'Historical meaning and ideological orientations of the Italian workers' movement', *Politics and Society*, **16**(1): 1–34.

Hammarstrom, O. (1987) 'Swedish industrial relations', in G. Bamber and R. Lansbury (eds) *International and Comparative Industrial Relations*, London: Allen & Unwin.

Hanley, D., Kerr, A. P. and Waites, N. H. (1988) *Contemporary France*, London: Routledge.

Jacobi, O. and Muller-Jentsch, W. (1990) 'West Germany: Continuity and structural change', in G. Baglioni and C. Crouch (eds) *European Trade Unionism: the Challenge of Flexibility*, London: Sage.

Jenkins, A. (1987) 'Work, new technology and the changing form of industrial relations in France', *Employee Relations*, **9**(6): 17–22.

Katz, H. and Sabel, C. (1985) 'Industrial relations and industrial adjustment in the car industry', *Industrial Relations*, **24**(3): 295–315.

164   *Responding Social Institutions*

Kendall, W. (1975) *The Labour Movement in Europe*, London: Allen Lane.
Kriele, M. (1988) 'The crisis of Italian trade unionism in the 1980s', *West European Politics*, 11(1): 54–67.
Lash, S. (1984) *The Militant Worker: Class and Radicalism in France and America*, London: Heinemann.
——(1985) 'The end of neo-corporatism? The breakdown of centralised bargaining in Sweden', *British Journal of Industrial Relations*, 23(2): 215–39.
Lucio, M. (1989) 'Union–worker relations in a transforming Spain', *Economic and Industrial Democracy*, 10(4): 423–46.
Moss, B. (1988a) 'Industrial law reform in an era of retreat: the Auroux laws in France', *Work, Employment and Society*, 2(3): 317–34.
——(1988b) 'After the Auroux laws: employers, industrial relations and the right in France', *West European Politics*, 11(1): 68–80.
Neal, A. (1987) 'Co-determination in the Federal Republic of Germany: an external perspective from the United Kingdom', *British Journal of Industrial Relations*, 25(2): 227–45.
Negrelli, S. and Santi, E. (1990) 'Industrial relations in Italy', in G. Baglioni and C. Crouch (eds) *European Trade Unionism: the Challenge of Flexibility*, London: Sage.
Peterson, R. (1987) 'Swedish collective bargaining – a changing scene', *British Journal of Industrial Relations*, 25(1): 31–48.
Regalia, I. (1988) 'Democracy and unions: towards a critical analysis', *Economic and Industrial Democracy*, 9(3): 345–71.
Rehn, G. and Viklund, B. (1990) 'Changes in the Swedish model', in G. Baglioni and C. Crouch (eds) *European Trade Unionism: the Challenge of Flexibility*, London: Sage.
Santi, E. (1988) 'Ten years of unionisation in Italy', *Labour*, 2(1): 153–82.
Schregle, J. (1987) 'Workers' participation in the Federal Republic of Germany in an international perspective', *International Labour Review*, 126(3): 317–27.
Schroder, K. (1989) *The Trade Unions in a Changing Society*, Bonn: Inter Nationes.
Segrestin, D. (1990) 'Recent changes in France', in G. Baglioni and C. Crouch (eds) *European Trade Unionism: the Challenge of Flexibility*, London: Sage.
Sellier, F. and Silvestre, J-J. (1986) 'Unions' policies in the economic crisis in France', in R. Edwards, P. Garrona and F. Todtling (eds) *Unions in Crisis and Beyond*, London: Auburn House, ch. 5, p. 173.
Smith, W. (1987) *Crisis in the French Labour Movement*, London: Macmillan.
Spineaux A. (1990) 'Trade unionism in Belgium', in G. Baglioni and C. Crouch (eds) *European Trade Unionism: the Challenge of Flexibility*, London: Sage, ch. 2, p. 42.
Streeck, W. (1984) *Industrial Relations in West Germany: a Case Study of the Car Industry*, London: Heinemann.
Svensson, L. (1986) 'Class struggle in a welfare state in crisis: from radicalism to neoliberalism in Sweden', in R. Edwards, P. Garrona and F. Todtling (eds) *Unions in Crisis and Beyond*, London: Auburn House.
Visser, J. (1989) *European Trade Unionism in Figures*, Deventer: Kluwer.
Weiss, M. (1987) *Labour Law and Industrial Relations in the Federal Republic of Germany*, Deventer: Kluwer.
Windolf, P. (1989) 'Productivity coalitions and the future of European corporatism', *Industrial Relations*, 28(1): 1–20.

CHAPTER 9

Crime and cross-border policing in Europe

MICHAEL LEVI AND MIKE MAGUIRE

Many of the broad sociological issues which are beginning to be re-examined in the context of the development of the European Community – questions about national identity, the formation and maintenance of norms and values, the role of formal and informal rules, and so on – are of obvious relevance to the study of crime and social control in the new Europe. However, the contribution of criminology to such debates has so far been negligible. Indeed, even at the level of mapping differences between countries in crime rates, in attitudes towards crime, and in specific forms of social control, much of the basic comparative work has yet to be done.

The reasons for this are fairly clear. First and foremost, communication between European criminologists has been seriously handicapped, not merely by language barriers, but also by the fragmented nature of the discipline of criminology itself. The subject embraces a wide diversity of intellectual and theoretical traditions, both between and within individual countries. Criminology can be a sociological subject, concerned with explanations of crime rates and forms of social control; a psychological subject, concerned with explaining differences in the propensity of individuals to commit crime and to respond to punishment; a social policy subject, concerned with the ethics and/or the effectiveness of measures to reduce crime; or a (socio-)legal subject, concerned with the scope and limits of the criminal law, and the relation of law to society. Indeed, it is largely true to say that the existence of criminology as a separate discipline is sustained as much by shared interest in the phenomenon under study – crime and modes of social control – as by any distinctive methodology or approach.

This being the case, it is unsurprising to find that, in some European countries, 'criminology' barely exists as a discipline in its own right, remaining a trade plied by lone academics in a variety of law, sociology or psychology departments, many of whom retain only a temporary interest in crime *per se*. Conversely, in other countries, it has become concentrated in a small number of specialist research institutes, often dependent on direct government funding, which tend to develop their own narrow focus and communicate only with similar groups elsewhere. Criminology also tends to follow the broader intellectual traditions and academic strengths of each country. Thus German criminology is dominated on the one hand by legal formalism and on the other by the sociological heritage of the Frankfurt school; French sociologists, steeped in the traditions of grand theory, have tended to take only a tangential interest in crime; Norwegian criminology, reflecting the more informal modes of conflict resolution associated with intimate societies, is highly critical of formal justice principles taken for granted in more anonymous urban societies, and so on.

In fact, although by no means immune from the problems of fragmentation and narrow specialisation mentioned above, British criminology is probably larger numerically, more broad-based and more integrated than its counterpart in any other European country. For much of the twentieth century, it was dominated by positivist schools of thought, seeking pathological explanations for individual criminal behaviour through a variety of quantitative methodologies. This tradition was seriously challenged in the 1960s by sociologists influenced by structuralist and interactionist approaches developed in the United States (anomie, subcultural theory, labelling theory, and so on) and again in the 1970s by Marxist and other radical schools. After a period of ferment, some reintegration has taken place, and it is fair to say that British criminology has emerged in a relatively healthy state. It has not only maintained its empirical tradition, establishing a reputation for high quality – if sometimes unimaginative – descriptive and evaluative research, but also has made advances in theoretical approaches to explaining crime control, influenced primarily by American sociology, but also to some extent by writers such as Gramsci and Foucault (for historical overviews, see Taylor, Walton and Young 1973; Rock 1988).

Unfortunately, this productive period has passed in almost total isolation from European concerns. With a few prominent exceptions. European theorists have been ignored, their work being alien to the American sociological approaches which have dominated criminological training and thinking in the United Kingdom. Where empirical work is concerned, a similar lack of British interest stems largely from the fact that few European countries have a tradition or output rivalling its own or that of the United States (exceptions being the Netherlands, Scandinavian countries and, to a lesser extent, Germany). Equally, many of the innovations in policy which attract attention in Britain – recent examples being Neighbourhood Watch, electronic tagging and private prisons – have originated in the United States, European developments being largely ignored.

The lack of British scholarly interests in Europe also reflects the fact that – with certain very important exceptions, to be discussed below – crime control has hitherto been an issue of relatively low priority among the mass of cooperative ventures associated with the growth of the European Community. The subject is not included in the Treaty of Rome, and most crime-related 'conventions', resolutions and agreements between member states have been made in a piecemeal, *ad hoc* fashion. The explanation for this lies partly in the fact that the great majority of criminal offences are committed within a few miles of the offender's home (Mawby 1979; Maguire 1982). Sophisticated travelling or 'cross-border' criminals are in a very small minority, and, for the bulk of criminal investigations, police forces see little need for communication with neighbouring forces, let alone forces in other countries. Equally important, each country has its peculiar legal and penological traditions, often defended by powerful interest groups resistant to change. Although the European Committee on Crime Problems at the Council of Europe in Strasbourg has for many years collated information, promoted exchanges of ideas and produced broad recommendations on criminal justice issues, its impact upon national policies – especially in Britain – has been modest.

Nevertheless, a number of developments can be mentioned in which trends towards harmonisation are clearly to be seen. Some of these appear to be gradual and long-term: for example, there has been a steady increase in recent years in international communication between practitioners in specialised fields such as crime prevention (Home Office 1988) and victim assistance (Waller 1988; VLOS 1989), helping to spread ideas about 'best practice'. Similarly, the advent of '1992' and its attendant publicity has at last begun to kindle British interest in comparative studies. Exchange visits and collaborative research are becoming more common, while conferences on European themes have brought European criminologists to the United Kingdom and disseminated their views through edited collections of papers (for example, Hood 1989; Heidensohn and Farrell 1991).

Much more important and fast-moving developments, however, can be found in a small number of areas arousing major political interest. By far the most governmental attention, unsurprisingly, has been lavished upon types of crime with a strong international or '*cross-border*' element which have been perceived as a serious threat to the 'fabric of the state'. These include large-scale drug-trafficking, terrorism and, latterly, the issue of illegal immigration. They also include, more modestly, various forms of business (or 'enterprise') crime. In such instances, 'harmonisation' means far more than simply the adoption of similar policies. It may entail the construction of international intelligence-gathering systems and data banks, the regular exchange of information, joint policing operations across borders, the allowance of 'hot pursuit' across frontiers and, increasingly, the use of new methods of surveillance and undercover policing. It may also entail the use and extension of EC powers originally granted for purposes other than crime control. A good illustration, discussed below, is provided by efforts to control 'money laundering' by major enterprise criminals. These have led to the imposition of criminal liability upon banks and other credit institutions if they knowingly assist money launderers, fail to keep specified information about their clients, or fail to inform the police about suspicious transactions – all of which challenge previously accepted principles of banking secrecy (Levi 1991).

Moreover, such developments have not been restricted to major forms of criminal activity. Growing concern about football hooliganism has also generated increased collaboration between European police and criminal justice authorities (Williams 1989), culminating during the 1990 World Cup in joint operations of a scale and intensity regarded by some commentators as wildly out of proportion to the problem (Armstrong *et al.* 1991). Such operations, some of the undercover methods used and the heavy-handed pre-emptive actions taken (for example, restrictions on movement and summary deportations) raise questions about the control and public accountability of cross-border operations of all kinds.

In this chapter, we can do no more than touch upon a few basic issues relating to crime and its control in Europe. We shall look, first, at the extent to which 'crime problems' – and perceptions of these problems – differ in the various European countries; second, at the nature and extent of 'cross-border' crime; and third, at trends in policing and criminal justice policies in different states and among transnational bodies, including the degree of 'harmonisation' so far apparent. Finally, we shall argue that, as cooperation between crime control agencies increases, civil-rights issues and questions about accountability are likely to assume more prominence.

Variations in crime levels and the 'crime problem'

To what extent is the 'crime problem' a similar phenomenon in different European countries? To answer this, one has to look both at comparable statistical material and at possible differences in attitudes and perceptions. It is also important to note any major variations in, for example, geography, population density, car ownership, alcohol consumption, or other factors which may affect levels of opportunity for the commission of crime or may help to generate particular patterns of criminal behaviour.

Official (police-recorded) statistics have indicated fairly uniform trends in crime levels throughout western European countries since the Second World War: stable or falling rates until the mid-1950s, very sharp increases throughout the 1960s and 1970s, and some flattening of these increases during the 1980s. In relation to population, Sweden, West Germany and England and Wales have generally exhibited the highest levels of recorded crime, while at the other extreme, Switzerland has always appeared from its official statistics to experience so little crime that a distinguished American academic was moved to write a book to try to explain the phenomenon (Clinard 1978). Clinard attributed it to the country's tight social cohesion, its conservative values, the absence of large cities, and the lack of a strong, separate youth culture. However, Balvig (1987) has cast doubt on Clinard's evidence and conclusions, observing that Denmark, which has traditionally liberal values, high social welfare, a large city, and a flourishing youth culture, also has an exceptionally low crime rate.

Of course, there are always serious doubts about the comparability of crime figures between countries, owing to differences in definitions and in reporting and recording practices. For this reason, the publication in 1990 of the first international crime victimisation survey (Van Dijk *et al.* 1990) marked an important step forward in the field of comparative criminology. The survey was conducted in eleven European countries, as well as the United States, Canada and Australia. It was based upon telephone interviews with members of representative samples of households in each country, all respondents being asked to recall any criminal offences whether or not reported to the police, committed against them or their household during the previous twelve months. The survey provides comparative data on the incidence of eleven different types of crime.

As Table 9.1 shows, the European countries emerging from this exercise with the highest crime rates (about 25 per cent of respondents reporting an offence against them) were the Netherlands, Spain and West Germany. At the other end of the scale came Northern Ireland, Switzerland, Norway and Finland (about 15 per cent). Generally speaking, the survey results confirm the rank order of the countries, in terms of volume of crime, as indicated by official statistics, but there are some exceptions. For example, England and Wales come lower down the table, and the Netherlands considerably higher up, than would be expected from their respective totals of crimes recorded by the police.

Again, though, global comparisons can be misleading and any serious comparative study has to examine carefully the component parts of each set of figures and to interpret them in the light of knowledge about particular conditions within the various countries. To take a simple example, Holland's relatively high crime rate is largely accounted for by the exceptional numbers of bicycle thefts, which, not unexpectedly, occur in a country where cycling is an important part of the culture. (The same, incidentally, can be said of Oxford and Cambridge!)

Where perceptions of crime problems are concerned, there are a number of areas in which very different attitudes prevail. A good example is drunk driving, an offence about which, despite a gradual hardening of public opinion, British attitudes have always been somewhat ambivalent. In Scandinavian countries, by contrast, and especially in Sweden, this has long been regarded as a very serious

Table 9.1   **Victimisation rates in Europe, 1988: selected offences and countries from 1989 International Telephone Survey**[1]

Country	Burglary/ attempted burglary	Theft from car	Bicycle theft	Attack or threat	Sexual offence	All crimes[2]
Netherlands	5.0	5.3	7.6	3.4	2.6	26.8
Spain	3.6	9.9	1.0	3.0	2.4	24.6
W Germany	3.1	4.7	3.3	3.1	2.8	21.9
England & Wales	3.8	5.6	1.0	1.9	1.2	19.4
France	4.7	6.0	1.4	2.0	1.2	19.4
Scotland	4.1	5.3	1.0	1.8	1.2	18.6
Belgium	4.6	2.7	2.7	2.0	1.3	17.7
Norway	1.2	2.8	2.8	3.0	2.1	16.5
Finland	1.0	2.7	3.1	2.9	0.6	15.9
Switzerland	1.2	1.9	3.2	1.2	1.6	15.6
N. Ireland	2.0	4.0	1.6	1.8	1.8	15.0
Europe	3.7	5.8	2.2	2.5	1.9	20.9

Notes:
1 Figures are percentages of respondents claiming to have been the victim of one or more crimes within 1988
2 Victim of any one or more of the eleven offences covered by the survey: those shown in the table, together with car theft, car vandalism, motorbike theft, violent theft and other theft
Source: Adapted from J.J.M. Van Dijk, P. Mayhew and M. Killias (1990) Experiences with Crime Across the World: Results of the 1989 International Telephone Survey, The Hague: Kluwer

offence, resulting in automatic imprisonment and producing social stigma comparable to conviction as a thief.

Another example is drug use and small-scale dealing in drugs. Whereas the British and the Germans tend to see such activities essentially as 'crime problems', the Dutch perception is of a health or education problem, to be met by policies based on harm reduction and normalisation. These include efforts to demythologise drug-taking, to present it to the public as a normal social problem, to discourage its glamorous image among the young, and to avoid driving the drug culture underground through police harassment and stigmatisation. City councils readily fund services such as syringe exchange and drop-in centres for addicts (Mol 1991). And, uniquely, Amsterdam has experimented with the decriminalisation of the consumption of cannabis: it is openly sold in small quantities in more than 250 coffee shops, the sales being technically illegal but rarely interfered with by the police. These policies reflect a traditionally liberal attitude towards crime (other than serious violent or sexual offences) peculiar to the Netherlands, which has been reflected over the past twenty years in distinctive sentencing policies and progressive experimentation in crime prevention, prison management and other areas of the criminal justice field.

The Amsterdam example, especially, illustrates the further general point that, while there are pressures towards conformity, there is still room for radically different thinking to be translated into action at a local level, and particularly at the level of local government in large cities. Even in Germany, where the national government fosters an unambiguously repressive approach to drugs problems, the level of police tolerance towards small-scale dealing and use varies widely between individual cities.

Cross-border crime

In contrast to the wealth of data collected about criminal offences, reported or not reported to the police, in every European country, there is almost no hard information available about cross-border crime for gain in Europe. Because police forces and national governments define their responsibilities for the production of statistics in terms of crimes occurring within their own jurisdictions, and because victimisation surveys exclude crimes against organisations (the main victims of cross-border criminals) and do not specify the origins of offenders, no data are collated routinely. Nor are there any specific research studies which demonstrate with any accuracy the proportion of all offences which possess a cross-border dimension.

There are individual forms of crime which constitute exceptions to this dearth of knowledge: especially terrorism cases, and – because the scope of customs agencies, and hence their statistics, is restricted to importation – drug-trafficking. For example, it is known that in Europe the total heroin seized rose from 1,850 kilos in 1985 to 6,100 kilos in 1990 (and that the proportion of this going through the Balkan route – from Turkey via Greece or Bulgaria and Yugoslavia – rose from 25–35 per cent to 70–80 per cent, partly reflecting the opening up of eastern Europe). Nevertheless, this is an unknown and possibly fluctuating proportion of the total amount smuggled. Although a certain amount of retrospective analysis can be done on the origins of drugs seized on the streets, it is generally true that the data on trafficking are less a reflection of underlying trading patterns than of where detection resources are put: clearly, if relatively few white people are searched, whites will be under-represented among the population of officially-defined drug-traffickers. Meanwhile, for burglary, robbery, vice, white-collar crime, and even frauds against the European Community, cross-border crimes simply merge into the general statistics of recorded crime.

The fact that *inter*-state crimes cannot be counted and tabulated in the same way as *intra*-state crimes does not mean that nothing can be said about these phenomena. On the contrary, a number of pioneering writers are beginning to piece together information from interviews with offenders, from police and customs sources, and from specialist agencies set up to control serious cross-border offending. Let us now look briefly at some of their findings.

Types of enterprise crime

In discussing serious cross-border offending, much of which takes place under the guise of legitimate business transactions, we shall use the term 'enterprise crime', because the conventional division into 'white-collar' and 'organised' crime (for example, Mack and Kerner 1975) is no longer appropriate, if it ever was. The term 'white-collar crime' may mislead the reader into assuming that business crime is committed only by members of the social elite. Conversely, 'organised crime' conjures up images of unambiguously criminal groups, composed of gangland figures whose practices routinely include the use of violence, extortion and the corruption of officials – personified in Al Capone and the 'Cosa Nostra' (Wolfgang *et al.* 1970; Cressey 1972).

We are not denying that many company fraudsters never commit any other types of crime, or that most drugs dealers, let alone other criminals, have no sophisticated business networks. But the realm of serious cross-border business crime is the place where the activities of 'professional criminals' and 'criminal professionals' increasingly intersect. Groups involved in large-scale drug-smuggling include ostensibly legitimate business people who also help to evade value-added tax, commit subsidies frauds against the European Community, dump toxic waste across or within borders, and evade excise duties on imported or exported goods such as tobacco (from Ireland to England via Holland). Again, armed robbers may operate to a limited extent in other countries, but for them, the main cross-border connection arises should they decide to move their money off-shore (Levi 1991; Van Duyne 1991) and/or flee abroad. Are any of the above groups white-collar criminals sometimes and organised criminals at other times? Such a demarcation has no point, for the crucial empirical question is what range of activities they embark upon and what affects that range of choices.

As a result of their banking secrecy rules, some European countries – Austria, Liechtenstein, Luxembourg and Switzerland – have a well-deserved global reputation for laundering the proceeds of crime (and of conduct that may later be viewed as crime if the Third World government official who is depositing the funds later falls). But it should be remembered that for persons outside Britain, the United Kingdom is an off-shore financial centre, and we too offer many services for foreign criminals. We shall devote special attention to money-laundering later. But looking at other crimes, the main ones with a cross-border component are smuggling (of legal and illegal goods), fraud and drug-trafficking. These can be illustrated with a few concrete examples.

1 Securities fraud

In the United Kingdom, the Financial Services Act 1986 made it illegal to make an unsolicited call to someone who has not requested financial services. Moreover, all people selling investments must be licensed by a state-authorised body, a Self-Regulatory Organisation. However, during the mid and late 1980s, groups of fraudsters – mainly Canadians – set up in Amsterdam and 'cold-called' people in Britain with 'wonderful' investment opportunities that later proved valueless. When the Dutch tightened up their law and enforcement, the fraudsters moved to Belgium.

The above frauds are termed 'boiler-room operations', and all they need is a respectable country and a good telephone system. Likewise, company directors, accountants, surveyors and bankers with inside information about a company's prospects can arrange, using overseas corporations, to purchase or sell that company's shares: the crime of insider-dealing. Of course, such operations, like many other kinds of major business crime (price-fixing cartels, for example), can be carried out within one country as well as internationally. However, using an overseas base (European or not) gives the perpetrators a major advantage in that effective mutual assistance between investigators from different countries is necessary to convict them – an objective difficult to achieve both in law and practice.

2 Toxic waste dumping

A Dutch company paid a Dutch transport company to dump waste containing the dangerous chemical PCB in Belgium. However, before crossing the border, the transporter covered the waste with a thin layer of earth and described the waste as 'loose earth from market gardening'. This was then dumped (more cheaply than if described accurately) in the Belgian site and elsewhere, even more cheaply. Either way, the environment was damaged.

3 European Community fraud

At the simplest, firms are paid subsidies for the production of vast quantities of wine, olives or other products that in reality do not exist. They can produce forms stamped by local officials (who are bribed) testifying to the cultivation of the vineyards or olive groves, but no one checks. In other, more complex cases, export subsidies are obtained on meat which is claimed to be produced for non-EC countries, whereas, in fact, it is either not produced at all, or is produced for home consumption (see, more generally, Tutt 1989). There is a vast amount of fraud, not only against the agricultural funds but also against the development funds of the EC: for example, Mafiosi in the Mezzogiorno simply take money for projects that they do not build, or at best construct with poor-quality materials. Such frauds are not inherently linked to the EC: they can be committed just as easily against domestic governments. However, because of the peculiar nature of its regulatory structure, and the fact that individual states who may not be harmed by fraud against the EC have sole charge over prosecuting it, the EC provides a particularly attractive target. Guesstimates of the extent of EC fraud vary from £2–10 billion, but there seem no valid basis for the calculations.

4 Value-added tax fraud

Here, pending VAT harmonisation within the EC, advantage is taken of differential VAT rates in European countries. Some good examples exist of trade between Northern Ireland and the Republic of Ireland, but a typical European situation is described by Van Duyne (1991) in relation to a Belgian–Dutch team:

Depending on the availability of forged customs stamps and the possibility of profitable disposal in Belgium, there was either a real export or only a transfer of invoices. The profits were realised by evading 25% VAT plus 8% luxury tax on the Belgian side, and 20% VAT on the Dutch side. . . .The same shipments were sometimes used a number of times before they were sold in the open market at a knock-down price. . . .Holland [company] 1 imports and sells to Holland 2, charging 20% VAT. Holland 2 exports (for the same price or at a loss) and reclaims the VAT from the taxman, because VAT is remitted on exports. Holland 1 does not pay the VAT it charged Holland 2. Holland 2 has sold to Belgium 1 and the same game is played, selling to Belgium 2, which exports the same batch back to Holland 1. Holland 1 and Belgium 1 are front companies designed to go bankrupt. In some cases the last act of the dying firm consisted of an ordinary long-firm [bankruptcy] fraud.

Modes of organisation

Although quite a lot is known about the modes of *operation* described above, the haphazard development of criminological research in different parts of Europe has meant that knowledge about the modes of *organisation* of crime remains very patchy. There has always been a tendency to contrast north European forms of criminal organisation with the 'crime corporation' – like structures supposedly existing in North America and southern Italy. For example, Mack and Kerner (1975) seemed to be obsessed with distancing north European crime from American organised crime, implying that if crime is not 'syndicated' (and supported by widespread police corruption), it cannot be 'organised'.

However, more recent work has demonstrated that the situation is by no means so clear-cut. For example, Reuter (1983) has characterised most US cities as having 'disorganised' crime. Equally, Kelly (1986), reviewing articles on organised crime in a number of countries, asserts:

In England there are no criminal syndicates of the size and scope of those in the United States. The reasons for this are mainly economic. Great Britain's legislators and law enforcement officials have recognized the public demand for certain goods and services (gambling and drugs) in a highly administered manner which has taken the market away from criminal organizations that would have developed to fill the gap. Criminals . . . tend to work in small groups but, nonetheless, maintain extensive networks of contacts through which they can procure wider services. . . .

[Sicilian] Mafiosi are not a residue of a state of lawlessness; they are not bandits or outlaws; Mafia groups are not outside the mainstream of social life living on its margins; rather they belong to, and often occupy, prominent positions in a reliable, protective and successful chain of patron-client relationships. . . . Mafiosi resemble local party bosses operating the urban political machines which for votes and support return favors and provide a range of services that the large municipal and state governments are incapable of performing.

From this juxtaposition, we can see the contrasts even within Europe in the forms of criminal organisation. In Italy, the weakness of the central state and peculiar historical characteristics have shaped the form of organised crime there, though even in Sicily 'the' Mafia really takes the form of networks of alliances rather than a line-management national criminal organisation (Arlacchi 1986; Hess 1986; Walston 1986). In Italy, as in many parts of the United States (Chambliss 1978), organised crime groups are linked heavily into the local and national political networks, frequently combining with right-wing political groups. They are involved also in international crime.

Perhaps a more fruitful way of looking at modes of criminal organisation is that adopted by McIntosh (1975), who distinguished them in terms of the technological and policing barriers the particular crime confronts. In short, as policing and prevention strategies improve, organisation shifts from routinised craft groups – such as pickpockets, and even safe-crackers – to looser, perhaps even one-off, alliances between *project* criminals. A further move in the game may be to extend operations across borders. As Levi (1981) points out, since the sixteenth century, bankruptcy ('long firm') fraudsters in particular have found cross-border crime attractive because it creates problems of legal jurisdiction, investigative cost, and practical interest by police, prosecutors and even creditors themselves.

European Community harmonisation does not itself make any difference to this, except in providing new pretexts or 'storylines' for fraudsters to use to get credit or investment, and inasmuch as it changes the structures of control: for example, reducing customs paperwork makes VAT evasion easier. (This will almost certainly become a bigger problem after 1992, when formal customs controls are greatly reduced.)

More recent comparisons between organised crime in America and western Europe (for example, Fijnhaut 1991) have not actually looked at cross-border crime, and even their comments about criminal organisation intra-nationally for different European countries are patchy. The lack of a research base on patterns of criminal relationships in most European countries – including, regrettably, the United Kingdom – means that we have little information about how domestic criminals meet and decide what to do, let alone how and to what effect, or lack of effect, 'Eurocriminals' meet. Major offenders do not advertise their services in the media, and apart from common holidays in Spain, marinas and casinos, such contacts – mediated no doubt by language difficulties – may often be tentative. Most plausible is the notion that Eurocriminals are either crime entrepreneurs who already exploit international trade for the purposes of fraud and/or smuggling, or money-launderers who put their clients in touch with one another.

The above comments, of course, remain substantially in the realm of speculation, and a great deal of research remains to be done. But it must be reiterated that, however important the activities of a few such major criminals, in most European countries almost all crime remains local in character, and is not highly organised in the sense of being conducted under the aegis of a crime syndicate. This does not mean that they are not small-scale 'syndicates' to be found, even involving systematic corruption of police and public officials in areas such as smuggling, toxic waste dumping, fraud, and narcotics distribution. In a sense, except where it is officially tolerated – as cannabis is in the Netherlands – 'service crime' almost requires such corrupt liaisons, for vice has to advertise in order for potential clients to know of its availability. But we ought to be careful in asserting that 'there is organised crime' in country X when all we mean is that some tiny proportion of criminal activity is run by a syndicate.

Crime control and criminal justice policy

Variation and convergence

Perceptions of the 'crime problem' differ between countries, as do ideas about ways to tackle it. This is reflected in differences in the allocation of resources between programmes or agencies, as well as in basic policing and criminal justice policies. As intimated earlier, there are still notable variations across Europe in, for example, crime prevention strategies, sentencing practice, attitudes to prison reform and levels of assistance to victims. On the other hand, the differences seem to be narrowing even in areas without high priority, as a result of increasing discussion and collaboration between government officials at a high level – for example, through meetings arranged by the Council of Europe (such as the Council of Europe 1985) and the United Nations (United Nations 1990). And whereas crime policy has traditionally been a matter of ideological difference between political parties (with, broadly speaking, conservatives favouring 'hard-line' deterrence-based strategies and socialists favouring strategies aimed at changing the social conditions thought to generate crime), there is already more consensus to be found, whatever the political orientation of the national government.

One area in which quite wide differences still exist is in the use of, and attitudes towards, imprisonment. Van Dijk (1991) provides some interesting figures comparing governments' relative expenditure upon different parts of the crime control system. He calculates that, in the mid-1980s, England and Wales were spending almost three times as much (per 100,000 inhabitants) upon prisons as France and considerably more than West Germany, but spending less than either upon police officers. Indeed, the ratio of expenditure on police to expenditure on prisons varied between 13:1 in France to under 3:1 in Sweden. Sweden's low ratio is explained mainly by its commitment to maintaining good conditions in prisons; it has also been a leader in the field of prisoners' rights. (A detailed comparative account of approaches to prisoners' rights in France, Germany and the United Kingdom can be found in Vagg 1991). On the other hand, a similarly high rate of spending on prisons in England and Wales (the police/prisons ratio being 4.5:1) reflects something quite different: one of the highest incarceration rates in Europe, combined with the legacy of a stock of ageing penal institutions in a poor state of repair and exceptionally expensive to staff.

Table 9.2 shows the prison population in most European countries, in relation to their overall population, as at 1 September 1989. It can be seen that the countries making up the United Kingdom led the table by some distance. (It should be noted that, two years later, the prison population in England and Wales had fallen by over 2,000, but even then it was proportionally higher than virtually all others.) Judges in the United Kingdom have traditionally resorted to sentences of imprisonment more readily, and for longer terms, than their counterparts in mainland Europe – a situation difficult to alter, partly because of their selection from a narrow social and professional background, and partly because of their jealous guarding of their constitutional independence, which has made them resistant to government attempts to introduce judicial training or to constrain their discretion (Devlin 1976; Ashworth 1983). They have been particularly harsh in dealing with young adult offenders, the proportion of prisoners under the age of 21 exceeding 20 per cent in England and Wales, compared with, for example, about 11 per cent in France and 7 per cent in Spain (NACRO 1991).

As Table 9.2 also shows, there is no clear relationship between crime rates and rates of imprisonment across the various countries: the Netherlands has a high crime rate and low imprisonment rate, Northern Ireland has the reverse, while in West Germany both rates are high and in Norway both rates are low.

Another important difference in emphasis noted by Van Dijk

Table 9.2   **Prison populations in Europe, 1 September 1989**

Country	Pop. at 14/6/89	Pop. per 100,000 inhabitants	Rank order of crime rates[1]
N. Ireland	1,780	112.8	11th
England & Wales	48,481	96.2	4th
Scotland	4,768	94.0	6th
Luxembourg	345	92.7	
West Germany	51,729	83.8	3rd
Turkey	48,413	83.5	
Portugal	8,458	82.0	
Spain	31,137	80.0	2nd
France	45,102	78.5	4th
Austria	5,771	76.0	
Switzerland	4,714	71.4	10th
Belgium	6,761	68.5	7th
Denmark	3,378	66.0	
Finland	3,103	62.3	9th
Sweden	4,796	57.0	
Ireland	1,980	56.0	
Norway	2,171	54.3	8th
Italy	30,594	54.0	
Greece	4,564	50.0	
Netherlands	6,461	44.6	1st
Iceland	113	44.6	
Cyprus	191	34.1	

Note:
1 Based on 1989 international victim survey (see Table 9.1)
Source: NACRO Briefing, June 1991

(1991) is between countries with a high and a low commitment to crime prevention programmes. Sweden and Denmark, who led the field in this respect, have had National Crime Prevention Councils for nearly twenty years, encouraging and evaluating local projects, stimulating research and collating and disseminating ideas and information (Jensen 1988). More recently, France has set up Prevention Councils at local, regional and national level, and the government has funded an impressive array of projects, involving a wide range of agencies and aimed especially at young people (King 1988).

The Dutch government, too, while deciding against such a council, has tended to put an exceptionally large proportion of its resources into crime prevention projects: in the mid-1980s it was spending nearly 3 per cent of its total crime-related budget on such projects, compared with only 1 per cent in England and Wales. This reflects its consistent policy, since the early 1970s, of seeking alternative crime-control strategies to that of incarcerating offenders: the Dutch were well in advance of other countries in taking seriously research findings which suggested that prison is ineffective as a deterrent or rehabilitative measure, and, in contrast to Britain, their judges have been persuaded to use custody only in the last resort.

In Britain, crime prevention has remained less institutionalised, but private agencies such as Crime Concern have received considerable government support, while research sponsored by the Home Office Crime Prevention Unit is receiving a higher profile than in the past. These developments, together with clear efforts in several countries to enhance the profile of crime prevention, has moved a former head of the Home Office Research and Planning Unit (Tuck 1988) to speak, in somewhat grandiose fashion, of a European-wide move away from the 'carceral' society towards 'a preventive, community-based approach to crime control'.

Whether this trend really signals the beginning of the end of the carceral society, or turns out to represent only the 'latest fashion' in the constant battle to find both cheaper and more effective responses to rising crime rates, remains to be seen. However, what is new is that governments are now watching more closely what is going on in the crime prevention field in other European countries and are reacting more quickly to new ideas. There is now a particularly strong consensus developing about the desirability of reducing prison populations and, in contrast to the lack of interest aroused by Holland's dramatic innovations in this area in the 1970s, the recent success of Germany in reducing its population of young prisoners in particular (Graham 1990) has stimulated plans to emulate it in several other countries.

In addition to increased interest in, and imitation of, other countries' policies, harmonisation is also being encouraged in a more formal way by the promulgation of Conventions, Recommendations and Resolutions by the Council of Europe. These are not binding on member states, and many are 'watered down' when implemented. Nevertheless, they have clearly had some influence on domestic policies in a number of crime-related areas. A good example is policies towards victims of crime, where two important Resolutions and a Convention have helped to stimulate advances in compensation, welfare support and victims' rights in several countries where there was previously virtually no provision (Waller 1988; Maguire and Shapland 1991).

Finally, mention must be made of the influence of the European Court of Human Rights, which, though so far limited to fairly narrow areas, has been of great importance in these areas, as its decisions are binding on national governments. In the field of prisoners' rights, for example, several key decisions have compelled the UK government to amend its policies. These include findings in the early 1980s that both the denial of access by prisoners to solicitors and the censorship of prison mail constituted breaches of the European Convention on Human Rights (Fawcett 1985): as a result, new Standing Orders were introduced, and a substantially different set of attitudes has grown up towards communications between prisoners and the outside world. More recently, the Court has found that parole decisions on the release of 'lifers' should not be taken by government ministers, and the UK government has agreed to cede full powers in this regard to the independent Parole Board.

Cross-border crime control

We turn now to the important question of the regulation of *cross-border* crime within Europe. We must first ask here what is special about Europe? The answer is that, with the exception of crime issues that are affected by the organisation and laws of the European Community, there is nothing special about Europe. Interpol (see below) is not restricted by its borders, and even the Council of Europe has links outside Europe. With the disintegration of Comecon and the transition of all former communist countries to market economies, the boundaries of Europe are once again problematical. It should also be noted that, in some important respects, Britain's common law tradition sets it apart from the other European nations which operate on strictly defined penal codes, and this – plus insular political attitudes which distrust all harmonisation as the 'thin end of the wedge' towards the acceptance of 'inferior' foreign justice – means that Britain finds greater difficulty in cooperating in the criminal justice sphere than do any other western European countries, members of the EC or not.

1. Police cooperation: the 'drugs war' and the legitimation of new tactics

The history of cooperation between European police forces can be traced back to the early nineteenth century, when it was concerned almost exclusively with political control. It continued mainly at an informal and secret level until 1923, when Interpol was created – albeit as a worldwide, not exclusively European agency. Interpol's first objective was to facilitate the exchange of intelligence, although over the years the volume of direct investigative assistance to national police forces increased.

Even so, Interpol has never developed into the powerful and effective international police force that some of its leading members have envisaged (Anderson 1989; Fijnhaut 1991). This is partly because of rivalry and lack of trust and cooperation between police forces in different countries, and partly because of its own internal politics and unwieldy bureaucracy. However, probably more important has been the lack of a totally clear role, combined with overlaps with other international agencies. Where the control of 'subversion', for example, is concerned, its role has always been limited by Article 3 of its constitution, which prohibits 'interference with political or military matters', and has consequently played second fiddle since the

Second World War to the secret intelligence services which mushroomed to meet the 'communist threat'.

A more important overlap is that with the intergovernmental group known as TREVI, which was set up in 1976 to facilitate cooperation to control a marked increase in terrorism (experienced especially in West Germany and Italy), but which has since expanded its role to include other forms of international crime, including drugs- and armssmuggling and armed robbery. In doing so, it has clearly trespassed upon areas squarely within Interpol's original terms of reference. Somewhat ironically, the formation of TREVI had originally been aided by the reluctance of Interpol to trespass beyond its own brief, seeing terrorism as excluded by the above-mentioned Article 3.

Interpol's basic intelligence-sharing role has also been superseded to some extent by more direct forms of bi-lateral or multi-lateral cooperation between police forces, as in agreements allowing 'hot pursuit' across borders between the Benelux countries (Fijnhaut 1991) and in high-level political and judicial, as well as police, planning of joint operations, such as the earlier-mentioned control of Dutch and English football fans in Italy in 1990.

However, perhaps the greatest push towards coordinated policy and operations – including the generation of legal changes and even changes in national policing traditions – has come from the 'war against drugs'. Ever since the elevation of this issue by the Nixon administration to a matter of global importance, the driving force has come from the United States, and, while we are here concerned with the European dimension, this can be properly understood only in the wider context of US foreign policy (Block 1991; Levi 1991).

The influence of the worldwide efforts of the US Drugs Enforcement Agency (DEA) to coordinate the fight against drug-traffickers (initially from South America, but latterly also from the Middle and Far East) has been felt by all European governments. One consequence has been a massive increase in the gathering and exchange of information about people suspected of involvement in the drugs trade. For example, the United Kingdom has set up its own centralised intelligence system (National Drugs Intelligence Unit: the NDIU), which will in turn feed into an increasingly sophisticated – and also recently centralised – European drugs intelligence network. Direct bilateral exchanges of information, as well as through Interpol and TREVI, are also becoming routine.

A second, increasingly controversial, consequence of the American-led push against drug-trafficking has been the employment – and gradual acceptance – of various forms of covert policing, now commonplace in the United States (Marx 1988), but traditionally alien in many European countries. These include wire-tapping, bugging, and the use of other sophisticated listening and recording devices, as well as deceptions by undercover agents such as 'bust-buy' and 'sting' operations. Some countries initially encouraged their police, customs and other enforcement agencies to expand their range of tactics in these directions, accepting the argument that sophisticated criminals can only be caught by sophisticated methods. Where the tactics were illegal, special legislation was sometimes introduced to legitimise them. However, as lawyers and civil-rights activists have begun to question their propriety and legality, and a number of associated scandals have emerged, there has been something of a counter-trend to place clear limits on their use. For instance in 1990 Belgium specified (albeit in unpublished government directives), that undercover policing can be used only in relation to offences of a certain level of seriousness and only when the goals cannot be achieved through other methods (Outrive and Cappelle 1991). Several countries have also sought to tighten controls on the use of wire-taps and have defined certain forms of sting operation as entrapment (Tollborg 1991).

However, even if (as is doubtful in such secret areas) controls of this kind are effective curbs on overenthusiasm by national police forces, it has to be remembered that under the Schengen agreement it has become increasingly easy for police forces and other agencies to operate in foreign countries, where they are not subject to the same regulation.

As important as, if not more important than, the spread of unconventional covert tactics in intelligence-gathering and investigation, has been the pressure for harmonisation of crime *policies*. This can be well illustrated in the Netherlands, which, as described earlier, has traditionally adopted a very liberal policy towards drug use, treating it essentially as a health, rather than crime, problem. Despite this, and despite the existence of strong support, even among senior police officers and government officials, for the gradual legalisation of drug use, the Dutch government has had little alternative to the adoption of a hard-line deterrent approach in relation to trafficking and sale. This has resulted in a somewhat schizophrenic policy, whereby one can openly buy and legally consume marijuana in Amsterdam, and heroin or cocaine addicts and small-time dealers are rarely pursued by the police, but at the same time the importation or manufacture of all kinds of drugs are subject to intensive policing and heavy penalties. Moreover, as 1992 approaches, the Netherlands is increasingly perceived by less liberal governments as a 'weak spot' in Europe's defences against the drugs trade, and groups supporting the current Dutch approach fear that their government will capitulate to foreign pressure and revert to more repressive policies (Mol 1991). There were signs of this in June 1991, when the Dutch Ministry of Justice announced that it was reconsidering its policy of decriminalisation of marijuana use in the light of the problem of 'drugs tourism' to Amsterdam, particularly by young people from Germany – an issue causing considerable concern in the German newspapers.

2. Money-laundering

Another area in which there is a strong trend towards harmonisation concerns the movement of money between countries, especially where this constitutes the 'laundering' of funds accumulated through crime. The regulation of international securities trading, like that of drugs-trafficking, tends to be conducted on a global basis, driven once again by US interests and passions for extra-territorial control. Even so, there are *some* – frequently overlapping – crime-control initiatives that emerge out of specifically European bodies, principally the Council of Europe and the EC. How, readers may ask, can we include the EC here, since it has no constitutional competence in criminal matters? The answer to this is that the EC's responsibility for ensuring harmonisation and free trade in the economic sphere has given it a lever to regulate financial institutions in respect of insider-trading, money-laundering, anti-competitive practices, and – ironically, least cogent in enforcement – frauds against the Community funds.

(*a*) *The European Community Directive on Money-Laundering.*
Criminal law matters are normally an issue reserved to member governments individually: they are not within the legal competence – in the technical rather than efficiency sense – of the Community as a whole. However, in the interests of developing a single European market in financial matters, the United Kingdom and other EC countries have agreed to treat attempts to combat money-laundering as being within the competence of the Community. The preamble to the Council Directive on Prevention of Use of the Financial System for the Purpose of Money Laundering of 31 May 1991 seeks to justify this competence by noting, *inter alia*, that:

When credit and financial institutions are used to launder proceeds from criminal activities . . . the soundness and stability of the institution concerned and confidence in the financial system as a whole could be seriously jeopard-ized, thereby losing the trust of the public.

When the Single Banking Licence comes into effect, it will no longer be possible for a member state of the EC to refuse a licence to a bank which has been given a licence in another member state. The costs of financial supervision in the money-laundering arena are very high, and if some countries act vigorously while others do not, this will distort competition between the member states. Consequently, some countries would enjoy unfair advantages over others: because laundering money gives banks extra profits, it is to the financial and social detriment of the country suffering from the crime whose proceeds are being laundered.

In the same way that the importance of 'crime prevention' can be used to justify almost any action by the police in interfering with the rights of citizens, this involvement in regulating money-laundering, together with the development of anti-drug initiatives described above, could become the 'thin end of the wedge' for Community interference in domestic criminal justice issues. This is because more major crime involves putting money into financial institutions at some stage (see, further, Levi 1991). Potentially, the ambit of money-laundering rules is very wide: Article 1 of the European Community Directive defines it – if 'define' is the appropriate word – *inter alia*, as the intentional

conversion or transfer of property, knowing that such property is derived from criminal activity or from an act of participation in such activity, for the purpose of concealing or disguising the illicit origin of the property or of assisting any person who is involved in the commission of such activity to evade the legal consequences of his action.

Except in so far as it will always include the proceeds of drug-trafficking, the definition of what criminal activities are to be covered by the Directive remains unresolved, with some countries currently wishing to restrict it to drug-trafficking and others to any other offences regarded as serious by the member states. There has been a gradual narrowing of its scope from all 'serious crime' to drug-trafficking and 'any other criminal activity designated as such for the purposes of this Directive by each Member State'. This reflects the wish of some countries to limit the degree of responsibility falling upon them for regulating the consequences of misconduct that does not occur within their own criminal jurisdiction.

Article 10 sets up (slightly ambiguously) the fabric of increased inter-agency cooperation by requiring that

Member States shall ensure that if, in the course of inspections carried out in credit or financial institutions by the competent authorities, or in any other way, those authorities discover facts that could constitute evidence of money laundering, they inform the authorities responsible for combating money laundering.

Will this apply to information coming into the possession of the Inland Revenue, which might be relevant to other agencies? In keeping with the 'crime prevention' approach discussed above, Article 11 requires all institutions to establish adequate procedures of internal control and communication 'to forestall and prevent operations related to money-laundering' and 'these measures shall include participation of their relevant employees in special training programmes to help them recognise operations that may be related to money-laundering as well as to instruct them as to how to proceed in such cases'. So what formerly was a largely private-sector matter has become a matter of public interest which is regulated by the criminal law.

(*b*) *The Council of Europe Convention on Laundering, Search, Seizure and Confiscation of the Proceeds of Crime.* The Council of Europe also has produced a Convention, signed (8 November 1990) by Belgium, Cyprus, Denmark, Germany, Iceland, Italy, Netherlands, Norway, Portugal, Spain, Sweden, and the United Kingdom, in relation to laundering, seizure and confiscation. Four other states – Finland, France, Ireland and Switzerland – declared officially that they would sign the Convention 'at an early date'. In addition to the twenty-five Council of Europe member states, the Convention is open for signature to Australia, Canada and the United States. Unlike the EC Directive, money-laundering is not restricted to drug-trafficking. There is no space here for detailed discussion of its provisions – see Levi (1991) – but Article 4 of the Convention provides that

Each Party shall adopt such legislative measures . . . to empower its courts . . . to order that bank, financial or commercial records be made available or to be seized in order to carry out [investigations, searches, seizures and confiscation]. A Party shall not decline to act under the provisions of this article on the grounds of bank secrecy.

So bank secrecy should not, at national level, present an obstacle to the carrying out of investigations, provisional measures and forfeitures in relation to the proceeds of crime.

There are several provisions to enhance mutual legal assistance in the seizing, freezing and confiscation of the proceeds of crime in Europe. The moral and political pressure is so great that it is hard for countries to resist agreement. How the formal rules work out in practice is another question. It should be noted, however, that if a regulatory 'level playing field' is to exist at a substantive rather than merely at a formal, symbolic level, more attention will have to be given by regulators to rule compliance if competitive under-enforcement is not to undermine the effect of these developing rules. This indeed is the rationale given by the European Commission for their intervention in money-laundering. However, international bodies are normally rather poor at evaluating rigorously the implementation of what they do.

Concluding remarks: harmonisation and the problems of regulation

The extent to which European 'harmonisation' is occurring in crime-related areas is a complex question. On the one hand, many aspects of the systems designed to combat crime bear witness to their piecemeal growth over the centuries, with major variations *within* countries, let alone between them. Policing remains primarily a local rather than national responsibility; sentencing is characterised by considerable individual discretion; the philosophy of imprisonment and attitudes to prisoners' rights vary widely across Europe (Vagg 1991); and strategic approaches to the prevention and control of individual forms of deviant behaviour show some striking contrasts – none more so than those concerned with soft drugs (compare the

Netherlands with Germany, or cities within Germany). More fundamentally, one can contrast the adversarial basis of the British system of criminal law with the inquisitional systems found on the Continent. The role of prosecutors in investigations has always been marginal in England and Wales compared with other countries, including Scotland – a situation obtaining even after the introduction of the independent Crown Prosecution Service in the mid-1980s. Priorities and strategies are still determined largely by the police.

On the other hand, while certain parts of the criminal justice system cling firmly to their own tradition, and although crime control is not formally in the province of the EC, the pressures towards homogeneity are clearly to be seen. These pressures may take the form of resolutions or recommendations from the Council of Europe, or, occasionally, opinions from the European Commission on Human Rights. If member states wish to oppose them, they can, if necessary, make use of the absence of crime policy from the Treaty of Rome to justify the assertion of individual states' rights and thus retention of the status quo. By contrast, where the issues are seen by most member states as urgent or important, the lack of a clear mandate in EC constitutional terms has not held back the harmonisation process. Europe-wide policies in relation to serious cross-border crime have been smuggled in through convenient back doors, as with the money-laundering initiatives described earlier, or through bi-lateral or multi-lateral agreements such as the Schengen Accord, or through the creation of new organisations such as TREVI and the recently-formed European drugs intelligence unit.

The latest 'crime'-related issue to be regarded by some member states – prominently, in this case, by the United Kingdom – as important enough to warrant special measures, is that of immigration, both legal and illegal. In June 1991, the British Prime Minister called for 'much greater collaboration between Europe's police forces to contain the flow of immigrants', and proposed a study of new procedures for cross-border policing, to be submitted to the European Council in 1992 (*Guardian*, 29 June 1991). However, he opposed a paper delivered at the same time by the German Chancellor, who proposed a European federal police force on the lines of the FBI. Police collaboration, Mr Major argued, should be 'inter-governmental, not supranational' (*ibid.*). This debate was linked to Britain's previous reluctance to sign the Schengen Accord, under which border controls on movements of EC nationals are waived. It was hinted that if a 'strong perimeter fence' against both legal and illegal immigration could be established, the United Kingdom might be willing to change its opposition to Schengen. The possibility of the introduction of identity cards is another thorny political issue underlying some of these negotiations.

To conclude, a fundamental point of concern about many of the developments in cross-border policing and crime control discussed in this article is that they have occurred quickly, without much public debate, and the resulting operations have been (to some extent necessarily) shrouded in secrecy. Legal and other forms of local control over actions of police, customs and other enforcement agencies have been eroded, the justification being the seriousness and the international dimension of the problems. There has been little serious discussion of what forms of behaviour actually merit drastic responses: if football hooliganism, for example, warrants massive surveillance, restrictions of movement, summary deportations, and so on, what other kinds of deviance may be subjected to such measures in the future? Above all, little thought has been given to effective international mechanisms of accountability to prevent abuses by the authorities, especially by supranational bodies. Some protection is given by the European Convention on Human Rights – the European Court has, for example, pronounced on the subject of the acceptable limits of telephone-tapping – but, considering that cases can take many years to reach the Court, this alone is scarcely an adequate safeguard in the rapidly-changing circumstances of international crime control.

References

Anderson, M. (1989) *Policing the World*, Oxford: Oxford University Press.

Arlacchi, P. (1986) *Mafia Business: the Mafia Ethic and the Spirit of Capitalism*, London: Verso.

Armstrong, G., Hobbs, O. and Maguire, M. (1991) 'The professional foul, covert policing in Britain: the case of soccer', Paper to Law & Society Association International Conference, Amsterdam 26–29 June.

Ashworth, A. (1983) *Sentencing and Penal Policy*. London: Weidenfeld & Nicholson.

Balvig, F. (1987) *The Snow White Image*, Oxford: Oxford University Press.

Block, A. (ed.) (1991) *Crime, Law and Social Change* 16 (1) (July 1991) special issue on the Politics of Cocaine.

Chambliss, W. (1978) *On the Take: from Petty Crooks to Presidents*, Bloomington, Indiana University Press.

Clinard, M. (1978) *Cities with Little Crime*, Cambridge: Cambridge University Press.

Council of Europe (1985) *Resarch on Victimisation*. Collected Studies in Criminological Research, vol. XXIII, Strasbourg: European Committee on Crime Problems.

Cressey, D. (1972) *Criminal Organisation*, London: Heinemann.

Devlin, Lord (1976) *The Judge*, Oxford: Oxford University Press.

Fawcett, J. (1985) 'Applications of the European Convention on Human Rights', in M. Maguire, J. Vagg and R. Morgan (eds) *Accountability and Prisons: Opening Up a Closed World*, London: Tavistock.

Fijnhaut, C. (1991) 'Police Co-operation within Western Europe', in F. Heidensohn and M. Farrell (eds), *Crime in Europe*, London: Routledge.

Graham, J. (1990) 'Decarceration in the Federal Republic of Germany; how

188   *Responding Social Institutions*

practitioners are succeeding where policy-makers have failed', *British Journal of Criminology*, 30 (2) (Spring): 150–70.

Heidensohn, F. and Farrell, M. (eds) (1991) *Crime in Europe*, London: Routledge.

Hess, H. (1986) 'The traditional Sicilian Mafia: organised crime and repressive crime', in R. Kelly (ed.) *Organised Crime: a Global Perspective*, Rowman & Littlefield, Totowa, New Jersey.

Home Office (1988) *Research Bulletin*, Special European ed, London: Home Office Research and Planning Unit.

Hood, R. (ed.) (1989) *Crime and Criminal Policy in Europe: Proceedings of a European Colloquium*, Oxford: Oxford University Centre for Criminological Research.

Jensen, L. (1988) 'Crime prevention in Denmark', in Home Office, *Research Bulletin*, Special European edn, London: Home Office.

Kelly, R. (ed.) (1986) *Organised Crime: a Global Perspective*, Totowa, New Jersey: Rowman & Littlefield.

King, M. (1988) 'Crime prevention in France', in Home Office, *Research Bulletin*, Special European edn, London: Home Office.

Levi, M. (1981) *The Phantom Capitalists: the Organisations and Control of Long Firm Fraud*, London: Heinemann.

——(1991) *Customer Confidentiality, Money-Laundering and Police – Bank Relationships*, London: Police Federation.

McIntosh, M. (1975) *The Organisation of Crime*, London: Macmillan.

Mack, J. and Kerner, H-J. (1975) *The Crime Industry*, Farnborough: Saxon House.

Maguire, M. (1982) *Burglary in a Dwelling: the Offence, the Offender and the Victim*, London: Heinemann.

——and Shapland, J. (1991) 'The "Victims' Movement" in Europe', in A. Lurigio, W. Skogan & R. Davis (eds) *Victims of Crime: Problems, Policies and Programs*, Newbury Park, California: Sage.

Marx, G. (1988) *Undercover: Police Surveillance in America*, Berkeley, CA: University of California Press.

Mawby, R. (1979) *Policing the City*, Aldershot: Gower.

Mol, R. (1991) 'The liberal image of the Dutch drug policy', *International Journal on Drug Policy*, 2 (5): 16–20.

NACRO (1991) *Imprisonment in Western Europe: Some Facts and Figures*, NACRO Briefing No. 25, London: National Association for the Care and Resettlement of Offenders.

Outrive, L. and Cappelle, J. (1991) 'Twenty years of undercover policing in Belgium: the regulation of a risky police practice', Paper to Law & Society International Conference, Amsterdam 26–29 June.

Reuter, P. (1983) *Disorganised Crime: the Economics of the Visible Hand*, Cambridge, Mass: MIT Press.

Rock, P. (ed.) (1990) *A History of British Criminology*, Special issue of *The British Journal of Criminology*, 28 (2) (Spring 1988).

Taylor, I., Walton, P. and Young, J. (1973) *The New Criminology: for a Social Theory of Deviance*, London: Routledge & Kegan Paul.

Tollborg, D. (1991) 'Covert policing in Sweden: the Swedish Secret Service', Paper to Law & Society International Conference, Amsterdam (26–29 June).

Tuck, M. (1988) 'Crime prevention: a shift in concept', in Home Office, *Research Bulletin*, Special European edn, London: Home Office.

Tutt, N. (1989) *Europe on the Fiddle*, London: Croom Helm.

United Nations (1990) *Crime Prevention and Criminal Justice Newsletter* Special Issue on the Eighth UN Congress on the Prevention of Crime and the Treatment of Offenders. Vienna: United Nations Office.

Vagg, J. (1991) 'A touch of discipline: accountability and discipline in prison systems in western Europe', in F. Heidensohn and M. Farrell (eds) *Crime in Europe*, London: Routledge.

Van Dijk, J. (1991) 'More than a matter of security: trends in crime prevention in Europe', in F. Heidensohn and M. Farrell (eds) *Crime in Europe*, London: Routledge.

——Mayhew, P. and Killiag, M. (1990) *Experiences with Crime across the World: Results of the 1989 International Telephone Survey*, The Hague: Kluwer.

Van Duyne, P. (forthcoming) 'Organised crime and business crime enterprises in the Netherlands', (1991) in *Crime, Law and Social Change*

VLOS (1989) *Guidelines for Victim Support in Europe: Report of the First European Conference of Victim Support Workers*, Eerbeek (Dec: 1987), Utrecht: Vereniging Landelijke Organisatie Slachtofferhulp.

Waller, I. (1988) 'International standards, national trail blazing, and the next steps', in M. Maguire and J. Pointing (eds) *Victims of Crime: A New Deal?* Milton Keynes: Open University Press.

Walston, J. (1986) 'See Naples and die: organised crime in Campania', in R. Kelly (ed.) *Organised Crime: a Global Perspective*, Rowman and Littlefield: Totowa, New Jersey.

Williams, J. (1989) *Hooligans Abroad*, London: Routledge.

Wolfgang, M. E., Savitz, L. and Johnston, N. (eds) (1970) *The Sociology of Crime and Delinquency*, New York: Wiley & Sons.

CHAPTER 10

From AIDS to Alzheimer's: policy and politics in setting new health agendas

BRIDGET TOWERS

This is an interesting time for sociologists to be studying the changes that are being wrought in the design and operation of health-care services in Europe. Assumptions about core concepts of 'health', 'illness', 'disease', 'medicine', 'care' and 'therapeusis' are being challenged, not just in the academic domain but also in the public forums of the media, the legislatures, political parties, trade unions and professional associations. Health issues are now high on the agendas of economists and accountants as they try to construct new measurements and forecasts for regulating the demand and supply of a major item of public spending. Health care is now a growing specialism within management as the organisational parameters of medical goods and services have become widened and bureaucratised. Political scientists and policy analysts are using questions of health-care decision-making to monitor and evaluate changes in power relationships between the central state and local organisations. Feminists have centred a large part of their critique of patriarchy upon scientific medicine's appropriation of their bodies, their selves and their knowledge. Even within the community of professional sociologists we can note the rapid expansion of 'medical sociology' as a legitimate and funded field of expertise.

In such a context perhaps one of the most useful contributions a sociological perspective can make is to do what we have always been best at and most unpopular for; namely, to stand back and study the process of the construction of the 'object'. In this case we can chart the making of a new 'discourse community' around health. In a rather obvious way it is about looking at who is sitting around what table, where, using what kinds of language and knowledge claims when something called a 'health issue' is on the agenda for discussion.

There is no shortage of detailed descriptive material on the present changes and developments in health-care policy in Europe, and it is not such a hard task to assemble charts and tables of comparative epidemiological data, per capita health-spending, ratios of health-sector funding, medical manpower or even consultation and referral rates. The OECD reports, *Measuring Health Care, 1960–83* (1985) and *Financing and Delivering Health Care* (1987), together with the WHO report on the European Region's health situation, *Evaluation of the Strategy for Health for All by the Year 2000* (1986) and its forthcoming update provide comprehensive data bases for such an exercise. The purpose, however, of this chapter is to explore critically only some of these developments and to see if a specifically sociological mode of analysis can yield any further understandings.

Health for all

Probably the most accessible starting point for considering the current trends and developments in health-care policy in Europe is the World Health Assembly's global strategy of 'Health for All by the Year 2000'. The strategy was built out of the Alma-Ata declaration of 1977 which located 'primary health care' as the bedrock of all future health-care planning. The strategic task was to ensure that by the year 2000 'all the people in all the countries should have at least such a level of health that they are capable of working productively and of participating actively in the social life of the community in which they live.'

The main objectives of the strategy were to promote healthy life-styles, to prevent preventable conditions, and to enable rehabilitation of those whose health has been impaired (Ashton 1990). In the language of WHO-speak, these millenarial objectives were clarified into the 'health goals' of health prevention and health promotion, and further focused by the European Regional Office into thirty-eight 'targets' accepted by all member states to be achieved by the year 2000.[1] These targets cover a wide range of conditions and activities, specifying particular levels of reduction in mortality rates from heart disease, lung and cervical cancer, infant and maternal mortality, and road traffic accidents; also included are reductions in life-style risk factors such as alcohol and tobacco consumption. However, the major emphasis within the targets is the reorientation of medical care towards health promotion, prevention and primary health care and its bearing on the need for community participation and inter-sectoral cooperation. Health-care planners distinguish between primary, secondary and tertiary models of medical care provision, in terms of emphasis upon specialist hospital, general hospital, and outpatient- or community-based treatment services.

There is a significant difference between the medical concept of 'primary *medical* care', which is individualistic in terms of the patient/practitioner treatment-specific base, and 'primary *health* care', which is a social concept involving a wide range of health providers in addition to medical personnel and focused upon whole communities and their general health status (Ashton 1990).

Whilst it has to be acknowledged that global policy objectives often command only lip-service application in collaborating countries, and that there are wide variations in the enthusiasm, manner, form and comprehensiveness with which they are implemented at the national level, nevertheless it is clear that there has been a radical shift in the direction of health-care planning. Up until the mid-1970s it had been assumed that the best model to be pursued was a specialist/hospital-based medical service and that the task of governments was to focus upon increasing access and utilisation.

In trying to account for this change it is tempting to have recourse to arguments of economic determinism. By the early 1970s health-care costs were presenting major problems for all European countries, regardless of the structure of their health services or methods of financing them, and in the context of what was called the 'fiscal crisis', redirecting spending from other public sectors was not an option that was believed to be available. Additionally, it was clear that the technological developments in treatment methods entailed a massive increase in future costs, together with a changed demographic profile that indicated a new heavy demand for medical care from the elderly. Whilst it is correct to say that the economic conditions provided the basic operational constraints, these were mediated by political and ideological factors which led to the selection of particular policy choices and the rejection of others.

Early responses to this concern over predicted increasing expenditure were focused upon policies of cost containment which involved, among other things, restrictions on the training and supply of medical manpower, limiting the purchasing power of providers of health care and restricting capital expenditure on high technology. This type of policy was still rooted in the model of equating good health care with the consumption of medical goods and services. The shift away from this way of thinking was influenced partly by the opposition of the medical profession to any attack upon their autonomy and their resistance to implementing policy, and also partly by the recognition that cost containment was an inadequate basis for long-term planning in so far as it was purely reactive. In the multi-national context of pharmaceutical companies and medical technology, price controls at the national level were inoperable, and so a major component of the increasing expenditure remained uncontrollable.

There is a paradox here, in that traditional accounts of historical changes in health policy have attributed the central role to developments in medical knowledge; that is, that the history of medical care can be seen as therapeutically led. This interpretation is no longer seen as adequate (Wright and Treacher 1982). And yet it appears that it was the new medical knowledge and practices which posed the financial problems even before the recession deepened.

The challenge to the legitimacy of this therapeutic optimism was already under way in the late 1960s from a variety of academic studies on psychiatry, public health and chronic disability which questioned both the efficacy of medically-based care and also its monopoly of the knowledge field. Taking a broad historical sweep, Thomas McKeown argued persuasively that improvements in health status could not be attributed to curative medicine and that personal behavioural and environmental changes were the key to past and future advances in health (McKeown 1976). These ideas were taken up and endorsed in Canada in the Lalonde Report 'A new perspective on the health of Canadians' (1974); probably the first modern community diagnosis, it stressed the primacy of preventive health care at the national level. It set an agenda for a new era of health policy in Canada and had a direct influence on the formulation of the WHO strategy.

The Lalonde Report was a powerful weapon for governments in their confrontation with medical establishments. As Jane Lewis has argued, it implied that 'if expansion of the health care system could not have much impact on mortality and morbidity, then neither could curtailing its growth' (Lewis 1987). Indeed, the very likelihood that a relatively small increase in expenditure on the public-health sector would result in a saving on total health-care costs made it a compelling option for European countries similarly placed with demands from high medical-care spenders.

Health-care systems

Although it is possible to identify this broad consensus of policy shift, we need to be aware of the differences between countries not only in terms of their health-care spending but also of where 'health' is situated in their wider social policy traditions and welfare systems. In Europe we find a diversity of patterns of origins and forms of health-care systems, and earlier forms established before the 1939–45 war have sometimes remained in central European countries as a legacy of an infrastructure despite changes in their geo-political boundaries and ideologies (Hellberg 1987).

There have been a number of attempts to categorise the European systems of health care, most of them drawing upon existing developmental and political classifications (Roemer and Roemer 1981; Maxwell 1980; Pyle 1979), and whilst they do generate clarity out of diversity, we should be mindful of the dangers in constructing rigid typologies and categories which iron out the overlaps and ambiguities that are so often the very substance of a system that is in a state of change. For instance, Pyle's (1979) five-fold classification of types of health-care systems – (1) free enterprise; (2) welfare state; (3) socialist; (4) transitional; (5) underdeveloped – fails to allow for the changing direction towards internal markets and privatisation within welfare state and socialist types.

Another approach is to construct a matrix of economic and political systems, which has been done by Roemer (1977). This identifies the importance of the degree of centralisation of decision-making in the

194   *Responding Social Institutions*

political apparatus of the state, and how within welfare states we can identify a spectrum from centralised to provincial to localised district structures. This allows us to make comparisons between the Scandinavian countries and Britain, which share the general characterisation of a welfare-state model of health care; it also allows for a more detailed consideration of the differences between the various eastern European socialist systems.

Babson (1972) focuses specifically upon the degree of centralised control of health services as a critical factor for comparison within Europe. He makes a four-fold classification: (1) the Scandinavian systems (Denmark, Finland, Norway and Sweden), typified by high levels of local autonomy; (2) the eastern European systems (USSR, Poland, Hungary and East Germany), which have a high level of centralised control and ownership; (3) the central European systems (Austria, Germany and Switzerland), which have provincial and regional decentralisation; and (4) the Latin–Benelux countries (Italy, Belgium, France and the Netherlands), which have great diversity of controls and ownership within different sectors.

There is a considerable difference, however, between a country which has historically built up a pattern of health care based upon a conscious policy of decentralisation and democratic decision-making, and countries such as Greece, Portugal and Spain where an historical legacy of inaction or political conflict has led to separatism or neglect of rural health services. Unless we take into account the methods of financing health care, it is easy to assume that decentralisation is a 'good thing' in that it allows for a more sensitive response to local 'need'. Decentralisation of decision-making may be simply the political rhetoric which justifies reductions in central government funding; and placing the responsibility for revenue-raising as well as budgetary management at the local level can lead to a decline in health-care provision, as has been painfully found to be the case recently in Poland, Hungary and the USSR.

Another axis for comparing health-care systems in Europe is their method of financing. All countries have some level of central exchequer funding of health care, but there are variations in where, when, to whom and for what these moneys are actually paid. Broadly, we can distinguish between countries which finance their health services mainly out of collective taxation (the United Kingdom, eastern Europe); those which are based on state-run health-insurance funds (Germany, Sweden, Norway, Denmark, Belgium); those based on a combination of private and state-run insurance (Ireland, France, Switzerland); and those based wholly on private insurance schemes (Greece, Austria, the Netherlands). In all countries there is some state regulatory control of insurance.

There is a wide literature on the complexities and mechanisms of health-care financing. A non-technical rehearsal of the debates is to be found in Binns and Firth (1988).

It is the method of financing which has been traditionally identified as a critical factor in explaining inequities in access and utilization of medical care. However, whilst studies in Switzerland would appear to confirm that insurance-based schemes result in health inequalities amongst poor and disadvantaged groups (Egger, Minder and Smith 1990), the evidence from the United Kingdom would suggest that the same pattern results even when a national health service operates (Townsend and Whitehead 1988). More complex models of explanation and redress (Phillips and Joseph 1984) are now being sought to deal with what is perceived as a major failure of the health-care system in the Netherlands to reach urban minority groups (WHO 1986). It is now recognised that the dynamics of individual health practitioner/patient consultations are mediated by a broad context of discriminatory attitudes and practices running through a wide spectrum of social institutions and not just limited to a cash nexus (Klein 1989; Defever 1990).

Much has been written about a new convergence of patterns of health and welfare provision, and whereas there are clearly discernible trends in the main economic determinants, there is wide diversity in the realised practice. Nobody constructing policy, unless they are an ideologial zealot or scenario-constructing academic can start from Year Zero. We ignore to our peril, or convenience, 'schemes on the ground' (SOGs), which are constructed and realised out of the messy business of trying to reconcile new programmes with past practices, existing buildings and real people who have to turn up for work on Day 1 of 'the new policy' with their everyday routines still intact.

Participant observer studies can be an important counterweight to some of the grandiose WHO reports given by member states on their radical restructuring of health care. A practitioner on an observation visit to the Soviet Union last year gives this account of the Moscow Accident and Emergency Service; 'Paramedics we accompanied on urban ambulance runs were rationed two to three reusable hypodermic needles and one syringe, necessitating mixing of medications before infusing. This practice is apparently common, judging from wall charts of miscible medications we saw on hospital walls' (Schultz and Rafferty 1990).

This is something that organisational analysts and health managers have begun to give attention to in their newly claimed knowledge field of the 'management of change'. But there is a considerable difference between the potentially controllable interests and concerns of health-care organisations and the worlds of service users. In Britain we are familiar with the length of time it took, sometimes generations, before service users stopped seeing the Poor Law ethic as implicit in their engagement with any public health and welfare service. So we should be mindful when we appraise a change in health policy and philosophy as to what its perceived implications are for service users. Not only is there often an information gap on what the changes are, but they may also be perceived purely in terms of the financial bite of increased insurance contributions and higher additional charges of goods and services. In Poland an attempt to build a direct line of communication with service users is found in a requirement that all local sector managers hold weekly complaints surgeries.

Cultural contexts

The material so far has been concerned with structures and policies, but medicine is also a culturally based ideology and practice, and despite its claims for a 'scientific' knowledge status it involves values and beliefs. How that involvement of culture with medicine can be theoretically explained and empirically validated is best approached by considering health-care systems as cultural systems (Fabrega 1973). Like other cultural systems, it is a symbolic system built out of meanings, values and behavioural norms. Being ill in a foreign country can make us acutely aware that there is no neutral, 'transcendent', scientific medical care. We know that the experience of sickness leads often to a need for security, familiarity and stability for recovery to take place.

In her comparative study of the influence of culture on medical practice in France, Germany and England, Lynn Payer (1989) attributes differences in the style, methods and forms of diagnosis and treatment to differences in national cultural epistemologies. She argues that French medicine is characterised by Cartesian thought and is reflected in the specific cultural concept of the 'terrain'; German medicine, by the influence of Romanticism and the concepts of synthesis and *Gestalt*; whilst English medicine is seen as rooted in empiricism and parsimony. Her evidence is illustrative and often anecdotal, but her approach provides an interpretative framework for variations in such things as surgical practice, radiography, diagnostic tests and prescribing practices. A particularly interesting link is made with these different intellectual traditions and doctors' responses to treatment evaluation based on preference for experimental (Germany), theoretical (France) or controlled trial (England) research methods. One might hypothesise that the failure to make a definition of 'brain death' in Denmark is similarly rooted in a national philosophical tradition.

Arthur Kleinman succinctly captures the comprehensiveness of this relationship between culture and medicine:

The health care system articulates illness as a cultural idiom, linking beliefs about disease causation, the experience of symptoms, specific patterns of illness behaviour, decisions concerning treatment alternatives, actual therapeutic practices and evaluations of treatment outcomes. Thus it establishes systematic relationships between these components.

(Kleinman 1986)

It is therefore not surprising that when health-education programmes target particular health-risk life-styles, they reflect the
different cultural values given to 'health' and 'risk'. This can be seen
in the comparison between the alcohol campaigns of France, the
Netherlands and the Soviet Union. France launched a health-based
campaign focused on alcohol-related disease. The Netherlands
focused upon the social costs of fractured lives and emphasised social
and collective responsibility; whilst the Soviet Union went for a
straight link between alcohol and social disorganisation in terms of
crime and lost production (Ivanets and Lukomskaya 1990).

Preventive policies

Health education is an important part of the package of the new
primary health care; it is linked to a philosophy which stresses
'individual responsibility' for one's own health. Many countries have
directly embodied this philosophy in their prologues to their health-
policy statements. The Danish statement clearly asserts, 'in the years
to come, health policy will aim, *inter alia*, at increasing recognition by
individuals of their responsibility for their own health' (WHO 1986).
In the 1984 legislation on patients' rights in the Netherlands, the
relationship between the rights of patients and the individual's
responsibility for his/her own health was fundamental. There is a long
history of health education in Europe, going back to the mobilising
role of the American-led League of Red Cross Societies and the
Rockefeller Mission to Europe during the First World War and in the
early 1920s, when it changed from being part of the package of
tuberculosis-control measures to a more general, healthy life-style
promotion. It was always an area of political sensitivity, and the
American dominance of both styles and materials led to cultural
misunderstandings, particularly in France (Towers 1987). Similar
conflicts are to be found in the present AIDS campaigns, although
this time there is less American dominance of both finance and
materials.

Health education is an interesting area of health policy despite its
low status in medical hierarchies of legitimacy. It commands support,
albeit sometimes sceptical, from all countries, as it is both a cheap
form of health care and has a high profile of visibility. It serves
perhaps the primary function of promoting the state's own commitment to health without necessarily entailing any follow-up expenditure. There is the additional attraction that it is an activity which can
be jointly funded by other public-service departments and voluntary
bodies. However, in Scandinavia there is an increasing scepticism of
its efficacy, and in Finland and Sweden there is a move towards more
formal methods of evaluating large-scale education campaigns.

In efforts to bypass even the expense of health education, some countries have simply introduced statutory controls to limit health-risk behaviours. Most of the eastern European countries as well as Italy, Norway and Finland have imposed total bans on all forms of cigarette promotion. Alcohol consumption can be similarly more cheaply controlled by statutory regulation of the supply or through tough fiscal measures. Drug dependency is also increasingly being tackled by focusing upon the supply and penalising providers, a policy which does not incur health-care costs of users, and effectively sheds this area of concern from the health domain. This is a marked change from the mid-seventies, when treatment and rehabilitation of drug related offenders was claimed as a health province.

There is a long tradition of coercive public-health powers in Europe rooted in the medical policing of infectious diseases (Towers 1980). Compulsory notification, isolation and treatment were the favoured measures in most countries' response to venereal disease and tuberculosis. At the Health Committee of the League of Nations during the inter-war years the case for compulsory powers was vigorously advanced, and many of the same arguments have been revitalised in formulating new public-health policies for AIDS.

Another element in the new health policies is the expansion of health-screening as a tool of preventive medicine. Again this is a health-care development which, although it can be expensive to mount, commands a high public visibility and appears to offer a service, but if there is no treatment follow-through then it similarly does not commit the state to further expenditure. The type of technology involved and its operating costs, the possibility of clinic and non-medical site location have the advantage of taking a health-care service away from more expensive hospital- and doctor-based services (Reisler 1978). From a case-finding function of screening, which had its origins in the early mass radiographic screening for tuberculosis, there has been an expansion of the programme towards 'multi-phasic' screening. In one comprehensive examination, a range of tests are now administered which not only identify communicable disease but also incipient chronic disease. It is claimed that this is the most cost-effective way of delivering preventive health care, since it saves the expense of separate campaigns, reduces administrative costs, saves both public and physician time and is adaptable for new tests. However, critics have demonstrated that the value of screening procedures vary greatly and that screening is only valuable as part of a larger health programme of follow-up diagnosis and therapy (Reisler 1978).

At a certain point, multi-phasic screening has become a parallel development to the battery tests which a number of countries find their doctors using on a routine basis. In Germany there is evidence that patient expectations of a consultation are that it should involve 'testing' and an element of laboratory science in order to legitimise the practitioner's own diagnostic skill (Payer 1989). Such tests inevitably throw up results that justify some medical intervention even though the condition may be pre-symptomatic and have a natural history of self-termination. It is a good example of the uncontrolled escalation of health-care demand that is generated by unrestricted medical practitioners operating even at the primary level of care. The introduction of HIV antibody testing has led to an additional demand for laboratory services, and a strengthening of the bargaining power of the public-health and laboratory sectors for a greater share of resources.

Health surveillance

The HIV epidemic has also effected an increase in manpower and services for epidemiological data collection and analysis. In France this has provided the foundation for a new set of organisations. These twenty-two regional health 'observatories' were designed to make use of new information science, employing statisticians and epidemiologists to construct data banks for health surveillance and forecasting, and eventually to operate a system of automatically processed individual health records.

Portugal, having had to make a very late start on constructing a national framework of health care, has decided to make information technology and epidemiology key features in a system-planned health service, and has invested heavily in linked computer systems.

These two examples illustrate an interesting change taking place within a knowledge field. There is a shift from the knowledge domain of traditional medical statistics as an aid to evaluating treatment outcomes to a broader social science domain of long-term forecasting of health demands based on complex matrices. The level and type of statistical techniques and modelling that are being developed and marketed through packages, means that this new 'knowledge object' is increasingly becoming a major influence on health-care planning. It shares a communicative language with the planners and lies outside of the professional monopoly on 'medical knowledge'. It has to be stressed, however, that where there is a coincidence of doubtful diagnostic practice, inappropriate statistical reasoning and an international climate in which data production is a necessary membership card for participation and credibility, then it may happen that the new epidemiology will resemble the Ten Year Plans of Stalin (Miles 1979). There is a hierarchy of credibility of epidemiological data at the unofficial level of international health policy, and there is a rigorous scepticism in most countries of their own data claims. However, the WHO statistics are still used as evidential material and often uncritically appended to the more rigorous economic reports of the OECD.

Medical practitioners

Medical monopolies have also been challenged and threatened by the political dynamics of decentralisation policies. More regional or local autonomy has meant in effect more managerial and bureaucratic control over health-care decision-making at levels which they had traditionally seen as their clinical monopoly. Previously they had more direct political influence on central government policy through professional state advisory bodies, or by direct roles within ministerial departments. However, as governments began to make economic policies of cutting public spending and targeting specifically the high costs of seemingly unregulated medical-care demands, so the vulnerability of their traditional power base in tertiary and secondary health-care systems became apparent. The new policy shift towards a lower-cost primary system to be managed and implemented locally became enthusiastically taken up and defended by these local authorities who were eager to manage their own restricted budgets. The primacy placed upon efficiency and the critical role of local health managers in implementing cost-effective services has threatened the power and authority of the medical profession. Doctors have been further weakened by the political culture within which local health policy is made. They have reacted to this by defending their traditional institutional base (the hospital) through populist appeals and not infrequently by direct political action.

The situation of the doctors in Spain is interesting in this light (Rodriguez and de Miguel 1990). The political role of the medical profession had a high profile in the opposition to the first socialist government and culminated in strike action in 1987. Under Franco the doctors had a monopoly of health care, but at the political price of being state-employed salaried officials. With the socialist government they found themselves lacking their political power and undercut by new emphasis upon regional and local decision-making, stressing primary care. Whilst the transition to the new system required their cooperation, they were still state employees and the old fascist controls still existed, their traditional if illusory claim of freedom of action was called into question and they resorted to populist appeals and strikes.

Sweden is an instance where doctors have retained their political power and inhibited any real change in reallocation of health-care resources. Here their base has been through tight control of the family practitioner and specialist services (Calltorp 1990). It would appear that where the family practitioner is used as the basic unit in primary-care organisation, then doctors are able to tie their specialist referrals into a network of mutual support for a private market which keeps the core hospital-based services well-funded.

Radical change

The effects of the fundamental economic restructuring and political changes in the Soviet Union and eastern Europe have had inevitably major implications for the organisation of health care. The overall impression that can be gained from the new reporting and availability of information is that the effects of economic recession have borne particularly heavily on the health-care services. At the same time there is evidence of the existence of a separate system of medical care available only to privileged or elite groups. There appears to be a breakdown in the provision and distribution of supplies and the development of a black market, which is tacitly endorsed by the authorities.

In the Soviet Union, recent reports suggest that the basic infrastructure of health care has all but collapsed in Moscow under the pressure of non-funding and shortages of basic supplies, whilst the new policies are still the subject of intense political debate and are not implemented (Schultz and Rafferty 1990). The issue appears to be that as the Soviet Union moves towards autonomy for the republics, so the financial and administrative responsibility for health care is decentralised. The problem is that without any start-up funding and the sudden withdrawal of central financing support, the first response to the financial crisis has been to move away from the Leninist tradition of centrally planned and fiscally financed health care available to all, and to move towards an insurance-based service with supplementary charges and fees. The effect of this rapid change-over has been to reinforce the *ad hoc* private markets for specialist services and to create separate occupationally-specific insurance and health-care schemes; the result is a picture of gross inefficiencies and inequities.

The shift away from centrally planned and funded health care towards local autonomy is also to be found in Poland and Hungary. Poland has had a longer period in which the restructuring of its political and economic system has been under way and, like Czechoslovakia, inherited from the prewar period an established system of institutionally based medical manpower which has continued to be focused upon the large and capital cities, with the result that geographical inequities are pronounced. In Czechoslovakia, the new government is considering introducing graduated insurance contributions and also allowing the development of a private market in insurance. Recognising the problems associated with stimulating a private health sector, strict controls on maximum insurance payments and fixed service pricing on treatment services are being introduced.

Yugoslavia had historically developed a strong political infrastructure of decentralised planning; regional and local autonomy was an integral part of the Tito ideology attempting to reconcile a mosaic of nationalisms. This has now clearly failed. It appears that although there are considerable regional variations of quality, a basic medical-care system is in place, and a far greater freedom of the private market has allowed it to be integrated into the public service in a formally-planned way. The central state is responsible for medical manpower planning and the public health network, but the increasing political autonomy and overt warfare means that the role of state planning is becoming minimal. Bilateral arrangements with western pharmaceutical companies has meant the freedom to work out local deals, and although the shortage of medical supplies is a chronic problem, it had not reached the crisis point or black market propor-tions before the outbreak of fighting that it had in the Soviet Union.

In eastern Germany, unification has meant the virtual abandonment of its socialist model of health care; however, no organisational change is to be implemented until 1992. In the meantime there is a prohibition on any West German doctor practising in the east. West Germany has made it clear that it will not simply take up the financial responsibility for the system, and that it must be anchored in the same pattern of contributional insurance and the private market that operates in the west. The future of the big 'polyclinics' which were the star in the crown of the East German system looks parlous, and the future of unemployment amongst health-care workers is projected to rise to 75 per cent (*Lancet* 1991).

Both systems have problems in trying to contain and reduce health-care costs, although there is a fundamental difference in their health-care models. The East German model has a large medical manpower base which is state-salaried, and the polyclinics with their specialist services are an expensive way of delivering health care; nor are they an efficient model for the development of a private market in specialist services, since there is no incentive for the containment of costs. In West Germany, however, the power of the medical establish-ment has led to a large manpower base that is in a secure position in so far as it is not state-salaried; costs are covered by both the private and state insurance funds, which has led to unrestricted pricing and escalating demand.

The drug companies are particularly concerned with the present period of indeterminacy. They are manoeuvring to make sure that the differential pricing of drugs in the east and west is resolved either by an acceptance of a common West German price in accordance with economic union or by government reimbursement for the 55 per cent lower price charged in the east. They have already threatened and enforced a freeze on further supplies until the issue is resolved. It would seem that whatever the resolution, the need to control clinical freedom of prescribing as well as cost containment will have a high priority in future health policy.

Southern Europe

A different set of problems faces countries like Portugal and Greece, which experienced their political revolutions in the 1970s and eighties and have commenced major economic and industrial development plans. These states have only recently begun to create state-funded health and welfare services, and are concerned to integrate themselves into the European market with all of its implications for harmonised social policy. In these countries medical manpower has been relatively uncontrolled, and capital city-based hospitals have retained specialist monopolies which led to gross imbalances in rural and regional provision.

The state's priority has been to build a framework of environmental and public health and to target the primary problems of illness and disease. Inevitably, this means that there are large gaps in service provision, particularly in the fields of mental health and chronic illness. Perhaps the opportunities are greatest for these countries in that they have not as yet revealed the high degree of modern chronic illness and have the chance to create health-care systems which are not hospital-intensive. However, forecasters look to the reductions in infant mortality and increasing life expectancy and anticipate that the future epidemiological profile will converge to the European norm.

The epidemiological picture

We have looked at the politics and organisation of health care, and now it is appropriate to consider the reported patterns of illness and disease in Europe. There is only space here to look at a few of the most prominent features of the picture. Tables 10.1–10.6 provide more detailed data which can be used for further comparative work.

Perhaps the most striking factor is that despite the prevailing media panics and concerns about communicable diseases and deaths from external causes, the predominant pattern of mortality and morbidity is from circulatory diseases and malignant neoplasms (cancers); (see Tables 10.1 and 10.2) in other words, the diseases of developed industrial societies. Although this is the overall pattern, there are considerable variations within each country. We find that in Poland, Norway, Greece and Italy lung cancer rates are rising, and in Spain, cervical cancer is rising; that in eastern Europe there is an increase in cerebrovascular disease (strokes), whilst this may be also accompanied by a decrease in ischaemic heart disease. Life-style and diet are identified as contributory factors in these diseases, and it is clear that countries with high rates of tobacco consumption appear to have higher lung cancer rates; but one must be careful of such gross patterns, particularly when there are likely to be additional factors such as industrial pollution and occupation-related bronchial diseases.

.1 **Standardised mortality rates for cardiovascular diseases, age group**
rs

Country	Historical year Year	Value	Last available year Year	Value	%
Austria	1973	101.92	1982	95.55	−6.23
Belgium	1973	109.70	1983	93.13	−15.10
Bulgaria	1973	115.20	1983	139.80	+21.35
Czechoslovakia	1972	140.40	1982	151.92	+8.21
Denmark	1972	96.50	1983	87.70	−9.12
Finland	1971	192.60	1981	133.60	−30.63
France	1972	73.60	1981	56.93	−22.65
German Democratic Republic	1973	84.40	1983	83.50	−1.07
Germany, Federal Republic of	1973	96.80	1982	87.48	−9.63
Greece	1972	69.90	1981	67.91	−2.85
Hungary	1973	139.50	1983	183.00	+31.18
Ireland	1971	143.60	1981	128.85	−10.27
Italy	1971	96.70	1979	85.47	−11.61
Luxembourg	1973	126.10	1982	103.80	−17.68
Netherlands	1973	91.90	1983	76.40	−16.87
Norway	1973	98.10	1982	84.69	−13.67
Poland	1971	118.80	1982	135.10	+13.72
Portugal	1971	109.00	1979	95.00	−12.84
Romania	1973	131.20	1983	146.00	+11.28
Spain	1970	93.30	1979	77.04	−17.43
Sweden	1973	85.60	1982	79.40	−7.24
Switzerland	1972	74.20	1981	64.72	−12.78
UK	1972	143.68	1983	118.04	−17.85
Yugoslavia	1972	103.90	1981	116.70	+12.32
European Region	1972	106.26	1981	99.22	−6.63

Source: World Health Organisation Regional Office for Europe

The development of anti-smoking campaigns in order to reduce both the mortality rates and the costs of chronic respiratory disorders is a feature of most European societies.

Cervical cancer rates show the steepest decline in most countries, although again there is a pattern of higher rates in those countries with the lowest GNP (see Table 10.3). There is evidence that there is a social-class gradient in all these rates. Circulatory diseases need also to be seen in a context of an ageing population; so whilst we find that in Greece the rates are lower, this is unlikely to be due to the same factors that we find in Norway. Austria is a good example of an ageing population, predominantly rural but with urban clusters. Here the circulatory disease rates are particularly high, and it is perhaps useful to compare Austria with Finland where, hitherto, high rates have been brought down apparently as a result of health promotion campaigns.

Infant mortality rates are used as a crude indicator of the level of development of a country, and we find that all European societies

Table 10.2 **Standardised mortality rates for cancer of the trachea, bronchus and lung, age group 0–64 years**

Country	Historical year Year	Value	Last available year Year	Value	%
Austria	1973	15.50	1983	16.92	+9.16
Belgium	1973	24.30	1983	28.32	+16.54
Bulgaria	1973	17.10	1983	18.90	+10.53
Czechoslovakia	1972	21.90	1982	29.99	+36.94
Denmark	1972	20.60	1983	25.50	+23.79
Finland	1971	22.90	1981	20.90	−8.73
France	1972	13.30	1981	16.90	+27.07
German Democratic Republic	1973	15.80	1982	16.64	+5.30
Germany, Federal Republic of	1973	13.90	1982	16.40	+17.99
Greece	1972	13.50	1981	17.10	+26.67
Hungary	1973	16.00	1983	27.90	+74.38
Ireland	1971	20.80	1981	22.03	+5.91
Italy	1971	16.20	1979	21.70	+33.95
Luxembourg	1973	20.70	1982	29.30	+41.55
Netherlands	1973	23.90	1983	22.70	−5.02
Norway	1973	8.90	1982	13.70	+53.93
Poland	1971	16.10	1980	23.80	+47.83
Portugal	1971	6.60	1979	8.60	+30.30
Romania	1973	14.00	1983	21.40	+52.86
Spain	1971	9.40	1979	12.76	+35.74
Sweden	1973	8.60	1982	10.80	+25.58
Switzerland	1972	16.90	1981	18.60	+10.06
UK	1972	30.10	1983	26.27	−12.72
Yugoslavia	1972	12.20	1981	18.50	+51.64
European Region	1972	16.68	1981	19.90	+19.30

Source: World Health Organisation Regional Office for Europe

show steep reductions in the last ten years (see Table 10.4). The eastern European planners attribute this to the high percentage of hospital births, but it is likely to be a more complex factor, and we can find countries where the highest rates of home births are accompanied by low infant mortality, such as the Netherlands and Scandinavia.

Maternal mortality rates are also falling (see Table 10.5), and this is unlikely to be attributable purely to hospital births; it is likely to be linked in part to the nutritional levels, the birth intervals and the availability of contraception. In some of the eastern European countries the use of abortion as a method of contraception results in very high figures for abortion-related maternal mortality. Also, it is the case that some countries like France and Greece invest highly in infant and maternal care, especially where there is a history of a declining population; this in turn can influence the whole skew of medical services towards issues of fertility as opposed to regulating and controlling the availability of reproductive technologies.

Table 10.3   **Standardised mortality rates for cancer of the cervix uteri, age group 0–64 years**

Country	Historical year		Last available year		
	Year	Value	Year	Value	%
Austria	1973	5.95	1983	3.55	−40.34
Belgium	1973	3.10	1983	2.13	−31.29
Bulgaria	1973	3.80	1983	3.08	−18.95
Czechoslovakia	1972	5.53	1982	5.78	+4.52
Denmark	1972	9.52	1983	7.13	−25.11
Finland	1971	4.92	1981	1.55	−68.50
France	1972	2.70	1981	2.55	−16.67
German Democratic Republic	1973	10.74	1982	6.60	−38.55
Germany, Federal Republic of	1973	6.22	1982	3.43	−44.86
Greece	1972	1.14	1981	1.32	+15.79
Hungary	1973	6.46	1983	7.49	+15.94
Ireland	1971	3.49	1981	3.64	+4.30
Italy	1970	1.69	1979	1.20	−28.99
Luxembourg	1973	8.47	1982	2.00	−76.39
Netherlands	1973	4.44	1983	2.60	−41.44
Norway	1973	6.54	1982	5.73	−12.39
Poland	1971	10.05	1980	9.09	−9.55
Portugal	1971	8.56	1979	4.35	−49.18
Romania	1973	10.98	1983	9.94	−9.47
Spain	1970	0.86	1979	1.08	+25.58
Sweden	1973	5.06	1982	3.29	−34.98
Switzerland	1972	5.20	1981	3.85	−25.96
UK	1972	6.12	1983	5.09	−16.83
Yugoslavia	1972	5.34	1981	5.37	+0.56
European Region	1972	5.23	1981	4.07	−22.18

Source: World Health Organisation Regional for Europe

There is a general tendency towards the expansion of non-hospital-based maternity-care units. In some countries this is a specific feature of the development of private market 'nursing homes', whereas in others it is an extension of the clinic principle. A parallel feature is the widely different pattern of midwifery. In some countries there has been a dramatic decine in the number of midwives. Where this is not accompanied by a decline in the overall number of nurses it seems likely to be part of the trend towards hospital-based births; in other countries, it may be associated with the surplus of doctors and the use of doctors for home births; in yet others the traditional demarcation of district nurse and specialist midwife may not have developed; and some countries (such as Portugal) are specifically training a paramedical nurse who is also qualified to deliver.

How can we account for changes in the policy and control of childbirth? In part it may be as a result of pressure from the women's movement, which is concerned about the medicalisation of childbirth (as has been the case in Germany and the United Kingdom); or it

Table 10.4 **Infant mortality per 100,000 live births**

Country	Historical year Year	Value	Last available year Year	Value
Albania	1972	58.90	1984	29.00
Austria	1970	25.90	1983	11.90
Belgium	1970	21.10	1984	10.10
Bulgaria	1970	27.30	1983	16.50
Czechoslovakia	1970	22.10	1983	14.20
Denmark	1970	14.20	1983	7.71
Finland	1970	13.20	1982	6.10
France	1970	18.20	1982	9.40
German Democratic Republic	1970	18.50	1984	10.00
Germany, Federal Republic of	1970	23.60	1983	10.20
Greece	1970	29.60	1982	15.10
Hungary	1970	35.90	1983	19.00
Ireland	1970	19.50	1984	10.10
Italy	1970	29.60	1982	13.00
Luxembourg	1970	24.90	1984	10.00
Netherlands	1970	12.70	1983	8.40
Norway	1970	12.70	1983	7.90
Poland	1970	33.20	1984	19.10
Portugal	1970	58.00	1984	16.70
Romania	1970	49.40	1983	23.90
Spain	1970	26.30	1982	9.60
Sweden	1970	11.00	1983	7.00
Switzerland	1970	15.10	1983	7.60
Turkey	1972	129.60	1982	95.00
UK	1970	18.50	1983	10.00
Yugoslavia	1970	55.50	1982	29.90
European Region	1970	49.34	1982	36.05

Source: World Health Organisation Regional Office for Europe

may be due to the overall rationalisation and concentration of health services in the one hospital/clinic; or again it may be due to the specialisms within medicine wishing to retain control of this clearly ongoing demand for health care. Another factor could be to do with the changing expectations about perinatal mortality: this is clearly true where developed systems have invested in special baby units or even high-technology paediatric care. The projections in Europe are for further reductions in infant mortality, but we should also be mindful of the high rates of external causes of death still in Europe through road traffic accidents, other accidents and poisoning.

Immunisation programmes show a fairly consistent pattern; where they are tied to infant care support, or the education system, some countries operate a policy of compulsory vaccination. Even the less economically strong countries have high rates of vaccination, possibly because of the WHO support for these basic health measures and the subsidised cost of vaccines. It is interesting therefore that the lowest

Table 10.5   **Maternal mortality per 100,000 live births**

Country	Historical year Year	Value	Last available year Year	Value
Austria	1970	25.82	1983	11.10
Belgium	1973	12.40	1982	7.21
Bulgaria	1973	34.40	1982	17.70
Czechoslovakia	1972	17.50	1983	10.02
Denmark	1972	4.00	1981	3.80
Finland	1971	8.20	1981	4.73
France	1970	28.10	1981	15.50
German Democratic Republic	1970	43.00	1981	14.73
Germany, Federal Republic of	1973	45.90	1984	10.78
Greece	1972	29.80	1981	11.40
Hungary	1973	37.80	1983	14.00
Ireland	1971	25.20	1981	4.16
Italy	1970	54.50	1979	12.20
Luxembourg	1973	52.60	1984	0.00
Netherlands	1973	10.30	1983	5.29
Norway	1973	3.30	1982	0.00
Poland	1971	22.40	1984	14.16
Portugal	1971	54.50	1982	22.51
Romania	1973	135.20	1983	170.14
Spain	1970	33.10	1979	10.40
Sweden	1970	9.90	1981	4.30
Switzerland	1972	21.90	1981	6.80
UK	1972	15.52	1982	6.95
Yugoslavia	1972	37.00	1982	15.05
European Region	1971	36.93	1982	19.75

Source: World Health Organisation Regional Office for Europe

rates of vaccination are in those countries like the Netherlands and the United Kingdom where parents may be exercising discretionary judgements about 'risk' in view of possible side effects. Some countries are persistent with BCG vaccination against tuberculosis. This is a good example of the heritage of past practice, for the efficacy of this method of tuberculosis control was always inconclusive, but very early on some countries adopted this measure and tied it to the school health service and it now appears to be a residual part of the vaccination battery (There is, however, an increase in the rates of tuberculosis, notwithstanding the possible increase attributable to the HIV virus). Nevertheless, in the context of renewed concern about infectious diseases environmental health policies may be the preferred route to provide a more powerful impact on tuberculosis, which is classically a disease occuring during periods of economic recession and depressed immunological status.

AIDS and HIV infection are the most topical disease that concerns both inter-country and domestic health policy. Because of the designation of AIDS as a global epidemic, the WHO has established

Table 10.6 **Reported AIDS cases, 1986–90**

Country	<1986	1987	1988	1989	1990[1]	Total
Austria	54	82	103	139	96	474
Belgium	258	115	137	147	107	764
Bulgaria	0	2	0	5	0	7
Czechoslovakia	6	2	4	7	5	24
Denmark	142	100	124	171	168	705
Finland	17	8	17	15	14	71
France	1,926	2,004	2,680	2,828	280	9,718
Germany[2]	1,083	1,036	1,250	1,406	725	5,500
Greece	35	53	82	107	98	375
Hungary	1	7	9	15	16	48
Ireland	17	20	37	50	37	161
Italy	688	994	1,728	2,335	1,831	7,576
Luxembourg	6	3	4	11	6	30
Netherlands	255	237	319	382	294	1,487
Norway	35	35	30	45	40	185
Poland	1	2	2	24	18	47
Portugal	57	58	95	150	162	522
Romania	6	4	14	198	833	1,055
Spain	637	900	1,825	2,162	1,523	7,047
Sweden	102	78	85	125	97	487
Switzerland	189	164	348	455	392	1,548
UK	802	631	790	833	828	3,884
Yugoslavia	8	18	39	44	49	158

Notes:
1 Provisional figures for 1990
2 Since 1990 the data for the former FDR and GDR have been amalgamated
Source: World Health Organisation Regional Office for Europe

special AIDS monitoring centres which produce detailed and voluminous epidemiological updates. It is not possible in this overview chapter to deal adequately with the complexities of this epidemic and the politics of its epidemiological mapping. Basic data on reported AIDS cases is given in Table 10.6.

One new disease that is responsible for a high consumption of health-care resources is Alzheimer's disease. There is some question about degree of overlap with other demanding conditions, and there are still considerable problems about its diagnostic reliability, except *post mortem*. We should therefore be reserved about the existing epidemiological data, which estimates a prevalence of between 2.5 and 5.6 per cent of the population over 65. Where health-care resources are specifically linked to diagnostically related groups and carry a price ceiling for insurance, then there may be an incentive in diagnosing a disease-specific category, rather than the open-ended general dementias. However, it does seem to be the case that many European societies are faced with an increase in the amount of resources they will need to find to cover this condition. Since it is a chronic degenerative condition and in the advanced stages needs a high level of care, the emphasis in most countries is to develop community-support services for home nursing for as long as possible. However, there is increasing concern that the burden of care is extreme, and the secondary carers' health-care costs are gradually becoming recognised. There is a convergence of research towards the development of drugs that will either delay its progress or the possible connection between its genetic base and other environmental factors.

Mental illness is still very much a low-profile area of health-care resource allocation, despite the fact that it accounts for a large share of most countries' stocks of hospital beds and that its incidence is rising. The pattern of care varies enormously, from minimal treatment or incarceration in hospitals or asylums (Greece), to an almost total outpatient community psychiatric service (Italy). The documentation of the Greek chronic hospitals with minimal living standards of care has prompted the government to divert resources towards the building up of a new community and clinic-based service. In many respects countries which had not developed the mental hospital pattern of institutional care are better placed than those who are having to shift towards decarceration policies. Again the costs of 'community care' can be passed on to families and a significant saving is made. Ireland is another country which is making a priority of developing community psychiatric services. At the other extreme, Germany and France have well-developed psychotherapeutic services within the insurance-based health services.

Where there is a private market for psychiatric services then there is likely to be an increased status for the medical specialism, a climate of research, and work opportunities that are treatment-based. This contrasts with eastern Europe where for a long time psychiatry was associated with state policies of social control and the morale and status of psychiatrists was low, even to the extent where they were somewhat regarded as international pariahs. There is an increasing pressure upon psychiatrists to reconcile treatment concerns with the legal rights of patients in western Europe, and the concomitant development of forensic psychiatry has become a new focus for those concerned with civil liberties, particularly in the context of the European Court of Human Rights.

This is a field which touches on changes within jurisprudential thinking that have occurred because of harmonisation; it is a development that has implications for an increasing range of medically controlled technologies which had hitherto not been subject to legal scrutiny. It is an example of both the medicalisation of law and the legalisation of medicine (Wynne 1989). Once we see medical issues in a broader frame than their familiar sectoral neighbours, we are not shocked to find that the issue of the regulation of cadaveric organs for transplant surgery is a question of 'trade' of commodity items, and that the present arrangements between countries are dangerously vulnerable to abuse (Defever 1990).

Environmental health

It would be absurd to talk about health and medicine without considering the relationship of health care to environmental health. We have seen that in some countries this is at the basic level of introducing access to main sewage and water supplies; in others it is at the level of monitoring and regulating atmospheric pollution. Throughout Europe there is a recognition that all aspects of economic and industrial development should be considered also in terms of their impact upon the health of the population. But this may well be more honoured in proclamation than in action; and although Chernobyl was a devastating example of the international health dangers caused by one country's nuclear capability, there has been a reluctance to link issues such as the transportation of hazardous materials, the regulation of chemical plants, the development of genetic engineering to main-stream health policy until after a catastrophe has occurred. This is well indicated in the secondary position in which health claims and concerns are treated in the context of food and agricultural policy, where national self-interest of the agro-business communities is pursued with little consideration of the impact that it might have upon health status and well-being.

Conclusions

What conclusions can be drawn from this overview? In many ways it is a paradoxical time of contrary trends in medicine and health care in Europe. On the one hand, there is the move away from secondary health care and the emphasis upon primary health care, and the attempt to move away from doctor-based medicine to see the overlap with other sectors of welfare work, to move away from single ministry planning and control. On the other hand, the developments within medicine itself indicate an increasing move towards higher and more expensive technology and more expensive treatments. The state and the insurance companies are locked into a conflict with the medical professionals, whom they see as equating health care with medical care, who defend their clinical judgement regardless of the costs involved; and yet as new therapies and interventions become available, then the impetus within the medical profession is to adopt them as part of their mandate to practise according to the possibilities within their grasp, and with that goes the patient's expectation that the doctor–patient relationship is based upon the clinical contract which stresses the primacy of the 'health need', not the adjudication of the health-care budget. Governments respond to their constituents in terms of rationing public spending in order to secure the economic strength of the country. They can reconcile this policy with the demands for greater decentralisation of government and diversity of service, by pushing the responsibility for health finance and management down to the local or regional level, or outwards to private insurance companies, whilst still retaining a central overview by fixing budget limits and subventions and price regulation. In this context doctors become potentially vulnerable and their control over health policy is weakened. In response they make populist appeals under the traditional banner of representing the 'health' interests of the people. However, it is clear that what is happening is that 'health' and 'medicine' are no longer the monopoly of doctors. The fight is about resources and also about legitimacy and the right to identify and control the process of demand.

Note

1 The thirty-eight targets of the European Region of the World Health Association are as follows:

1 By the year 2000, the actual differences in health status between countries and between groups within countries should be reduced by at least 25%, by improving the level of health disadvantaged nations and groups.

2 By the year 2000, people should have the basic opportunity to develop and use their health potential to live socially and economically fulfilling lives.

3 By the year 2000, disabled persons should have the physical, social and economic opportunities that allow at least for a socially and economically fulfilling and mentally creative life.

4 By the year 2000, the average number of years that people live free from major disease and disability should be increased by at least 10%.

5 By the year 2000, there should be no indigenous measles, poliomyelitis, neonatal tetanus, congenital rubella, diphtheria, congenital syphilis or indigenous malaria in the Region.

6 By the year 2000, life expectancy at birth in the Region should be at least 75 years.

7 By the year 2000, infant mortality in the Region should be less than 20 per 1,000 live births.

8 By the year 2000, maternal mortality in the Region should be less than 15 per 100,000 live births.

9 By the year 2000, mortality in the Region from disease of the circulatory system in people under 65 should be reduced by at least 15%.

10 By the year 2000, mortality in the Region from cancer in people under 65 should be reduced by at least 15%.

11 By the year 2000, deaths from accidents in the Region should be reduced by at least 15% through an intensified effort to reduce traffic, home and occupational accidents.

12 By the year 2000, the current rising trends in suicides and attempted suicides in the Region should be reversed.

13 By 1990, national policies in all Member States should ensure that legislative, administrative and economic mechanisms provide broad intersectoral support and resources for the promotion of healthy lifestyles and ensure effective participation of the people at all levels of such policy-making.

14 By 1990, all Member States should have specific programmes which enhance the major roles of the family and other social groups in developing and supporting healthy lifestyles.

15 By 1990, educational programmes in all Member States should enhance the knowledge, motivation and skills of people to acquire and maintain health.

16 By 1995, in all Member States, there should be significant increases in positive health behaviour, such as balanced nutrition, nonsmoking, appropriate physical activity and good stress management.

17 By 1995, in all Member States, there should be significant decreases in health-damaging behaviour, such as overuse of alcohol and pharmaceutical products; use of illicit drugs and dangerous chemical substances; and dangerous driving and violent social behaviour.

18 By 1990, Member States should have multisectoral policies that effectively protect the environment from health hazards, ensure community awareness and involvement, and support international efforts to curb such hazards affecting more than one country.

19 By 1990, all Member States should have adequate machinery for the monitoring, assessment and control of environmental hazards which pose a threat to human health, including potentially toxic chemicals, radiation, harmful consumer goods and biological agents.

20 By 1990, all people of the Region should have adequate supplies of safe drinking-water, and by the year 1995 pollution of rivers, lakes and seas should no longer pose a threat to human health.

21 By 1995, all people of the Region should be effectively protected against recognized health risks from air pollution.

22 By 1990, all Member States should have significantly reduced health risks from food contamination and implemented measures to protect consumers from harmful additives.

23 By 1995, all Member States should have eliminated major known health risks associated with the disposal of hazardous wastes.

24 By the year 2000, all people of the Region should have a better opportunity of living in houses and settlements which provide a healthy and safe environment.

25 By 1995, people of the Region should be effectively protected against work-related health risks.

26 By 1990, all Member States, through effective community representation, should have developed health care systems that are based on primary health care and supported by secondary and tertiary care as outlined at the Alma-Ata Conference.

27 By 1990, in all Member States, the infrastructures of the delivery systems should be organized so that resources are distributed according to need, and that services ensure physical and economic accessibility and cultural acceptability to the population.

28 By 1990, the primary health care system of all Member States should provide a wide range of health-promotive, curative, rehabilitative and supportive services to meet the basic health needs of the population and give special attention to high-risk, vulnerable and underserved individuals and groups.

29 By 1990, in all Member States, primary health care systems should be based on cooperation and teamwork between health care personnel, individuals, families and community groups.

30 By 1990, all Member States should have mechanisms by which the services provided by all sectors relating to health are coordinated at the community level in a primary health care system.

31 By 1990, all Member States should have built effective mechanisms for ensuring quality of patient care within their health care systems.

32 Before 1990, all Member States should have formulated research strategies to stimulate investigations which improve the application and expansion of knowledge needed to support their health for all developments.

33 Before 1990, all Member States should ensure that their health policies and

strategies are in line with health for all principles and that their legislation and regulations make their implementation effective in all sectors of society.

34 Before 1990, Member States should have managerial processes for health development geared to the attainment of health for all, actively involving communities and all sectors relevant to health and, accordingly, ensuring preferential allocation of resources to health development priorities.

35 Before 1990, Member States should have health information systems capable of supporting their national strategies for health for all.

36 Before 1990, in all Member States, the planning, training and use of health personnel should be in accordance with health for all policies, with emphasis on the primary health care approach.

37 Before 1990, in all Member States, education should provide personnel in sectors related to health with adequate information on the country's health for all policies and programmes and their practical application to their own sectors.

38 Before 1990, all Member States should have established a formal mechanism for the systematic assessment of the appropriate use of health technologies and of their effectiveness, efficiency, safety and acceptability, as well as reflecting national health policies and economic restraints.

(*Evaluation of the Strategy for Health for All by the Year 2000*, WHO Copenhagen, 1986)

References

Ashton, J. (1990) 'Public health and primary care: towards a common agenda', *Public Health*, 104: 387–98.

Babson, J. H. (1972) *Health Care Delivery Systems: a Multinational Survey*, London: Pitman.

Binns, T. B. and Firth, M. (1988) *Health Care Provision under Financial Constraint*, London: Royal Society of Medicine.

Calltorp, J. (1990) 'Physician manpower politics in Sweden', *Health Policy*, 15: 105–18.

Defever, M. (1990) 'The politics of organ transplantation in Europe: issues and problems', *Health Policy*, 16: 95–103.

Egger, M., Minder, C. and Smith, D. (1990) 'Health inequalities and migrant workers in Switzerland', *Lancet*, 29 Sept.: 816.

Fabrega, H. (1973) *Health and Social Behaviour*, Cambridge, Ma: MIT Press.

Hellberg, H. (1987) 'Health for all and primary health care in Europe', *Public Health*, 101: 151–7

Ivanets, N. and Lukomskaya, M. (1990) 'The USSR's new alcohol policy', *World Health Forum*, 11: 246–51.

Klein, R. (1989) *Infertility*, London: Pandora.

Kleinman, A. (1986) 'Concepts and a model for the comparison of medical systems as cultural systems', in C. Currer and M. Stacey (eds) *Concepts of Health, Illness and Disease*, Oxford: Berg.

Lalonde, M. (1974) *A New Perspective on the Health of Canadians: a Working Document* Ottawa: Ministry of National Health and Welfare.

Lancet (1991) 5 Jan.: 38. Report.

Lewis, J. (1987) 'What has become of public health? past patterns and future prospects in England, Ontario and Quebec', *Public Health*, 101: 357–68.

McKeown, T. (1976) *The Modern Rise of Population*, London: Arnold.

Maxwell, R. (1980) *International Comparisons of Health Needs and Services*, London: King's Fund.

Miles, I. (1979) 'The development of forecasting towards a history of the future', in T. Whiston (ed.) *The Uses and Abuses of Forecasting*, London: Macmillan pp. 5–42.

OECD (1985) *Measuring Health Care, 1960–83*, Paris.

——(1987) *Financing and Delivering Health Care*, Paris.

Payer, I. (1989) *Medicine and Culture*, London: Gollancz.

Phillips, D. and Joseph, A. (1984) *Accessibility and Utilization*, New York: Harper & Row.

Pyle, G. F. (1979) *Applied Medical Geography*, New York: Wiley.

Reisler, S. J. (1978) 'The emergence of the concept of screening for disease', *Millbank Memorial Quarterly*, 56 (4): 403–25.

Rodriguez, J. and de Miguel, J. (1990) 'The case of Spain', *Health Policy*, 15 119–142.

Roemer, M. (1977) *Systems of Health Care*, New York: Springer.

Roemer, M. and Roemer, R. (1981) *Health Care Systems and Comparative Manpower Politics*, New York: Marcel Dekker.

Schultz, D. and Rafferty, M. (1990) 'Soviet health care and Perestroika', *American Journal of Public Health*, 80 (2) 193–196.

Towers, B. A. (1980) 'Health education policy 1916–1926: venereal disease and the prophylaxis dilemma', *Medical History*, 24: 70–87.

——(1987) 'The politics of tuberculosis in Western Europe 1914–40', Unpublished MS, London University.

Townsend, P. and Whitehead, M. (1988) *Inequalities in Health*, London: Penguin.

WHO (1986) *Evaluation of the Strategy for Health for All by the Year 2000*, vol. 5, Copenhagen.

Wright, P. and Treacher, A. (1982) *The Problem of Medical Knowledge*, Edinburgh: Edinburgh University Press.

Wynne, B. (1989) 'Establishing the rules of laws: constructing expert authority', in Smith R. and Wynne B (eds) *Expert Evidence*, London: Routledge.

CHAPTER 11

God and Caesar: religion in a rapidly changing Europe

GRACE DAVIE

This chapter falls into three sections. The first examines in some detail the broad outlines of religious life in western Europe. In other words, it concentrates on what Europe has in common, not least its shared religious heritage. The second section adopts a rather different focus. It looks at the way in which such common patterns as can be established have been differently refracted across a variety of European countries. A whole range of factors comes into play in this section, the differing combinations of which account for the religious diversities of western Europe rather than its unity. One theme of this chapter – balancing unity against diversity (across time as well as space) – begins to emerge as the two sections are drawn together.

The third section not only introduces a second theme; it also adopts a more explicitly theoretical framework. More particularly, it aims to set the religious data presented in the first two sections within a theoretical discussion of modernity. In so doing it shifts the principal focus away from the secularisation debate and introduces theoretical approaches developed initially among French sociologists of religion.

It is necessary to make one further (rather extended) point at the outset. This chapter, like the others in this book, will deal with western Europe rather than a wider definition of the continent. It is, however, important to remember that the relatively recent division between east and west (communist and non-communist) Europe pales into insignificance compared with the split between Roman Catholicism and Orthodoxy that divided the continent a millennium ago. Indeed the terms 'east' and 'central' Europe have significance in this respect, for east Europe (Romania, Bulgaria and most of European Russia) belong to the Orthodox tradition, whereas the central European countries (Poland, Czechoslovakia, Hungary and what was East Germany) developed within western Catholicism. The position of the Baltic states is equally revealing. Roman Catholic Lithuania and Poland are closely linked historically; in contrast, Latvia and Estonia belong to northern Europe.

We would do well to remember these distinctions in our discussions about the future of Europe. The countries which shared the experience of postwar communist domination represent very different religious traditions (Walters 1988). These traditions are likely to have contemporary significance. Countries that belonged – and continue to belong – to western rather than Orthodox Christianity may well find it easier to realise their political and economic aspirations. Despite their very real economic difficulties, their aim is to *re*-establish western traditions; they are not learning something totally new.[1]

The vicissitudes in the Balkans in the summer of 1991 exemplify – albeit rather differently – the same point. For the entity known as Yugoslavia has attempted to combine within one country not only contrasting Christian traditions but a sizeable Muslim presence as well. For a relatively short space of time (two generations, perhaps), the country held together under the personal authority of President Tito. As that authority – and the creed that underpinned it – collapses, it is hardly surprising that Yugoslavia's pseudo-unity begins to fall apart. Ethnic nationalisms, bolstered by religious differences, interact with a multiplicity of factors (linguistic, historical and economic) to create an explosive situation. At the same time, the presence of sizeable ethnic minorities within the borders of each state renders the dissolution of the country as problematic as its retention.

In more ways than one, Europe reaches its limits in the Balkans; the essentially European patterns that will emerge in the following section start to disintegrate at the margins of the continent.

The European framework

What, then, do the countries of western Europe have in common from a religious point of view? There are several ways of looking at this question.

First, the historical perspective. O'Connell (1991) (amongst others) identifies three formative factors or themes that come together in the creation and re-creation of the unity that we call Europe: these are Judaeo-Christian monotheism, Greek rationalism and Roman organisation. These factors shift and evolve over time, but their combinations can be seen forming and re-forming a way of life that we have come to recognise as European. The religious stand within such combinations is self-evident.

It is, however, equally important to grasp from the outset the historical complexity of European identity. O'Connell approaches this question by introducing a series of interlocking and overlapping blocs which exist within the European whole. There are seven of these: the western islands, western Europe, central Europe, the Nordic/Baltic countries, the Mediterranean group, the former Ottoman territories and the Slav peoples. Not all of these will concern us in this chapter, but the 'building bloc' approach underlies a crucial aspect of modern as well as historical Europe:

If I have taken this building bloc approach, it is to make clear, on the one hand, how closely knit Europe comes out of its history and how important it may be to make a future unity, and to suggest on the other hand, how complex Europe is and, in consequence, how varied might future unity mosaics prove to be.

(O'Connell 1991: 9)

There is nothing deterministic about the future shape of Europe: several approaches are possible; so too are several outcomes.

For the time being, however, we need to stress one point in particular: the shared religious heritage of western Europe as one of the crucial factors in the continent's development – and, possibly, in its future – and the influence of this heritage on a whole range of cultural values. Other very different sources reinforce this conclusion. One of these, the European Value Study Group (EVSG),[2] provivdes a principal source of data for this chapter.

In contrast with O'Connell's primarily historical approach, the European Value Study exemplifies – for better or worse – sophisticated quantitative social science methodology.[3] Using careful sampling techniques, the EVSG aims at an accurate mapping of social and moral values across Europe. It has generated very considerable data and will continue to do so. It is essential that we pay close – but at the same time critical – attention to its findings.

Two underlying themes run through the EVSG study. The first concerns the substance of contemporary European values and asks, in particular, to what extent they are homogeneous; the second takes a more dynamic approach, asking to what extent such values are changing. Both themes involve, inevitably, a religious element. The first, for example, leads very quickly to questions about the origin of shared value systems: 'If values in Western Europe are to any extent shared, if people from different countries share similar social perceptions on their world, how had any such joint cultural experience been created?' (Harding *et al.* 1986: 29). As the European Value Study indicates, the answer lies in deep-rooted cultural experiences which derive from pervasive social influences which have been part of our culture for generations, if not centuries. A shared religious heritage is one such influence.

Both in historical and geographical terms, religion – or, more specifically, the Christian religion – provides an example of an agency which through the promulgation of a universal and exclusive faith sought to create a commonality of values and beliefs across Europe, and elsewhere. A shared religious heritage based on Christian values, therefore, may be seen as one formative cultural influence at the heart of and giving substance to 'European' civilisation.

(*Ibid.*)

So much is unproblematic and confirms O'Connell's historical conclusions. On the other hand, as soon as the idea of value change is introduced, the situation becomes more contentious. A series of unavoidable questions immediately present themselves. How far is the primacy given to the role of religion in the creation of values still appropriate? Has this role not been undermined by the process known as secularisation? Can we really maintain in the 1990s that religion remains a central element of our value system? The influence of religion is becoming, surely, increasingly peripheral within contemporary European society. Or is it?

It will be these questions that preoccupy us in the final section of this chapter. In the meantime it is important to indicate the principal findings of the 1981 EVSG survey for a variety of religious indicators. (For a fuller picture of these data – essential for any detailed work – see Harding *et al.* 1986 and Stoetzel 1983, together with the analyses for each European country involved in the survey.)

There are, broadly speaking, five religious indicators within the data: denominational allegiance, reported church attendance, attitudes towards the church, indicators of religious belief and some measurement of subjective religious disposition. These variables have considerable potential: they can be correlated with one another and with a wide range of socio-demographic data. In this respect the survey shows commendable awareness of the complexity of religious phenomena and the need to bear in mind more than one dimension in an individual's (or indeed a nation's) religious life.

However, what emerges in practice with respect to these multiple indicators is a clustering of two types of variable: on the one hand, those concerned with feelings, experience and the more numinous religious beliefs; on the other, those which measure religious orthodoxy, ritual participation and institutional attachment. It is, moreover, the latter (the more orthodox indicators of religious attachment) which display, most obviously, an undeniable degree of secularisation throughout western Europe. In contrast, the former (the less institutional indicators) indicate a remarkable persistence in some aspects of religious life.

In particular, some form of 'religious disposition' and acceptance of the moral precepts of Christianity continues to be widespread among large numbers of Europeans, even among a proportion for whom the orthodox institution of the Church has no place.

(Harding *et al.* 1986: 70)

The essentials of this contrasting information are presented in Tables 11.1, 11.2 and 11.3, reproduced from the EVSG study. These tables can be used in two ways: either to indicate the overall picture of the continent or to exemplify some of the national differences to which we shall refer in the second section of this chapter.

First, though, the trends common to the continent as a whole. We should start, perhaps, by echoing one conclusion of the European Value Study itself: that is, to treat with considerable caution statements about the secularisation process – particularly unqualified ones – either within Europe or anywhere else. For the data are complex,

Table 11.1 **National variations in denominational affiliation and reported church attendance (%)**

Country	Predominant Denomination	Denominational Affiliation Catholic 7071	Protestant 3214	None 1607	Others and no answers 1940	Church Attendance Weekly or more often 3073	Monthly 1456	Never 4267	'Score'[1]
Eire	Catholic	95	3	0	2	82	6	4	9.8
Italy	Catholic	93	0	6	1	36	16	21	4.6
Spain	Catholic	90	0	9	1	41	12	25	5.2
Belgium	Catholic	72	2	15	10	30	8	34	3.6
France	Catholic	71	2	26[2]		12	6	57	1.6
Denmark	Protestant	1	92	1	6	3	9	43	0.9
Britain	Protestant	11	74	9	5	14	9	46	2.0
N. Ireland	Protestant	24	66	0	9	52	15	11	6.7
W. Germany	Mixed	41	48	9	1	21	16	20	3.0
Holland	Mixed	32	26	36	6	27	13	41	3.5
West European average		57	28	12	2	32	13	30	3.2

	Weekly or more often	Monthly	Never	'Score'
All Catholics (N = 7,071)	37	14	22	4.6
All Protestants[3] (N = 3214)	9	12	35	1.5
All non-affiliated (N = 1607)	1	1	87	0.2

Notes:
1 Weighted average across all church attendance categories
2 Two categories coded together
3 Excluding Nonconformists (N = 239)

Source: Harding et al. (1986: 36–7)

Table 11.2 **Traditional beliefs, with trend comparisons**

% Believing in	Europe 1981	France 1947	France 1968	France 1981	Great Britain 1947	Great Britain 1968	Great Britain 1981	Holland 1947	Holland 1968	Holland 1981	W. Germany 1968	W. Germany 1981	Eire 1981	N. Ireland 1981	Belgium 1981	Spain 1981	Denmark 1981	Italy 1981
God	75	68	73	62	84	77	76	80	79	65	81	72	95	91	77	87	58	84
A soul	58			46			59			59		61	82	80	52	64	33	63
Sin	57	59		42	49		69			49		59	85	91	44	58	29	63
Life after death[1]	43		35	35		38	45	38	50	42	41	39	76	72	37	55	26	47
Heaven	40		39	27		54	57		54	39	43	31	83	81	33	50	17	41
The devil	25		17	17		21	30		29	21	25	18	57	66	20	33	12	30
Hell	23		22	15		23	27		28	15	25	14	54	65	18	34	8	31
Re-incarnation	21		23	22		18	27		10	10	25	19	26	18	13	25	11	21
A personal God	32			26			31			34		28	73	70	39	55	24	26
Some sort of spirit or life force	36			26			39			29		40	16	18	24	23	24	50
Don't really know what to think	16			22			19			17		17	6	8	15	12	22	11
Don't think there is any sort of spirit, God or life force	11			19			9			12		13	2	1	8	6	21	6

Note:
1 The question in the 1947 survey was worded, 'Do you believe in the immortality of the soul?' Trend data from J. Stoetzel (1983) *Les Valeurs du Temps Présent* (Paris: Presses Universitaires de France), p. 115

Source: Harding *et al.* (1986: 46–7)

Table 11.3 **Percentages of people not belonging to a religion and never attending church, national differences by age group**

	Europe	France	Great Britain	N. Ireland	Eire	Holland	Belgium	Spain	Denmark	W. Germany	Italy
Percentage not belonging to a religion											
Age											
18–24	18	38	14	5	2	47	24	15	6	9	9
25–34	20	45	10	7	2	45	16	19	9	15	12
55–64	7	16	4	5	1	26	13	5	4	8	4
Percentage saying that they never attend church											
Age											
18–24	43	63	59	20	5	44	41	39	53	31	26
25–34	45	72	54	16	7	52	38	39	52	28	31
55–64	29	50	36	5	5	30	34	16	36	22	19

Source: Harding et al. (1986: 42)

contradictory even, and clear-cut conclusions become correspondingly difficult (Harding *et al.* 1986: 31–4).

Bearing this in mind – together with the clustering of the variables that we have already mentioned – it seems to me more accurate to suggest that west Europeans remain, by and large, unchurched populations rather than, simply secular. For a marked falling-off in religious attendance (especially in the Protestant north) has not resulted, yet, in a parallel abdication of religious belief. In short, many Europeans have ceased to belong to their religious institutions in any meaningful sense, but they have not abandoned, so far, many of their deep-seated religious motivations.[4]

Two short parentheses are important in this connection. The first may seem obvious, but the situation of believing without belonging (if such we may call it) should not be taken for granted. This relatively widespread – though fluctuating – characteristic within European religion in the late twentieth century should not merely be assumed; it must be examined, probed and questioned.

The second point illustrates this need for questioning. It introduces two contrasting situations where believing without belonging is not the norm. Indeed, in east Europe prior to 1989, the two variables were (in some places at least) reversed, for the non-believer quite consciously used Mass attendance as one way of expressing disapproval of an unpopular regime. The second, very different, contrast comes from the United States. Here religious attendance has maintained itself at levels far higher than those that prevail in most of Europe; at least 50 per cent of the American population both believe and belong. Once again the situation should not be taken for granted; it must be examined, sociologically as well as theologically.

If we return now to the west European data and begin to probe more deeply, we find further evidence of consistency in the shapes or profiles of religiosity which obtain across a wide variety of European countries. One very clear illustration of such profiling can be found in patterns of religious belief, about which Harding *et al.* make the following observation:

Varying levels of belief in each country are similar to those seen on other indicators. Interestingly, irrespective of level of belief, the rank order among items is almost identical across Europe. The one exception to a consistent pattern, paradoxically, is the higher ranking given by English speaking countries to heaven than to life after death.

(1986: 47)

This kind of consistency is persuasive, the more so in that it is not easily predictable.

Correlations between religious indices and socio-economic variables confirm the existence of socio-religious patterning across national boundaries. For throughout west Europe, it is clear that religious factors correlate – to varying degrees – with indices of occupation, gender and age (social class as such is more problematic). The correlation with age is particularly striking, and raises once again the future shape of European religion (see note 4). Indeed, it prompts the most searching question of the study: are we, in west Europe, experiencing a permanent generational shift with respect to religious behaviour, rather than a manifestation of the normal life-cycle? The EVSG findings seem to indicate that this might be so:

The survey data are consistent with the hypothesis that there has been a degree of secularization in Western Europe. Markedly lower church attendance, institutional attachment, and adherence to traditional beliefs is found in younger compared with older respondents, and data from other sources support the notion that these are not life-cycle differences.

(1986: 69–70)

If this really is the case, the future shape of European religion may be very different indeed. We shall come back to this point.

So much for the similarities across west Europe. What about the differences? The first, and most obvious, of these lies between the notably more religious – and Catholic – countries of southern Europe and the less religious countries of the Protestant north. This variation holds across almost every indicator; indeed, they are interrelated. Levels of practice, for example, are markedly higher in Italy, Spain, Belgium and Ireland (closer in its religious life to continental Europe than to Britain) than they are elsewhere. Not surprisingly, one effect of regular Mass attendance is a corresponding strength in the traditional orthodoxies through most of Catholic Europe.[5]

There are, however, exceptions to this rule, and at this point it is necessary to anticipate the discussion in the second part of this chapter. For France displays a very different profile from the other Catholic countries, a contrast that cannot be explained without reference to the particular history of the country in question. The distinctiveness of France's religious history will form one focus of the second section.

Other exceptions to a European pattern, or patterns, should be looked at in a similar light; notably, the countries which do not conform to the believing without belonging framework. Conspicuous here are the two Irelands. Once again, the particular and problematic nature of Irish history accounts for this; for religion has – regrettably – become entangled with questions of Irish identity on both sides of the border. The high levels of religious practice as well as belief in both the Republic and Northern Ireland are both cause and consequence of this situation. In the Republic especially, the statistics of religious practice remain very high indeed.

Before such particularities are explored in detail, one further variation within the overall framework is important. In France, Belgium, the Netherlands and, possibly, Britain (more especially England) there is a higher than average incidence of no religion, or at least no denominational affiliation. Indeed Stoetezel (1983: 89–91) – in the French version of the EVSG analysis – distinguishes four European types in terms of religious affiliation rather than three:[6] The Catholic countries (Spain, Italy and Eire); the predominantly Protestant countries (Denmark, Great Britain and Northern Ireland); the mixed variety (West Germany); and what he calls a '*région laïque*' (that is, France, Belgium, the Netherlands and, possibly, England) where those who recognise no religious label form a sizeable section of the population. In many ways this analysis is more satisfying than groupings suggested elsewhere in the European Value material (see note 6), where countries which have very different religious profiles find themselves grouped together.

In anticipating the following section, we have already indicated one of the severest limitations within the EVSG data. There is no way of telling from the data *why* a particular country should be similar to or different from its neighbours. Apparently, similar statistical profiles can mask profound differences, a point that we shall explore in some detail with reference to France and Britain. Before doing so, a second drawback must also be mentioned. The EVSG sample sizes for each country are too small to give any meaningful data about religious minorities. It would, however, be grossly misleading to present an image of Europe at the end of the twentieth century without any reference to these increasingly important sections of the European population.

The first of these minorities, the Jews, has been present in Europe for centuries; a presence, moreover, that has been inextricably bound up with the tragedies of recent European history. Nor can it be said, regrettably, that anti-Semitism is a thing of the past. It continues to rear an ugly head from time to time right across Europe, itself a pretty accurate indicator of wider insecurities. Estimations of numbers are always difficult, but there are, currently, around 1 million Jews in west Europe, the largest communities being the French (500,000 – 600,000) and the British (300,000). French Judaism has been transformed in the postwar period by the immigration of considerable numbers of Sephardim from North Africa.[7]

Former colonial connections also account for other non-Christian immigrations into Europe. The Islamic communities are, probably, the most significant in this respect, though Britain also houses considerable numbers of Sikhs and Hindus. Islam is, however, the largest other-faith population in Europe, conservative estimates suggesting a figure of 6 million.[8] Muslims make up approximately 3 per cent of most west European populations (Clarke 1988).

More specifically, the links between France and North Africa account for the very sizeable French Muslim community (2–3 million). Britain's equivalent comes from the Indian subcontinent (1.5 million). Germany, on the other hand, has absorbed large numbers of migrant workers from the fringes of south-east Europe, and from Turkey in particular. The fate of these migrants in the face of growing numbers of east Germans looking for work within the new Germany remains to be seen.

Whatever the outcome of this particular situation, however, one fact remains increasingly clear: the Islamic presence in Europe is here to stay. It follows that Europeans can no longer distance themselves from the debates of the Muslim world. Whether they like it or not, the issues are present on their own doorstep. Admitting that this is the case is not easy for many Europeans, for the Islamic factor undoubtedly challenges the assumptions of European life, both past and present. Peaceful coexistence between Islam and Judaeo-Christian Europe cannot – and never could be – taken for granted.[9] Nor can Muslims accept unequivocally the live-and-let-live religious attitudes assumed by the majority of contemporary Europeans. This, surely, was the problematic at the heart of the Rushdie controversy.

One further source of diversity remains: the presence of new religious movements. The significance – or otherwise – of such movements remains, however, a controversial issue, with some commentators suggesting that they may have rather less influence, in the long run, than the other-faith communities of west Europe.[10] Be that as it may, we should note, none the less, the very particular resonance that new religious movements have for the sociologist. Inadvertently, they have become barometers of the changes taking place in contemporary society (Beckford 1985, 1986). New religious movements 'represent an "extreme situation" which, precisely because it is extreme, throws into sharp relief many of the assumptions hidden behind legal, cultural, and social structures' (1985:11).

We can use this perspective to examine one of the most urgent questions facing Europe at the present time; the need to create and to sustain a truly tolerant and pluralist society, both in Europe as a whole, and in its constituent nations – a society, that is, which goes well beyond an individualised live and let live philosophy; a society able to accommodate 'that unusual phenomenon' in contemporary Europe, the person (of whatever faith) who takes religion seriously (*The Times*: 6 February 1989). By examining the divergent attitudes displayed towards new religious movements in different European countries, we can learn a great deal about underlying attitudes. After all, tolerance of religious differences in contemporary Europe must mean tolerance of *all* religious differences, not just the ones we happen to approve of. If a country 'fails' in its tolerance of new religious movements, it is unlikely, or at least very much less likely, to succeed with respect to other religious minorities.

Unity and diversity

The third chapter of David Martin's *General Theory of Secularization* (1978) focuses on the tensions between religion and nationhood within the European situation. It starts from the following premise:

> Europe is a unity by virtue of having possessed one Caesar and one God, i.e. by virtue of Rome. It is a diversity by virtue of the existence of nations. The patterns of European religions derive from the tension and the partnership between Caesar and God, and from the relationship between religion and the search for national integrity and identity.
>
> (1978: 100)

The second section of this chapter will examine these relationships with particular reference to France and to Britain.[11]

It will also suggest that recent shifts in perspective – shifts that derive both from the implementation of the Single European Act and from the revolutions in east Europe – need to be taken into account in an up-to-date assessment of the tensions or partnerships between Caesar and God in contemporary Europe. Will there, for example, be more room for regional or subcultural identity if national profiles in west Europe diminish, relatively speaking? Conversely, will the re-emergence of nationalisms all over east Europe alter the patterns established – or rather, imposed – in the postwar period? The religious factor, suppressed along with so much else under communism, is a crucial element in these unpredictable events.

But, first, Britain and France.[12] If we look at statistics for believing and belonging in France we find, superficially at least, a pattern rather similar to that in Britain. Around 80 per cent of the French call themselves Roman Catholics, whereas regular weekly attendance at Mass is as low as 13 per cent. A further 7 per cent attend Mass once or twice a month (Hervieu-Léger 1986). The figures for Britain are not dissimilar (Brierley 1988; 1991), though the denominational mix is, clearly, quite different. Only 15 per cent of the British population attend church with any regularity, and even fewer in England, but nominal allegiances (especially to the national churches in England and Scotland) remain moderately high.

Such statistics must, however, be carefully interpreted. Why is it, for example, that almost all the indices of secularity are higher in France than in Britain? (Despite the apparent Catholicism of the French, the EVSG data tell us that only 62 per cent of the French say that they believe in God.) Why, if we look at another set of comparisons, do British Roman Catholics not only practice with greater enthusiasm than French ones, but behave quite differently from a political point of view? Conversely, the French Protestant minority, though tiny, has been disproportionately influential in many aspects of French life.[13] It has, moreover, voted to the Left traditionally, quite unlike its counterpart in Northern Ireland. These differences can only be explained sociologically; that is, by taking into account a whole series of interrelated contextual variables (economic, social and political) that derive from a particular national or regional context.

This is the essence of Martin's thesis: that broad social processes – among them the secularisation process – must always be considered in relation to particular historical situations. What, then, are the key contextual variables that have operated so decisively on either side of the Channel?

The greater prominence of secularity in France derives from a religious history quite different from that in Britain. Despite our persistent quarrels about various forms of Christianity, Britain has never experienced a major religious split that corresponded with a political divide. In contrast, the French were for generations politically divided about religious questions rather than anything else. The animosity of the early years of the Third Republic culminated in the separation of church and state and the establishment of an emphatically secular public-school system. The residual bitterness of these quarrels can still be felt; it accounts for the higher profile of anti-religion as well as non-religion in France. It also accounts for the persistence of political allegiances along religious lines right through the first half of the twentieth century.

In Britain, a considerably greater degree of pluralism was established at an earlier stage (our Roman Catholic and Nonconformist minorities are substantial). The existence of such minorities permitted a certain amount of choice between different flavours of Christianity, a choice quite unlike the French obligation to accept Catholicism or nothing at all. This is one reason, a major one, why the 'feel' of our religious life remains qualitatively different from the French, a contrast which persists despite a marked decline in institutional religion on both sides of the Channel.

Two relatively recent episodes exemplify these differences. The first, the controversy surrounding the publication of Salman Rushdie's *The Satanic Verses* was, initially, a British affair. Very quickly, however, the episode escalated to the point where it attracted considerable international attention. The French critique reflects very clearly French preoccupations about religious matters.

For a start, the divisions in France were far more clear-cut than those in England. Cardinal Decourtray (the president of the French Bishops' Conference) called *The Satanic Verses* 'an offence against religious faith', and lost no time in drawing the comparison with Martin Scorsese's film, *The Last Temptation of Christ*. President Mitterrand responded in similar vein: 'All dogmas which through violence, violate the freedom of the human spirit and the right to self-expression represent, in my eyes, absolute evil.' The controversy was, it seems, gradually translated into French terms; in other words it became 'part of France's hallowed battle between Christian and

Freethinkers' (*Independent*: 23 February 1989 and 10 February 1990; see also Appignanesi and Maitland 1989). In Britain the response was far more pragmatic, a question of both/and rather than either/or. Much of the debate concerned the law against blasphemy. The Archbishop of Canterbury called for a strengthening of this law to cover religions other than Christianity (*Independent*: 22 Feburary 1989); others insisted that we should abolish laws concerning something as outmoded as blasmphemy altogether. The French, understandably, were mystified by the domestic implications of these exchanges.

A second episode, or rather pair of episodes, confirms these impressions. Not long after the Rushdie controversy became headline news, two or three Muslim girls began to attract attention – on either side of the Channel – by wearing the traditional Muslim scarf (or *foulard*, to use the French term) within school. So much for the similarities. The differences arise in the reactions of each country to the initial gesture. The French were offended, above all, by the wearing of a religious symbol within the public-school system: that is, within the *école laïque*.[14] The British, in contrast, were unlikely to be bothered about religious symbols *per se* in state schools, for a certain degree of religious life (including religious symbols) forms an integral part of our educational system. Instead, we became concerned about school uniform, a peculiarly British preoccupation. Muslim scarves must be rejected because they do not conform to school uniform regulations. Mercifully, the school governors in the British case found satisfactory a compromise: navy-blue scarves would, after all, be acceptable.

There is, however, a more serious aspect to the British situation, for we have in this country denominational schools that are, very largely, funded by the state – a situation unthinkable in France.[15] And if the French were preoccupied about the wearing of a religious symbol in their state schools, we have to face the anomaly of refusing to the Muslim minority what we have allowed, and continue to allow to Anglicans, Roman Catholics and Jews. Such a policy is at best illogical, at worst discriminatory.

If these, very recent, events exemplify the continuing religious (even ideological) differences between two neighbouring European countries, are there, perhaps, aspects of the present situation which do the reverse? What, to be more precise, will be the effect of greater European unity on this kind of situation? Common rulings from Strasbourg or Brussels on the rights of religious minorities might, for example, iron out some of the anomalies. On the other hand, individual nations could resist such interference, feeling that the regulation of religious minorities is a purely domestic affair. One way or another, we find ourselves returning to one of the recurrent themes in the religious life of contemporary Europe: the problematic of a truly pluralist society.

We need now to set this problematic into a broader perspective and reconsider, more generally, the relationship between God and Caesar in a rapidly changing Europe. Such an exercise will also enable us to draw some of the threads in this chapter together.

Setting or resetting the tensions between God and Caesar in the context of contemporary Europe requires, first of all, that an important theoretical assumption within this chapter be properly articulated. This can be stated quite simply. Just how far does the religious life of a country (or indeed of a continent) reflect a context rather than create one? In other words, is religion primarily a reactive rather than proactive sociological variable? In my opinion, the potential for proactivity lies at the heart of the matter.

Looking back, for example, it is clear that the religious factor played a crucial part in the forging of something that we recognise as a European. At the same time, this common historical heritage has, undoubtedly, been moulded by a great diversity of contextual factors into a number of subtypes or national variations, some of them (not least the British case) very distinct indeed. In the 1990s, as the Single European Act becomes reality, the situation alters once again. Bearing this in mind, two lines of thought suggest themselves. First, we need to ask whether the religious factor has – in the supposedly secular late twentieth century – the capacity to do anything effective at all. And second, we must examine not only the degree of independence of the religious factor, but the direction in which it might operate.

Paradoxically, the first of these questions will be kept until last: it forms the focus of the third section. The second can be elaborated as follows. On the one hand, we need to ask what 'use' might be made of the religious factor, either by the state or by any number of interested parties. Can, for example, the religious element be pressed into service by pro-Europeans to emphasise what Europe has in common, or will it be used by their opponents to provide support for discrete and independent nations each with its own, carefully circumscribed religious sphere, possibly a national church? Either scenario is possible.

The argument, can, however, be turned the other way round. For the churches (national or otherwise), religious individuals or a wide variety of religious organisations may themselves attempt to initiate – rather than reflect – shifts in public opinion. In other words, the religious factor may operate as an independent variable in bringing about a greater European consciousness, or, conversely, in resisting just such a move.

It seems to me that a theoretically informed examination of contemporary events, bearing this framework (or these frameworks) in mind, is one of the most urgent empirical tasks of the sociology of religion in the 1990s.

The British case is particularly apposite, the more so if a Northern

Irish perspective is also included.[16] For we have, then, not only a
considerable denominational mix but four distinct national perspectives as well. It is, for example, hardly surprising that the Northern
Irish treat Europe with considerable suspicion. They are only too well
aware of Catholic majorities in Ireland, let alone in Europe, to risk
much down that road. In contrast, the Scots – and to some degree the
Welsh as well – have everything to gain, for greater European
integration necessarily diminishes English domination. The Scots,
moreover, have a national church (the Kirk), which belongs, both
theologically and organisationally, to one of Europe's major spiritual
traditions, Calvinism.[17] In Scotland, therefore, economic, political
and religious factors are mutually reinforcing.

The English case is altogether more complicated, but two factors
are, perhaps, crucial. The Church of England is exactly what that
name implies; it is the national church of England and can still, at
times, operate very effectively in that capacity (Davie 1990; 1991). It
has, in addition, been inextricably linked to our colonial past, for
missionaries followed the flag, or vice versa, for centuries. One very
obvious consequence of this past has been a multiplicity of organisational links with churches overseas. But neither the essential English-
ness of the domestic church nor its imperial connections are going to
be much help in forming effective and creative links with Europe;
they may well, in fact, be a hindrance. It remains to be seen whether
the English churches have either the will or the capacity to overcome
this situation.

Careful comparative work can reveal similar tensions elsewhere in
Europe; the tensions between regional and national loyalties are one
example. For the former may well find greater room for manoeuvre
as national identities diminish, relatively speaking. There are certainly
parts of Europe where the regions are claiming greater autonomy.
The affirmation of Scottish and Welsh identitiy is mirrored elsewhere:
in Catalonia and the Basque country, or in the Italian autonomous
regions, to name but a few. But it is in east Europe that ethnic
nationalisms are the most potent force. A detailed examination of
these is beyond the scope of this chapter, but the religious factor is,
clearly, of immense importance in such struggles. They should,
certainly, be borne in mind in the theoretical discussion which follows.

Religion and modernity in contemporary Europe

There have been a number of references to secularisation, or to the
secularisation process, in this chapter. We have seen, for example,
that the authors of the European Value Study evaluate much of their
religious data with this framework in mind. Their conclusions are far
from clear-cut. None the less, the importance of the age factor in the
EVSG analysis suggests a crucially significant change with respect to

the secularisation process; the possibility of a generational shift towards a more secular frame of reference far more deep-seated than the expected life-cycle differences.

Martin's thesis – the focus of the second section – finds its fullest expression in a book entitled *A General Theory of Secularization* (1978). The 'theory' that Martin puts forward is by no means deterministic; nor does he propose that secularisation is 'a very long term or inevitable trend'. Rather Martin describes a particular period (varying from two to four centuries) in which 'certain tendencies can be noted . . . with regard to the role, power and popularity of religious beliefs and institutions' (1978: 12). These tendencies are described in considerable detail. Secularisation is, however, the dominant theme; the material – subtle, perceptive and nuanced though it is – is ordered with this, rather than another, framework in mind.

In some ways, it is hardly surprising that ideas about secularisation have dominated thinking about Europe both in the sociology of religion and elsewhere (Edwards 1987), for the evidence is, in many respects, overwhelming. Something, in Owen Chadwick's phrase (Chadwick 1975), has happened to European society – to the European mind – in the last 200 years. Exactly what this was, and why it came about, must remain a matter of much enquiry by students of many disciplines, but an unmistakable shift has, undoubtedly, taken place. For want of a better word, we label this shift 'secularisation'.

On the other hand, if the impetus towards secularisation is as strong as some commentators imply (not, on the whole, those so far mentioned), a very great deal of explaining remains to be done. For not everything seems to be working in this direction. Indices of religious belief, for example, have not dropped in a way that might have been predicted a generation or so ago. Nor have religious controversies ceased to catch the public's imagination; the Rushdie controversy dominated the media for weeks. And governments – far from denying the existence of the sacred – are, increasingly, faced with moral, ethical, even religious, decisions as they grapple with the consequences of scientific advance. Bio-ethical and environmental issues remain at the forefront of public controversy, for science, it seems, has become the creator just as much as the solver of society's problems.

Indeed, just as it seemed possible that secularisation might, all other things being equal, begin to assert itself in a big way, all the other things have ceased, increasingly, to fulfil that condition. Sociologists are left trying to readjust their frameworks.

At least, they are left trying to come to terms with a great deal of conflicting evidence. Is there any way, for instance, in which we can hold together the persistence of religious belief in contemporary Europe alongside the marked decline – but not the disappearance of – religious practice? Can we find satisfactory explanations for the

prevalence of Christain nominalism alongside the hardening of religious boundaries associated with the growth of evangelical (even
fundamentalist) tendencies within Christianity, and with the increase
in other faith communities across contemporary Europe? What about
the disturbing evidence of fundamentalisms worldwide? And what
about the increasing tendency for politicians and other public figures
to consult the 'religious sector' about matters that they know to be
beyond their competence? Diverging and conflicting data make heavy
demands on sociological theorists.

One line of thinking has been to abandon the idea of an overall
framework altogether; a trend which can be illustrated both within
sociological theory and within the religious phenomena that such
theory seeks to explain. For 'postmodern' sociology is as much subject
to the relativisation process as postmodern theology or religion; both
involve parallel rejections of the all-explaining, all-encompassing
meta-narrative. Postmodern individuals, including sociologists, must
evolve whatever explanations of life – and death – that they can, from
whatever is available at the time.

In many ways notions of believing without belonging (the dominant
mood, perhaps, of European religion) fit quite well into this kind of
framework; for the phenomenon of detached belief, of privatised
religion, permits us, surely, to select at will from the religious goods
on offer and mould these into personal packages that suit our
particular life-styles and subcultures. At the same time, the institutional features of religious life representing orthodoxy become less
and less important as we set and reset the parameters of faith
according to whim. That the so-called theological certainties are also
under attack need not concern us unduly.

If we look at the evidence, however, this approach becomes
increasingly hard to sustain. For the phenomenon of detached belief,
though prevalent, is not the only religious phenomenon in contemporary Europe. The existence of significant other-faith communities
alongside an active, sometimes demanding Christian minority, have
to be taken into account. Indeed, the all-too-evident need to create
in modern Europe a pluralist society capable of accommodating such
elements is paramount. It requires, moreover, that differing religious
creeds are treated with considerably greater seriousness than inter-
changeable supermarket alternatives.

Hervieu-Léger (1986, 1990: see also Davie 1992) offers a rather
different approach. Her analysis suggests an open-ended concept of
modernity which almost – if not completely – renders a postmodern
dimension unnecessary. *Vers un nouveau christianisme* focuses on the
relationship between religion and modernity in advanced western
societies, a relationship which is both complex and paradoxical. The
argument works at two levels: it begins by acknowledging the contradictory features within contemporary religious life (and in particular

within the French situation); and it continues by relating these contradictions to the tensions within the concept of modernity itself. Hervieu-Léger underlines the dilemma facing those who try to understand the nature of contemporary religious life. On the one hand, there is no lack of data to support the secularisation thesis; a fall in religious practice, a drop in clergy vocations (a truly dramatic one in the French Catholic church) and a crumbling of traditional morality. On the other hand, we cannot deny the evidence of religious renewal, notably the emergence of a whole range of 'warm', emotional communities both within and outside the traditional churches. The latter aspect has been further documented by Hervieu-Léger in a series of case studies (for the most part French ones) published under the title *De l'émotion en réligion* (Hervieu-Léger and Champion 1990).

The 'paradox of modernity' – the second level – attempts to make sense of these contradictions by examining them in relation to strains within the concept of modernity itself. The paradox is defined in the following terms:

modernity destroys religion as a system of meaning and as a motivator of human effort, but – at the same time – modernity creates the time-space of a utopia which, through its very structure, remains attached to the religious problematic of fulfilment and salvation.

(Hervieu-Léger 1986: 224)

In other words, modernity, at the same time as it destroys traditional religious forms, creates an ongoing requirement for something beyond itself. If religion – in an infinite variety of forms – provides one response to this ongoing requirement, it follows that religion as such will continue to persist despite the destructive aspects of modernity. The secularisation process is, therefore, something far more complex than the notion of religion giving way to rationality; it becomes 'a process of permanent reorganisation in the function of religion, within a society which is structurally unable to fulfil the expectations that it must create in order to continue in existence' (1986: 227). Following this argument, the persistence of religion becomes an integral part of modernity rather than an antithetical or postmodern reaction to it.

This, skeletally, is the essence of Hervieu-Léger's analysis, an analysis that has emerged primarily within a French context. We need now to switch back to the European material and to examine the relevance of this argument to the principal focus of this chapter: the unity and diversity of European religion.

One area of research is, perhaps, crucial. Religious membership is, very often, most effective at a local or community level. In this way it becomes an increasingly significant way of preserving aspects of life threatened by the ever-increasing scale of modern economics, indeed of modernity itself. This facet of religious life can be found in many parts of the contemporary world. It has, none the less, particular resonance in Europe in the 1990s. For we find ourselves asking once again how the religious dimension will respond to the increasingly European stress within economic, social and even political life. Are we likely to see a corresponding homogeneity in Europe's religion, particularly in styles of belief (see Willaime 1989: 247–7)? If so, will such homogeneity extend to east European countries? Or will the religious factor take a rather different form; a form which bolsters national, regional and even local boundaries rather than European ones? In other words, will the religious life of Europe (east and/or west) reinforce the step towards wider boundaries; or will it counteract such pressures, and continue to give meaning to a more immediately accessible level of life?

We have already suggested that careful empirical work in this area is a priority for the European sociologist of religion in the 1990s. It assumes, moreover, that the sociologists involved will appreciate the continued importance of religion as a salient variable in their analysis. Despite the decline in conventional forms of religiosity, especially among the young, religion as such (following Hervieu-Léger) will continue to play a significant part in the development of modern Europe.[18] Discovering how is part of the empirical enquiry.

Notes

1 The situation is, however, far from predictable. Greece, for example, (an Orthodox country) is already a full member of the European Community. In the meantime Austria continues to wait.

2 The European Value Study was a major cross-national survey of human values, carried out in Europe in 1981, and then extended to other countries worldwide. It was designed by the European Value Systems Study Group (EVSSG). The material used in this chapter covers ten western European countries: Belgium, Denmark, France, Great Britain, Holland, the Republic of Ireland, Italy, Northern Ireland, Spain and West Germany. Analyses of the European material are available in Harding and Phillips, with Fogarty (1986) and in Stoetzel (1983). The British material is written up in Abrams, Gerard and Timms (1985). Other national studies are listed in Harding *et al.* (1986: xv).

A re-study is in process. Outline figures have appeared in the press; published material will be available in 1993.

3 The European Value Study reveals both the advantages and limitations of survey methodology. These are discussed in the introductory sections of Harding *et al.* (1986). Particular difficulties for the religious material will be highlighted in this chapter.

4 One of the crucial questions raised by the EVSG material concerns the future of European religion. Are we on the brink of something very different indeed: a markedly more secular twenty-first century? It is, however, very difficult to tell how the relationship between believing and belonging will develop. Nominal belief could well become the norm for the foreseeable future; on the other hand, the two variables may gradually

move closer together as nominal belief turns itself into no belief at all. At the moment we can only speculate.

5 In many ways, Protestant Europe is more secular. On the other hand, the loss of traditional orthodoxies does not necessarily imply the adoption of secular alternatives; increasingly, heterodox belief is equally likely.

6 Halsey (1985), for example, places British attitudes in a European perspective, offering three categories: Scandinavia (Denmark, Sweden, Finland and Norway); northern Europe (Northern Ireland, Eire, West Germany, Holland, Belgium and France); and Latin Europe (Italy and Spain). The northern Europe category includes some very different religious contexts.

7 Information (including statistics) about the Jewish communities in west Europe can be found in Lerman (1989).

8 Estimates of the size of Europe's Muslim population are, inevitably, related to questions about immigration. Statistics relating to illegal immigrants are particularly problematic.

9 The outstanding example of creative toleration comes from medieval Spain, where Jews, Muslims and Christians lived harmoniously for four centuries. The forcible expulsion of both Jews and Muslims from a re-Catholicised Spain in 1492 renders the 1992 celebration of this year a very ambivalent European anniversary.

10 There is a curious imbalance in the sociological literature with respect to new religious movements. Much has been published on these movements despite the relatively small numbers of people involved. Their importance has, at times, been correspondingly inflated.

11 France and Britain have been selected as examples of the secularisation process in west Europe in view of the author's familiarity with source material. The process could, equally well, have been documented for other European nations, though up-to-date material in English is not always available.

12 Detailed information on the French situation can be found in Hervieu-Léger (1986) and Michel (1985); for the British case, Brierley (1988 and 1991) and Hastings (1986) are invaluable. In the main these sources support the EVSG analysis, though the detailed statistics may vary from study to study.

13 In the early years of the Reformation, however, the spread of Protestantism within France was considerable. Though Protestants were reduced to a minority, the subsequent tenacity of French Protestantism through centuries of persecution has coloured much of French history.

14 The words '*Laïcité*', or '*laïque*' have no equivalent in English. The British have no need for such terms, given our very different religious culture.

15 This does not mean that there are no denominational schools in France; simply that they exist outside the state system of education.

16 For a more detailed discussion of the British churches in the European context, see Davie (1991).

17 The other two spiritual traditions of west Europe are Lutheranism and Catholicism. The Anglican church, in contrast, has no roots on the European mainland.

18 Beckford (1989) offers a similar, but none the less distinct analysis of religion in advanced industrial society. He argues (1989: 170) that religion has come adrift from its former points of anchorage (amongst others, the institutional churches) but is no less powerful as a result. 'It remains a

potent cultural resource or form which may act as the vehicle of change, challenge or conservation.' It can be 'used' in a wide variety of ways, not all of which are predictable.

References

Abrams, M., Gerard, G. and Timms, N. (eds) (1985) *Values and Social Change in Britain*, London: Macmillan.

Appignanesi, L. and Maitland, S. (1989) *The Rushdie File*, London: Fourth Estate.

Beckford, J. (1985) *Cult Controversies*, London and New York: Tavistock Publications.

——(ed.) (1986) *New Religious Movements and Rapid Social Change*, London: Sage/UNESCO.

——(1989) *Religion and Advanced Industrial Society*, London: Unwin Hyman.

Brierley, P. (1988) *UK Christian Handbook 1989/90*, London: Marc Europe.

——(1991) *Christian England*, London: Marc Europe.

Chadwick, O. (1975) *The Secularization of the European Mind*, Cambridge: Cambridge University Press.

Clarke, P. (1988) 'Islam in contemporary Europe', in S. Sutherland, S. Stewart, L. Houlden, P. Clarke and F. Hardy (eds) *The World's Religions*, London: Routledge.

Davie, G. (1990) 'An ordinary God: the paradox of religion in contemporary Britain', *British Journal of Sociology*, 41: 395 – 421.

——(1991) 'The British churches and Europe', Paper presented to a Conference on 'Le facteur réligieux dans la construction de l'Europe', Strasbourg (to be published in the Proceedings of the Conference).

——(1992) 'Religion and modernity in Britain', *International Journal of Comparative Religion*, 1: .

Edwards, D. (1987) *The Futures of Christianity*, London: Hodder & Stoughton.

Halsey, A. H. (1985) 'On methods and morals', in M. Abrams, G. Gerard and N. Timms (eds) *Values and Social Change in Britain*, London: Macmillan.

Harding, S., Phillips, D., with Fogarty, M. (1986) *Contrasting Values in Western Europe*, London: Macmillan.

Hastings, A. (1986) *A History of English Christianity*, London: Collins.

Hervieu-Léger, D. (1986) *Vers un nouveau christianisme*, Paris: Cerf.

——(1990) 'Religion and modernity in the French context: for a new approach to secularization', *Sociological Analysis*, 51S: 15 – 25.

Hervieu-Léger, D. and Champion, F. (eds) (1990) *De l'émotion en religion*, Paris: Centurion.

Lerman, A. (1989) *The Jewish Communities of the World*, London: Macmillan.

Martin, D. (1978) *A General Theory of Secularization*, Oxford: Blackwell.

Michel, P. (ed.) (1985) 'Religions et société en France: problèmes politiques et sociaux', *La Documentation Française*, 518.

O'Connell, J. (1991) The Making of Europe: Strengths, Constraints and Resolutions, Paper presented to a conference at St George's House, Windsor.

238 *Responding Social Institutions*

Rushdie, S. (1988) *The Satanic Verses*, London and New York: Viking-Penguin.

Stoetzel, J. (1983) *Les Valeurs du Temps Présent*, Paris: Presses Universitaires de France.

Walters, P. (ed.) (1988) *World Christianity: Eastern Europe*, London: Marc Europe.

Willaime, J. P. (ed.) (1988) *Vers de Nouveaux Oecuménismes*, Paris: Cerf.

CHAPTER 12

Leisure – *jeux sans frontières* or major European industry?

STAN CLARK

Leisure might be considered the climax of industrial society, the aspect of life which, for most people, makes it all worthwhile. It has however, a protean nature. A first attempt to define leisure might be to see it in terms of non-work, yet there are activities going on in the workplace – for example, chatting during tea-breaks – which have a clearly recreational character. Leisure activities are often divided from those necessary to personal care, but eating and drinking and care of the body may also share, to a greater or lesser extent, characteristics typical of leisure activity. Going out to a restaurant for a meal or to a pub for a drink would seem to be primarily leisure activities, and visiting a hairdresser may also have a recreational component for some people. In this chapter I shall simply choose four areas of activity which are commonly regarded as leisure, which I think are important. In discussing them I hope to make clear that such activities are bound up with and influenced by other areas of people's lives: work, religion, maintenance of health, family life.

Problems in defining leisure are one reason for the considerable theoretical controversy surrounding this field. Sociologists are, however, also uncertain of how important it is. For some sociologists work, not leisure, remains the key to understanding society. Work is the precondition for life and leisure, and the generator of capital. The relationships entered into at work are said to determine social classes, which themselves influence social conflict and societal evolution. For theorists of postmodern society, however, such views belong to an obsolete paradigm. In postmodern society individuals define themselves by leisure activities and choices, creating styles and identities from the artefacts and culture of a pluralist society. There are also differences of approach amongst those who take leisure seriously as a social phenomenon. I make no attempt in this chapter to deal systematically with these theoretical issues, but I do hope to demonstrate that whatever one's theoretical position within the sociology of leisure, the study of leisure is important as well as interesting.

Finally, it is necessary to justify a comparative approach to the study of leisure. The case for a European framework of analysis in approaching sociological phenomena has been stated in the general introduction, and should emerge in this essay as well as in others. It is only necessary, therefore, to state here that I hope to demonstrate the continuing relevance of divisions into rural and urban, rich and poor, Catholic and anti-clerical, in the study of leisure activity, though the effect of such divisions is being modified by continuing processes of modernisation and economic integration. The study of society in a European perspective, interesting and important in itself, is necessary to gain an accurate understanding of the distinctiveness of British experience and the extent to which this distinctiveness is likely to survive.

Festivals

Two features of other western European societies when compared with that of Britain – later urbanisation and industrialisation, and the greater significance of the Catholic church – may be held responsible for an important difference in leisure patterns; namely, the greater prominence of traditional communal celebrations in the public life of the Continent. This is despite the fact that, for the most part, the close organic connection which marked the relationship between work and leisure in pre-industrial Europe has disappeared, and also despite the decline in religious belief. This greater prominence of festivals is true, I believe, not just in the less urbanised and industrialised countries like Spain and Portugal, but also in highly urbanised and industrialised countries like Germany and the Netherlands.[1]

Spain and Portugal are, however, particularly interesting in this respect. One author has written about Portugal: 'With the arrival of Easter and of Spring the whole of Portugal enters into a rhythm of the festa until the first approach of autumn. A rhythm which moreover hardly slows down during the winter months' (Sanchis 1983: 15).[2]

The study from which this quotation is taken provides a detailed anthropological account of the *romarias*, popular pilgrimages which are found throughout Portugal, though they are more common in the north. The essence of the *romaria* is religious and involves a promise made to a local 'saint'. The saint in question can be a relic or an image of a saint but equally an image of Christ or the Virgin Mary. It is typical for the images to be in churches or chapels on the outskirts of towns or villages, or in the countryside beyond, and there is often a procession of pilgrims to these chapels. The pilgrims pray for aid of various kinds, and make a promise to bestow a 'gift' next year if their prayers are heard. The gift may take the form of money or agricultural produce, but it may also take such forms as proceeding to the church or going around it on one's knees, or being carried to the church in a coffin. Gifts may be repeated over many years. The main focus of the analysis is how the *romaria* has become a struggle for control between the church authorities, who tend to see it primarily as a celebration of the saint's day, and the strength of popular religiosity which stresses the bargain struck between devotee and saint.

Our focus of interest, however, is the *romaria* as an occasion for communal festivities, which may last for two or three days. A typical element in such festivities is firework displays. Gifts may take the form of money for fireworks, an outcome apparently not very agreeable to the church, which prefers money for Masses or upkeep of the sanctuary. Sometimes special cakes may be baked and sold, or there may be bullfights. Almost invariably there is music and dancing. The exact form of festivities varies, as does the nature of the requests for aid. Some saints are seen as particularly helpful for certain types of medical problems, others for aiding the harvest or the fishing. What is common to all the *romarias*, however, is the combination of religion and popular festivities, a combination characteristic of leisure in pre-industrial Europe, which still survives today.

Sanchis concludes:

> It would be a total mistake to imagine the romaria as an assembly of 'believers', exclusively devoted to formal religious activities. The romaria is lived and experienced as a festival, that is a total event, which is constituted as a break in everyday life, an irruption of another world.
>
> (1977: 76)

Another important type of celebration is the political festival. Rearick has shown how the leaders of the Third Republic in France sought to legitimise it by festivals: annual festivals, such as Bastille Day on 14 July, and exceptional festivals, such as the funeral of Victor Hugo in 1885 (Rearick 1977). These activities took their inspiration from the political festivals of the First Republic. Such festivals were matched by those of the workers on 1 May and by those on the nationalist Right celebrating Joan of Arc.

A particularly interesting example of political festivals in modern Europe, which have been consciously set up in opposition to traditional religious ones, is the *feste* of the Italian Communist Party (PCI). These are discussed by Kertzer in his study of the PCI organisation in Albora, a *quartiere* of Bologna (Kertzer 1980). As part of the national and local battle for supremacy between Communists and Catholics in postwar Italy a sharp struggle took place between the two groups as to who could mount the most attractive festivals. As each parish had its own *festa*, so each section of the PCI developed a rival celebration. In Albora there was no doubt about the winner. Whereas only a few hundred people continued to participate in the church festivals, thousands attended the sectional *feste* of the Communist Party. Such festivals lasted for three to four days and were held outdoors. There were political speeches, but the main activities were eating and drinking. A highlight of one of the Albora festivals was the traditional goose-pull in which youths tried to win a goose by pulling off its head whilst it was suspended above them.

Kertzer argues that the *festa* was the one time in the year when all the community had the opportunity to come together and share common activities. The normal social barriers were broken down, men and women worked together in the kitchen, and party leaders took on the role of waiters. Political loyalty was cemented indirectly by leisure:

Alborese, who because of their lack of formal education, disinterest, timidity, or feelings of inferiority, participate in none of the specifically political activities of the Party, can and do, through the festa identify themselves with the PCI and are made to feel a part of it.

(Kertzer 1980: 157)

It would be misleading, however, to ignore the effects of secularisation, official regulation and tourism, on the character of many traditional festivals. An article in the *Guardian* claims that in much of Spain, though to a lesser extent in Seville, Holy Week has lost a good deal of its traditional mystical value, being seen nowadays primarily as a period of family holidays.[3] Under the impact of tourism many festivals, where they have not disappeared altogether, have become to an increasing extent commercial spectacles.

Norman Lewis has related the abandonment of the festival of *Sa Cova* (the Cave) in the village where he was living in Catalonia (Lewis 1984). This festival had involved a large, particularly rich meal, and a parade through the village to the church, but it had been proceeded by a strange ceremony, perhaps a relic of some ancient fertility rite. The women and girls made a trip by boat to a nearby sea-cave, which was entered only by them, the boatmen remaining outside. One girl, who had been chosen to lead the festivities, would be lightly smacked by her mother, 'the child pretended to cry, and that was the end of the thing . . . absolutely meaningless . . . but it was far and away the most important event of the year for the people of Farol'.[4] After the abandonment of the festival the cave became a place visited by tourists, taken there by local fishermen. In the space of a few years, then, we have the transformation of the cave from the centrepiece of a pre-industrial ritual to that of a postmodern spectacle.

Tourism

In the context of a European-wide study of leisure the subject of tourism is of major importance. A number of countries, such as Spain, Greece, Italy and Austria, have economies which are highly dependent upon the industry, most of their visitors coming from other European countries. Tourism is indeed of great importance virtually everywhere in Europe, as more and more people each year travel away from home to subject foreign places and people to the 'tourist gaze' (Urry 1990). Travellers from Europe are also an important element in the increasing invasion of Third World countries for purposes of recreation.

Tourism is an interesting industry in that the contact between tourists and locals, whether as producers (that is, servicers of tourists) or as picturesque bystanders (objects of the tourist gaze), is an important part of the experience. Relationships should not be purely functional, at least from the standpoint of the tourist, but should involve an aesthetic or fantasy element. What can be said objectively, however, about these human contacts? It appears to have been a fairly general view in the nineteenth century that the growth of travel would lead to the breaking down of prejudice, even perhaps to the elimination of war, as increased human contacts led to a growth of understanding between nations and peoples.[5] Such a view seems implausible today. Some tourists indeed, like many football support-ers, seem to regard foreign travel as an opportunity to engage in national or quasi-tribal hostilities (Williams *et al.* 1989). Perhaps such a view of the consequences of travel was always naïve, however. After all, Smollett in the eighteenth century suffered a good deal, according to his own account, at the hands of rapacious landlords (Smollett 1766).

The relations between tourists and locals, due perhaps to cultural, linguistic or economic differences, often seem to lend themselves to interactions which are perceived as exploitative on one side or the other. The sheer volume of tourists in many places also no doubt makes it impossible to react to them as individuals. The situation is a fertile one for negative stereotyping. Local people may appreciate the economic benefits of tourism although they bemoan the changes that result.[6] Sex-tourism seems to be the ultimate form of exploitation by tourists. Its worst manifestations probably occur in the Third World rather than in Europe (Stolle 1990).

A cynical view of the relationship between tourists and foreign cultures is too one-sided, however. Travel may indeed broaden the mind – or the appetite. English food and drink have undergone something of a transformation since the beginning of mass tourism to Europe, with vastly increased consumption of wine and garlic. It is difficult to imagine most English people taking foreign languages seriously, yet a visit to any bookshop will reveal many language courses for sale – not just in the more usual languages, but also in Greek, Turkish and Portuguese, presumably intended for, and bought by, prospective tourists.

Let us look at material from and about two European countries: Spain, a leading 'producer' nation, and Germany, a leading 'con-sumer' nation. Spain is above all the country of mass foreign tourism. Unlike Italy, it does not have a long history of receiving visitors from abroad. The phenomenon only took off in the sixties, and Spain now has the greater number of foreign visitors. Spanish tourism is notable for its extreme degree of regional concentration and its strongly marked seasonality. Although there is some visiting of cities in the centre of the country, this sector is still underdeveloped. The vast mass of foreign tourists visits the coastal regions and the islands and does so during the summer. Tourism has had a massive and beneficial effect on the Spanish economy. It is the country's major industry, and has provided much of the funds for general economic development and capital formation over the last three decades. It is a major source of employment and foreign-exchange earnings: 1,234,000 jobs and 44.6 per cent of the value of exports in 1986. Spain had, then, the largest positive balance of tourist expenditure in Europe.[7]

Germany, by contrast, is Europe's leading consumer nation, with the largest deficit on tourist expenditure: DM27.9 billion in 1986. The percentage of holiday travel involving foreign destinations rose from 15 per cent in 1954 to 66 per cent by 1985. Indeed, West Germans have secured the reputation of being 'the world champions of travelling'. Despite the overriding importance of foreign travel, and the large deficit stemming from it, tourism within Germany is by no means unimportant. Thus in 1986 about 1.5 million jobs depended on tourism, some 6 per cent of all gainful employment (Schnell 1988).

Like other industries, tourism involves disproportionate consequences for producers and consumers. Producers become dependent for their livelihood on the desires of consumers, for whom the interactions involved in tourism are of sharply limited duration. The seasonal character of tourism can have deleterious consequences for the livelihood of producers, and likewise its disruption due to political events, the Gulf war being a striking example. Apart from the economic consequences of tourism, considerable attention needs to be paid to its ecological and cultural impact. It has become a commonplace that tourism is destroying the very things that tourists want to see: ancient buildings, unspoilt nature and 'authentic' human life. It is true, of course, that not everyone is interested in such things; some people are more interested in lying on beaches and drinking in bars. Even in the market for old buildings and unspoilt nature the impact of tourism may not always be harmful. Tourism can preserve as well as destroy, though the preserved object may undergo more or less significant changes.

According to a Spanish author, German tourists in Spain distinguish themselves from those of other nations by their '*ecological pre-occupation* . . . they want to know if the water where they intend to swim is pure or the beauty spots they plan to visit are free from contamination' (Diaz Alvarez 1989). This concern is present in a different way at the theoretical level, in German analyses of the phenomenon of tourism. Academics and publicists have become acutely aware of the real dangers to the ecological balance and cultural integrity of tourist destinations.[8] These problems may be particularly acute in the Third World but they also affect regions of Europe such as the Mediterranean and the Alps. German tourists in

Spain face a dilemma; they want pure water for swimming, but their very presence may overload inadequate sewerage systems, leading to pollution. The market and the local authority may deal with this problem in time. They are less likely to be successful in coping with the destruction of flora and fauna and peaceful, traditional ways of life.[9]

In the face of continued market growth one cannot be too optimistic about the long-term cultural and ecological impact of tourism in many areas. One can only hope that the desire to maintain a lucrative industry will call forth both market solutions and sensible planning to cope with *some* of the problems posed by such a momentous physical and social phenomenon as modern tourism (Diaz Alvarez 1989: ch. 6). From the standpoint of the consumer nations, the best hope would seem to be the gradual development of *sanfter Tourismus* – gentle/ soft tourism, a style characterised by a non-exploitative, accommodating rather than arrogant attitude towards foreign people and places (Krippendorf *et al.* 1988). Tourism, however, seems here to stay, despite temporary recessions due to economic difficulties and political factors (Lanfant 1989).

Sport

Sport is a traditional topic for writers on leisure, and another major industry. A look at sport in a European context provides us, first, with some interesting historical material. There is, for instance, the question of international borrowing or influence. One may compare the development of sport in different countries, noting the similarities, differences and influences.

This can be done quite easily for Britain and France, for we have detailed studies of sporting developments in the two countries produced by the same author, Richard Holt (1981; 1989). Chapter 4 of Holt's book on France is devoted to the impact of 'English sports' (football, Rugby and athletics) at the end of the nineteenth century. The initial impetus behind the introduction of English sports was patriotic and upper class in character. Following the nation's defeat in the Franco-Prussian war, a section of the French elite began to consider that useful lessons could be learnt from the English educational system in terms of the fostering of desirable moral qualities such as courage, leadership and initiative. A large element in the development of such qualities was ascribed to the influence of sport at the public schools and universities. With the encouragement of a few determined propagandists, of whom the best-known was the Baron de Coubertin, a number of lycée students in Paris began to set up sporting clubs in the early 1880s. Within a short period these sports spread geographically, partly because of the presence of expatriate Britons in the wine trade. It was football, however, which became the most popular of the English sports, spreading especially to the industrial areas of the north, and the north of Paris, as well as to Marseille and the south-east. The sport soon lost its upper-class and bourgeois character and became popular with workers, both as an activity, and more especially as a spectacle. Commercialism and professionalism soon followed in the period between the First and Second World Wars.

French sport, however, has its own strengths and specialities. Why did cycling become a major commercial spectacle in France, but never developed to the same extent in Britain? Holt suggests that cycling came on to the scene in France before the other major spectator sports were introduced. Initially it took the form of track races in specially built *vélodromes*, but after a while the popularity of track racing began to decline in comparison to that of the English sports. Long-distance races, however, especially the Tour de France which began in 1903, revived the popularity of cycling and made it into the premier French sporting spectacle. The great advantage of cycling was that road races cost nothing to the spectators, the costs being met by manufacturers, newspapers and advertisers. In a large country with a big rural population and comparatively few large towns, cycling proved to be a viable spectacle, where other sports made less headway due to lack of adequate demand. Commercialisation was thus integral to the sport from the beginning, and this was reflected in the cut-throat competition. Apparently there were complaints of drug-taking even before the First World War. Henri Desgrange, the organiser of the Tour de France, was an outspoken nationalist, and attempted to make the Tour a patriotic event by staging it in German-occupied Lorraine before the First World War and routing it through the battlefield areas in 1919 (Holt 1981: ch. 5).

Politics also comes into focus, if we turn to the major international sporting spectacle of the Olympic Games. The Baron de Coubertin, mentioned above, is of course famous as the founder of the modern Olympic movement. The attack on Israeli athletes at the Games in Munich in 1972, the boycott of the Games in Moscow in 1980 by several nations, and athletes protesting against the Russian involvement in Afghanistan, must have made clear to everyone that international sport is intimately and inescapably bound up with politics.[10] The Olympic Games in Berlin in 1936, however, had already provided a clear example of the politicisation of sport, having been orchestrated to provide favourable propaganda for the recently installed Nazi regime (Hart-Davis 1986; Mandell 1972).

Germany provides us wtih another fascinating example of the politicisation of sport. The reunification of Germany in 1990 brought to an end one of the most remarkable of sporting phenomena, the creation of a sports regime in East Germany, the former GDR, which was outstandingly successful at the level of international competition. East German sports policy was avowedly political in terms of the ideological goal of demonstrating the superiority of the socialist way of life, but also in narrower diplomatic terms, for sporting contacts formed one of the means by which the GDR hoped to overcome its diplomatic isolation by western states. Having achieved this, sport remained an important element in relations with foreign states (Holzweissig 1991). Despite the GDR's avowed linkage of sport with health and physical fitness, the spectacular propaganda value of sporting success clearly won out in the sense that Olympic achievements were based not on superior sports provision for the population as a whole, but on channelling resources into the production of elite performance. Levels of general participation in sport were higher and facilities more widespread in West Germany, which in the 1970s and 80s was far less successful in international competition, at any rate in Olympic sports.[11]

Turning to modern trends in sport, perhaps the simplest way to approach the issue is to look at a recent comparative account which examined trends in fifteen countries, five of which are in western Europe (France, Italy, Portugal, the Netherlands and Britain) (Kamphorst and Roberts 1989). The main focus of these reports is not on international sport but on 'sport for all', on levels of popular participation. Statistics vary between countries and comparisons are therefore difficult, but trends can be ascertained. In general, there was a trend towards increased participation in sport in the 1970s and 80s in western Europe.

Different reasons were given for these increases. For the author, Maria Carmen Belloni, writing about Italy the reason was seen to be bound up with the modernisation of Italian society, indeed to provide an index of such modernisation. The increases in participation in France were seen as due, above all, to increased leisure time. How then are we to explain increased participation between 1979 and 1987 in the Netherlands, where the growth in free time was unequally distributed, and where free time actually decreased slightly between 1975 and 1985 for the population up to age 50?

Although increased leisure time may be linked with increased participation in sport, it seems that it cannot be the only reason. It appears that values must have changed as well as opportunities. It Italy, there was a relative shift away from the more traditional sports of hunting, fishing and football, and in the case of hunting an absolute decline. In all three countries, indeed, there was a relative trend away from traditional and team sports towards individual and unorganised sports. The British data were congruent with these results. Apparently there were insufficient data in Portugal to permit analysis of trends. Western European trends towards increased participation in sport, found also in Finland, were not true of all areas of the world.

From this study, sports participation in eastern Europe, as well as in India and Nigeria, seemed to be in decline, which perhaps reflected the growing economic problems in these areas in the 1980s. Nevertheless, even in western Europe many people appeared to take no part in sport at all. Non-participants in Italy comprised 77.8 per cent of the population in 1985. This may be thought a more significant fact than that the figure apparently dropped from 84.6 per cent three years before. It was evident that women everywhere participated less in sport than men, but also that these differences had been decreasing in recent years.

An interesting issue raised by the Dutch contribution (Kamphorst and Roberts 1989) concerns the effects of socialisation. Studies of participation in sport tend to look to aspects of an individual's present situation such as education, income or marital status to explain differences in participation. Studies in the Netherlands, however, seem to show that differences can be better explained in terms of past influences. Thus children who played soccer in childhood, and who were members of clubs at that time, were much more likely to be engaged in the game as adults than those who had had no contact with the sport as children. This may seem an unsurprising finding, but it is perhaps of important general significance for leisure studies.

Why is non-participation in sport seen as a problem by sports authorities and by some sociologists? Is such a view reasonable? Sport as a form of leisure is an ambiguous phenomenon. Like the other forms of leisure discussed in this chapter, it has been subjected to political regulation and to commercialisation. Top sport has become a major spectacle, whether watched directly or on TV and is thus an important element in mass culture and indeed in international politics. Participant sport is in a different situation. Sport, unlike drinking, attending festivals or even tourism, is felt to be good for people, not primarily as a form of relaxation but as a means of maintaining health. This view is undoubtedly correct in general, but it results in sport being undertaken and supported for utilitarian reasons as well as for fun. This has been the case throughout the entire history of sport, which in the past was largely encouraged for military and nationalistic reasons. To regard as problematical the fact that a large proportion of the population does not engage in sport at all may be correct from a medical or public health perspective, but it makes little sense in the context of the sociology of leisure. While the promotion of 'sport for all' may be desirable, it should perhaps be recognised that sport is only one leisure option amongst many others. Perhaps the basic problem is that there are just too many sedentary occupations in the modern world.

Drinking and socialising

I have left this section to the last because drinking raises in a particularly clear way a number of issues which are central to the analysis of leisure and, I suspect, to its essence. In a survey into the sporting activities of Portuguese students, reported by Machado Pais, they were asked what afforded the greatest pleasure in free-time activities. The most frequent answer (60.2 per cent) was 'to be together with friends'. When asked the reasons for keeping up sports activity, only 19.6 per cent mentioned 'being together with friends' whilst 69.9 per cent mentioned 'to keep healthy.' Machado Pais commented that this implied that the social rewards from sport were relatively small, and hence that it was quite likely that it would always lose out as a leisure activity with many people in comparison to other activities which involved greater social rewards (Kamphorst and Roberts 1989: 261–76). I suggest that he is correct, and that sociability and the opportunities for it are among the most essential and sought-after qualities of leisure. This is not to deny that solitary leisure activities – reading, gardening, knitting, watching TV or listening to radio and records – are not important. Furthermore, these activities are not necessarily solitary: they can occur in the presence of other members of the family. The trend towards family-based leisure has been a marked one in recent years.

Nevertheless, I believe that sociability outside the family circle is of the essence of leisure and that the pursuit of it is important in both work and recreation. The booze-up after the Rugby match is often as important as the game itself. *Après ski* seems as important as, or more important than, skiing to some people. Social solidarity among members of the peer group is perhaps more significant to so-called hooligans than the football. How many people choose to travel abroad as part of a tourist group not just to see the sights, or for convenience, but because of the enforced intimacy and social contact involved in a fortnight's tour? If visits to the hairdresser have a recreational component, as I suggested at the beginning of this chapter, where can this come from except from sociability, or social interaction of a particular type? If I am correct, then the rigid distinction between work and leisure made by some sociologists and thought to be characteristic of industrial society is only true up to a point.

Recreation in the sense of sociability, non-functional or non-focused social interaction, is present in the workplace as well as in the leisure centre, and forms an important part of the rewards of work. Of course sociability can itself become a necessary ingredient of work. Certain professions and occupations may need to develop in trainees an ability to engage in non-functional social interaction because this is sought or demanded by customers and clients. Hairdressers, shopkeepers, doctors (the bedside manner) all need to develop this skill, the exercise of which may be rewarding or may be felt as a constraint, no doubt depending on personality.

From this standpoint, drinking has a particular interest and central-ity in the study of leisure, for clearly the essence of drinking is sociability *per se*. It is thus a particularly 'pure' form of leisure activity. Of course there are people for whom the consumption of alcohol becomes a physical need. Alcohol addiction and abuse is a serious and growing social problem, though a modest one in Britain in comparison with most of its European neighbours (Davies and Walsh 1983). The vast majority who drink alcohol and visit pubs, however, do not end up as alcoholics. Alcohol of course acts as a depressant, weakening inhibitions and thus facilitating social interaction, but the sociability associated with drinking as an activity does not necessarily depend on the ingestion of alcohol. In Muslim societies men drinking coffee together may do so for much the same social reasons as men in Europe gather in a pub or café. The female *Kaffeeklatsch* may also be a broad functional equivalent to the male pub group. Drinking tea provides the occasion for social interaction also (Hazan 1987). Let us concentrate, however, on the phenomenon of drinking alcohol.

There is space for only one case study: the German pub. In Germany, unlike most of southern Europe, there is a rough equivalent to the British pub (*die Kneipe*), a place essentially intended for socialising and drinking alcohol. In the past such pubs were largely seen as the preserve of workers, whereas the middle classes visited restaurants. From the late 1960s, however, pubs for students, intellectuals and the new middle classes began to appear in growing numbers. It is interesting to compare such pubs with those frequented by workers. Workers' pubs conform very largely to the traditional picture of male-dominated pub culture which is familiar from British studies.[12] This is particularly evident in those pubs near to the workplace. In the evening just after work has finished, such pubs will be invaded by workers seeking to refresh themselves and relax after the day's work. This is a world of beer, conversation and perhaps games, in an exclusively masculine atmosphere, more so than in the neighbourhood pub later in the evening, when one or two workers may bring their wives along with them (Droege and Kraemer-Badoni 1987).

Intellectuals' pubs are unlike this in a number of respects. First, the motives for going there are different. This is expressed very well in a study of pubs frequented by those in the left-wing subculture of Berlin:

An intellectual going to a pub does so only rarely with the feeling of having done a day's work . . . rather as a rule he flees from demands which he thinks he hasn't fulfilled or which he is unable to fulfill . . . every project seems impossible to finish. The compelling will to work necessary to finish it off permits no interruption of working time, but precisely for that reason it is more and more frequently interrupted.

(Laermann 1974)

Thus those who won't arrange to go for a walk or accept an invitation because it will interrupt their work are overcome by the rigours of their task and the need for distraction, and end up spending a few hours in the pub. Another reason to visit pubs is to meet members of the opposite sex, for in this type of pub women are (almost) as numerous as men and can visit them alone, for a characteristic of such places is that they are always crowded and anyone can engage anyone else in conversation. Women are to be found in such pubs sitting alone at the bar, which is still scarcely imaginable in workers' or socially mixed pubs. Nevertheless, according to Droege and Kraemer-Badoni, women still do not like to visit pubs by themselves. Even in intellectuals' pubs the atmosphere is still dominated by male preoccupations, though in a subtle way (Droege and Kraemer-Badoni 1987: 236). In this connection it would be interesting to compare the sociology of the pub with the sociology of the party, another context in which men, women and alcohol come together. Europe, particularly France, provides us with quite a different historical model of male – female social interaction in the institution of the salon.

These accounts of pubs illustrate the familiar sociological necessity to examine a phenomenon in relation to social class and gender. They also illustrate that what appears to be the same form of leisure behaviour can have a different meaning and quality for its participants because it stands in a different relationship to work.

Perhaps the most interesting aspect of these accounts is their analysis of the nature of sociability and communication in the pub. In workers' pubs work is a main topic of conversation, along with sport, drinking, other customers and the pub itself. Telling jokes, and jokes and conversation about sex tend to be the specialities of a few people, but common with such men.[13] Politics is also discussed. In the socially and sexually mixed pubs the conversation is similar and equally varied: politics, work, sport, eating and drinking, holidays, personal relations. Sex, however, plays a subordinate role.

More significant than the topic is the nature of conversation in pubs, and the kinds of unwritten rules it seems to follow. One sometimes thinks of pubs as places where arguments are conducted, but the view could be put forward that pubs are places where on the whole serious arguments are avoided. According to this view arguments in pubs largely take the form of subjective assertions. Explicit arguments involving lengthy elaboration of the grounds for an opinion would destroy the social atmosphere of the pub. This atmosphere is built up of tolerance, freedom and equality, in the sense that everyone has the right to speak, and expects to speak, and to have her/his opinion heard and considered sympathetically. Pubs are not places where people's illusions about themselves are shattered, but where they are accepted and tolerated, if not encouraged. Despite considerable drinking, conversations in pubs rarely end in ill-will, let alone fights. On the contrary, the attraction of the pub lies in the mutual recognition, trust and warmth generated by the atmosphere of sociability, but this depends paradoxically on people keeping a certain distance from one another and following the unwritten rules of pub conversation:

One may . . . certainly talk at length about oneself but not become personal with others. One may not give orders to others or ask them too many questions. One may only question ironically, not categorically, their competence to express themselves about practically everything. Contradicting too strongly must be avoided for it would put in question the expected tendency towards consensus held internally by all those engaged in the conversation.

(Laermann 1974: 178)

Thus sociability has its rules, which are generally observed even when inhibitions are weakened by alcohol. It is this sociability, even though it may be ephemeral, which is the attraction of pubs and which, I believe, epitomises the attraction of a wide range of leisure activities.

Despite this, visiting pubs, like sport (though in a different way), is an ambiguous leisure activity. People can become addicted to alcohol, and frequenting pubs can become expensive in terms of the time and money allocated to it. To the extent that pub-going is primarily a male phenomenon it may arouse the anxiety or hostility of wives who resent the diversion of resources from the household. Thus sociability between males may be paid for in terms of difficulties in, or destruction of, other relationships.[14]

The state has also concerned itself with drinking at various times, seeing pubs and taverns as centres of political propaganda and social disorder, and serious competitors to work (Brennan 1988). There is still official concern with drinking related to crime, especially perhaps motoring offences, and clearly it is likely to remain an activity which the state will consider it necessary to regulate.[15]

Conclusion

I trust that this chapter has given the reader some idea of the variety, and the interest, of the sociology of leisure. In conclusion I shall consider briefly the overall importance of the subject. There is a basic division in the sociology of leisure between those who lay emphasis on constraint in relation to leisure activities, and those who stress choice. For 'radical' theorists, leisure, like other aspects of life, is a field of activity structured by fundamental class, gender and ethnic inequalities. Furthermore, the activities of powerful private leisure providers, and of the state – indeed, the general ethos of capitalist society – create patterns of leisure which owe as much or more to the interests of producers as to the wishes of consumers. According to this perspective, those who stress freedom of choice and pluralism in relation to leisure are ignoring history, theory and the constraints of capitalist society, and producing for the most part naïve and urelated empirical studies.[16] It is not my intention here to examine in detail the plausibility of such a general view of leisure.

Clearly, ethnic and gender-based inequalities are important in relation to leisure opportunities (Clark 1990). Equally, emphasis on the role of providers is necessary and valuable. Sport, tourism and drink are all major industries – tourism is well on the way to becoming the world's biggest industry – and analysis of the phenomena in terms of industrial structure and provision is indispensable to a proper understanding.

Within this general approach to leisure the value of a European focus, rather than a narrowly British one, should need little demonstration. Sport and tourism are international as well as national phenomena, and it is the international dimension which has strenghtened concern about such problems as football hooliganism and the impact of tourism, and made them into very significant public issues. Furthermore, a comparative approach to leisure provision invariably opens up the need for historical enquiry. If we wish to know why Spaniards watch bullfights and the French watch cycling, whilst Britons on the whole watch neither, or why the British shoot grouse and the Italians shoot songbirds, then historical explanation is required.

Leisure still remains, however, an area where people can exercise considerable freedom of choice. Sport, drink and tourism are major industries because people choose to consume their products. There is no compulsion to do so, and substantial sectors of the population in all countries choose not to consume these services, though obviously many cannot afford to do so.

It might be argued that all mature individuals have to come to terms with four areas of life: work, leisure, personal relationships and some sort of general philosophy of life or *Weltanschauung*, in the broad sense a religion.[17] Work and personal relationships obviously involve choices as well as constraints, but the choices having been made, individuals become locked into networks of commitments and obligations. Leisure and religion are not like this, or are so to a lesser extent. One might argue that the nature of modern society is to make genuinely free choice in these areas more available than at any time in the past, though the price for this has been no doubt a weakening of the bonds of community. In an interesting article on the future of research in the sociology of leisure, Dumazdier has drawn attention to the similarity between leisure and religion in the context of a 'cultural revolution of free time', and has also pointed out that they may be rivals in this search for identity. There is a field for parallel research between the sociology of religion and the sociology of leisure (Dumazdier 1990).

Such a view of leisure as choice offers a perspective for research which is surely a legitimate one. In this connection it would seem important to look at the influence of socialisation, which, as we have seen above, seems more important in some circumstances to participation in sport than present influences. This type of research could be extended to other areas of leisure. Such research would not necessarily be deterministic in its implications but could contribute to the notion of the individual as a 'productive processor of reality' (Hurrelmann 1988). This perspective on leisure also benefits from an international focus. Leisure practices are cultural forms which can be adopted, adapted and transformed, and there are significant international borrowings in this area as we have seen. International borrowings depend on international contacts, however, and thus we come finally to another form of constraint on leisure behaviour which is of vital importance; namely, the nature and performance of the political and economic systems of nation states. It still makes a great difference to the general leisure potentialities of individuals, and their opportunities to travel in particular, whether they reside in Germany or Czechoslovakia, in France or in Poland.

Notes

1 See, for example, the wide range of festivals mentioned in Russ (1982).
2 See also Sanchis (1977) and Veiga de Oliveira (1984).
3 *Guardian*, 26 March 1991.
4 Lewis, (1985 Penguin ed), p. 62.
5 The Spanish writer Azorin (1912) has an interesting discussion of such ideas in relation to the development of railway travel. See 'Los ferrocarriles' in *Castilla*.
6 See Pi-Sunyer (1978); also Lewis (1985 edn), p. 180.
7 Valenzuela (1988); see also Diaz Alvarez (1989).
8 See Ludwig *et al.* (1990); also Krippendorf *et al.* (1988), which contains an exhaustive bibliography on 'gentle tourism'.
9 Tourism in Africa may be playing an important role in the preservation of the more obviously spectacular 'big game'.
10 See Holt (1981: ch. 10) and Holt (1989: ch. 4) for illuminating discussions on the political context and implications of sport in general in France and Britain in the nineteenth and early twentieth centuries.
11 Childs (1983: 186 – 7); see also Knecht (1978).
12 Hey (1986), but also see note 13.
13 Droege and Kraemer-Badoni (1987: 211). There appears to be nothing equivalent to Hey's secondary account of a rural pub in Herefordshire, where 'the main topic of conversation in the pub is women's sexuality and the effective male control of it' Hey (1986: 66).
14 Hey (1986: 71). In eighteenth-century France married women could apply directly to the commissaire of police for a separation from their husbands on the ground that their dowry portion needed to be protected from the effects of their husbands' dissipation in taverns; Brennan (1988: ch. 5).
15 Davies and Walsh (1983). Many leisure activities, including sporting events and festivals, are perceived as having a tendency to get out of control.
16 For an example of such an approach, see Clarke and Critcher (1985).
17 See Luckmann (1967) especially chapters 5 and 6 on the relation between religion and personal identity.

References

Azorin, Martinez Ruiz J. (1976) *Castilla*, Madrid: Biblioteca Nueva. Originally published in 1912.

Brennan, T. (1988) *Public Drinking and Popular Culture in Eighteenth Century Paris*, Princeton NJ: Princeton University Press.

Childs, D. (1983) *The GDR: Moscow's German Ally*, London: Allen & Unwin.

Clark, S. (1990) 'Shiftwork and leisure behaviour of ethnic and gender groups in the British textile industry', *Le Travail Humain*, 53 (3): 227 – 44.

Clarke, J. and Critcher, C. (1985) *The Devil Makes Work: Leisure in Capitalist Britain*, London: Macmillan.

Davies, P. and Walsh, D. (1983) *Alcohol Problems and Alcohol Control in Europe*, London: Croom Helm.

Diaz Alvarez, J. R. (1989) *Geografía del Turismo*, Madrid: Editorial Sintesis.

Droege, F. and Kraemer-Badoni, I. (1987) *Die Kneipe: zur Soziologie einer Kulturform*, Frankfurt am Main: Suhrkamp, p. 264.

Dumazdier, J. (1990) 'Pour un renouveau de la recherche en sciences sociales du loisir', *Loisir et Société*, 13 (1): 63 – 76.

Hart-Davis, D. (1986) *Hitler's Games: the 1936 Olympics*, New York: Harper & Row.

Hazan, H. (1987) 'Holding time still with cups of tea', in M. Douglas (ed.) *Constructive Drinking: Perspectives on Drink from Anthropology*, Cambridge: Cambridge University Press.

Hey, V. (1986) *Patriarchy and Pub Culture*, London: Tavistock.

Holt, V. (1981) *Sport and Society in Modern France*, London: Macmillan.

——(1989) *Sport and the British: a Modern History*, Oxford: Oxford University Press.

Holzweissig, G. (1981) *Diplomatie im Trainingsanzug: Sport als Politisches Instrument der DDR*, Munich: Oldenbourg.

Hurrelmann, K. (1988) *Social Structure and Personality Development: the Individual as a Productive Processor of Reality*, Cambridge: Cambridge University Press.

Kamphorst, T. J. and Roberts, K. (eds) (1989) *Trends in Sports: a Multinational Perspective*, Culemborg: Giordano Bruno.

Kertzer, K. I. (1980) *Comrades and Christians: Religion and Political Struggle in Communist Italy*, Cambridge: Cambridge University Press.

Knecht, W. (1978) *Das Medaillenkollektiv*, Berlin: Holzapfel.

Krippendorf, J., Zimmer, P. and Glauber, H. (eds) (1988) *Für einen Andern Tourismus*, Frankfurt am Main: Fischer.

Laermann, K. (1971) 'Kneipengerede: zu einigen Verkehrsformen der Berliner linken Subkultur', *Kursbuch*, 37: 172 – 3.

Lanfant, M-F. (1989) 'International tourism resists the crisis', in A. Olszewska and K. Roberts *Leisure and Life-style: a Comparative Analysis of Free Time*, London: Sage.

Lewis, N. (1984) *Voices of the Old Sea*, London: Hamish Hamilton.

Luckman, T. (1967) *The Invisible Religion*, London: Macmillan.

Ludwig, K., Has, M. and Neuer, M. (Hrsg.) (1990) *Der Neue Tourismus*, Munich: Beck.

Mandell, R. D. (1972) *The Nazi Olympics*, London: Souvenir Press.

Pi-Sunyer, O. (1978) 'Through native eyes: tourists and tourism in a Catalan maritime community', in V. L. Smith (ed.) *Hosts and Guests*, Oxford: Blackwell.

Rearick, C. (1977) 'Festivals in modern France: the experience of the Third Republic', *Journal of Contemporary History*, 12: 435 – 60.

Russ, J. M. (1982) *German Festivals and Customs*, London: Oswald Wolff.

Sanchis, P. (1977) 'Les romarias portugaises', *Archives de Sciences Sociales des Religions*, 43 (1): 53 – 76.

——(1983) *Arraial: festa de um povo*, Lisbon: Publicacoes Dom Quixote, p. 15.

Schnell, R. (1988) 'The Federal Republic of Germany: a growing international deficit?' In A. M. Williams and G. Shaw *Tourism and Economic Development*, London and New York: Belhaven Press, ch. 11.

Smollett, T. G. (1766) *Travels in France and Italy* (many modern editions).

Stolle, C. (1990) 'Sex-tourismus', In K. Ludwig, M. Has, and M. Neuer, (eds) *Der Neue Tourismus*, Munich: Beck.

Urry, J. (1990) *The Tourist Gaze*, London: Sage.

Valenzuela, M. (1988) 'Spain: the phenomenon of mass tourism', in A. M. Williams and G. Shaw *Tourism and Economic Development*, London and New York: Belhaven Press.

Veiga de Oliveria, E. (1984) *Festividades Ciclicas em Portugal*, Lisbon: Publicacoes Dom Quixote.

Williams, J., Dunning, E. and Murphy, P. (1989) *Hooligans Abroad*, London: Routledge.

SELECT BIBLIOGRAPHY

Each chapter in the book has attached a set of references. These are the most useful bibliographies for those readers intending to pursue particular issues. They form an excellent starting point both as guides to secondary data sources and as lists of the main writers and researchers to read.

This additional short bibliography is a supplement to those in the separate sections and is a starting point for those who need more general reading or who want to know more about particular societies as well as more general topics.

These are books by sociologists or by other social scientists and are written in a way that is relevant to and supportive of a sociological position. But they are just a brief guide, a starting point for those wishing or needing to find out more.

Generally on Western Europe

Archer, M. S., Giner (eds.) (1971) *Contemporary Europe: Class Status and Power*, London: Routledge and Kegan Paul.

British Journal of Sociology 1990 Vol. 41 no 3 Issue *Britain in Europe.*

Calvocoressi, P. (1991) *World Politics Since 1945*, (6th ed) London: Longman.

Commission of the European Communities (1988) *Social Europe: the Social Dimension of the Internal Market*, Luxembourg: Directorate General for Employment, Social Affairs and Education.

European Social Charter (1981) Strasbourg: Council of Europe Directorate of Press and Information.

S. Giner, M. S. Archer eds. (1978) *Contemporary Europe: Social Structure and Cultural Patterns*, London: Routledge and Kegan Paul.

Harding, S., Philips, D. with Fogarty, M. (1986) *Contrasting Values in Western Europe*, London: Macmillan.

Lane, J.–E., Ersson, S. (1991) *Politics and Society in Western Europe* London: Sage.

Teague, P. (1989) *The European Community: the Social Dimension*, London: Kogan Page.

Urwin, D. (1991) *The Community of Europe: A History of European Integration since 1945*, London: Longman.

Vandamme, J. ed. (1985) *New Dimensions in European Social Policy*, London: Croom Helm.

The State

Bornstein, S., Held, D., Krieger, J. (eds) (1984) *The State in Capitalist Europe: A Casebook* London: Allen and Unwin.

Hayward, J., Berki R. (eds) (1979) *State and Society in Contemporary Europe* Oxford: Martin Robertson.

Scase, R. (ed) (1980) *The State in Western Europe*

The Economy

Davis, H., Scase, R. (1985) *Western Capitalism and State Socialism* Oxford: Blackwell.

Therborn, G. (1986) *Why Some People Are More Unemployed Than Others* London: Verso.

Armstrong, P., Glyn, A., Harrison, J. (1988) *Capitalism Since World War II* Oxford: Basil Blackwell.

Scase, R. ed (1980) *The State in Western Europe*

France

Ardagh, J. (1977) *The New France* (3rd ed) Harmondsworth: Penguin.

Boltanski, L. 1987 *The Making of a Class: Cadres in French Society*, Cambridge: Cambridge University Press.

Gallie, D. (1983) *Social Inequality in France and Britain*, Cambridge: Cambridge University Press.

Hanley, D., Kerr, A., Waites, N. (1984) *Contemporary France: Politics and Society Since 1945*, London: Routledge and Kegan Paul.

Hantrais, L. (1982) *Contemporary French Society*, London: Macmillan.

Germany

Ardagh, J. (1988) *Germany and the Germans*, London: Penguin Books.

Childs, D., Johnson, J. eds. (1981) *West Germany: Politics and Society*, London: Croom Helm.

Dahrendorf, R. (1968) *Society and Democracy in Germany*, London: Weidenfeld and Nicolson.

Hulsberg, W. (1988) *The West German Greens: A Social and Political Profile*, London: Verso.

Krejci, J (1976) *Social Structure in a Divided Germany*, London: Croom Helm.

Italy

Ballamy, R. (1987) *Modern Italian Social Theory*, Cambridge: Polity/ Blackwell.

King, R. (1987) *Italy*, London: Harper and Row.

Pinto, D. ed (1981) *Contemporary Italian Sociology*, Cambridge: Cambridge University Press.

Sassoon, D. (1986) *Contemporary Italy: Politics, Economics and Society Since 1945*, London: Longman.

Sweden

Korpi, W. (1983) *The Democratic Class Struggle*, Routledge and Kegan Paul London

Scase, R. (ed) (1976) *Readings in the Swedish Class Structure*, Oxford: Pergamon.

Southern Europe

Mouzelis, N. (1978) *Modern Greece: Facets of Underdevelopment*, London: Macmillan.

Seers, D. *et al.* (1979) *Underdeveloped Europe: Studies in Core-Periphery Relations*, Hassocks: Harvester Press.

Williams, A. (ed) (1984) *Southern Europe Transformed: Political and Economic Change in Greece, Italy, Portugal and Spain*, London: Harper and Row.

INDEX

All page references in italics refer to tables.

Italy,
  abortion law, *78*
  attitudes to inequality, 25, 26
  attitudes to women, 96
  child care, 82, *83*, 84
  dependent population, 80
  divorce rates, 54
  education and training, 126,
    133, 134
  extent of poverty, 22
  female employment, *86*, *87*, *89*,
    90
  feminist movement, 75, 76, 77
  fertility rates, 55, *56*
  festivals, 241–2
  health-care, 210
  household structure, 57
  immigration to, 106–7, 111–12
  imprisonment policies, *178*
  income distribution, 21
  internal divisions, 125
  maternity and parental leave, *82*
  organised crime, 174, 175
  part-time employment, 88, *89*
  religion, 224
  social mobility, 29
  sport, 247, 248
  tourism, 242, 243
  trade unions, 147, 152–6, 160
  unemployment, 129
  welfare spending, 23, 24
Ivanets, N. and Lukomskaya, M.,
  on health-care, 197

Jacobi, O. and Muller-Jenitsch,
  W., on trade unions, 150
Jallade, J-P., on education and
  training, 123
Jeffcutt, P., on education and
  training, 140–1
Jenkins, A., on trade unions, 159
Jenkins, Roy, on multi-
  culturalism, 112–13, 114,
  118–19
Jensen, L., on crime prevention,
  178
Jones, G. and Wallace, C., on
  youth transitions, 126
Jones, K., on British education
  and training, 128
Joshi, H., on female employment
  and fertility rates, 63

Jowell, R. *et al*, 25–6, 129
Judaism, 225

Kamphorst, T.J. and Roberts, K.,
  on sport, 247, 248, 249
Katz, H. and Sabel, C., on trade
  unions, 151
Katzenstein, P., on Germany
  industry, 41
Kelly, R., on organised crime,
  174–5
Kendall, W., on trade unions, 156
Kertzer, K.I., on festivals, 241–2
King, M., on crime prevention,
  178
Klein, A., on health-care, 195
Kleinman, Arthur, on health-care,
  196
Klinger, A., on fertility rates, 65
Kocka, J., on German industry, 37
Kriele, M., on trade unions, 154
Krippendorf, J. *et al*, on tourism,
  245
Kruger, H-H., on youth
  transitions, 126

Laermann, K., on pubs, 250, 252
Landes, D., on French industry,
  38
Lane, C., on industry 5, 10, 42, 46
Lane, J-E., and Ersseon, S.O., on
  income distribution 20, *21*, 27
Lanfant, M-F., on tourism, 245
Lash, S.,
  on trade unions, 159
  and Urry, J., on patterns of
    social organization 6
Lawson, R. and George, V., on
  income distribution, 21
Lawton, D., on education and
  training, 131
Layton-Henry, Z., on
  immigration, 115
Le Bras, H., on immigration, 59
legislation, 'harmonisation' of 6
leisure 10, 239–56
  family-based, 249
  inequalities in, 252–3
  and religion, 253
  and sociability, 248–52
  sociological research, 239–40,
    253–4